# A Life Apart

# A Life Apart

## The English Working Class
## 1890-1914

STANDISH MEACHAM

HARVARD UNIVERSITY PRESS

Cambridge, Massachusetts · 1977

Copyright © 1977 by Thames and Hudson Ltd

All Rights Reserved

Library of Congress Catalog Card Number 77-72673

ISBN 0-674-53075-6

Printed in Great Britain

# Contents

Preface 7

1 The working class 11

2 House, neighbourhood and kin 30

3 Women at home 60

4 Working wives and mothers 95

5 Husbands and fathers 116

6 Children 156

7 A view of life 194

Chapter references 221

Bibliography 264

Sources of illustrations 268

Index 269

# Preface

TO PENETRATE the 'mind' of any particular collection of men and women at any particular period in history demands an ability to perceive evidence thoughtfully and with some measure of imagination. It requires, as well, a willingness to acknowledge that one's understanding will remain clouded, at least to some degree, by the nature of the evidence itself – who produced it and for whom; and a readiness to accommodate to the inevitable contradictions and variations that such evidence will always adduce. W. L. Burn, writing of the Victorian middle class in his masterful survey, *The Age of Equipoise*, encourages his readers to welcome complexity, as does Walter Houghton, in his equally impressive *The Victorian Frame of Mind*. Yet neither historian, despite an unwillingness to settle for simple explanations or single causes, leaves his readers bewildered by trees as he searches out the shape of the forest. Complexity is not permitted to deny pattern.

As I have traced what I perceive to be the patterns of working-class consciousness during the years before the First World War, I have tried to follow their example. In the case of this study, however, the task is complicated by the fact that so much of the evidence about workers' consciousness comes to us from the writings of middle-class men and women, through the filters of middle-class perception. Investigators like Charles Booth, Seebohm Rowntree, M. S. Pember Reeves and Clementina Black hoped that the facts they unearthed would speak the truth about the way workers lived, and thought about, their lives. Yet they were writing not just to record facts but to urge reform, or at least to make a reformer's point: the extent of hidden poverty in the midst of apparent plenty; the degree of working-class female servitude in a period caught up in the middle-class struggle for female emancipation.

Private surveys, like officially commissioned reports, are an invaluable tool for historians. The facts they provide on subjects such as budgets, diets, housing, work and wages are a reliable source for information obtainable in no other way, on nothing like the same scale. Yet valuable though the yield may be, it must not be judged apart from the reasons for its initial harvesting. Even when the surveys allow workers to speak for themselves, one must ask: to what extent is this testimony typical of a more general experience? A working mother's evidence about her daily schedule must be measured against what can be learned elsewhere about hours of work, family size, and average income before it can be accepted as in any sense 'typical', or instead discarded as an attempt by the investigator to arouse sympathy.

Sympathy can lie perilously close to patronage, a habit of mind the most well-intentioned reformers fought but seldom completely conquered. They wanted working-class men and women to lead not only 'better' lives, but lives defined as 'better' according to the standards and assumptions of the middle class. What they described as the dreary monotony of working-class weekends, for example, was luxury to a man compelled to work fifty-five or sixty hours a week. Their annoyance at the housewife's compulsion to scour and polish ignored her even more compulsive and very understandable desire to be looked upon as respectable. Recent inquiries into the nature of working-class life by sociologists are freer from the bias that marks the works of earlier pioneers, and have been of great use to me. The publications of Michael Young and Peter Willmott's Institute of Community Studies have helped me especially to discern the nature of a 'classic' working-class community, and have allowed me to place the communities with which I am concerned within a larger time span.

Novelists, again almost all of them middle class, brought their particular artistic concerns to bear upon their observations of working-class life. When they wrote about those who led that life, they expressed their fear that the anonymous, alienating city might smother the spirit of the people condemned to live confined within it. The Victorian novelist's central concern remained individual character. That concern might lead him to exaggerate – as George Gissing appears to exaggerate – the power of the city to defeat human will. The one genuinely working-class novel of the period, Robert Tressell's *The Ragged Trousered Philanthropists*, must be read with the author's equally insistent didacticism in mind, his disgust with workers' acquiescence in their own manipulation and degradation by the middle class. The writing of Gissing, Tressell, Arthur Morrison, Edwin Pugh and others can tell us a great deal about working-class life in the years before the First World War. To ignore it as a source would be as foolish and as unnecessary as to ignore the evidence in the novels of mid-Victorians such as Charles Dickens and Elizabeth Gaskell for that earlier period. It must simply be handled with the attention to motive, experience, and point of view that historians turn upon all their evidence.

The same is true, of course, of reminiscence. In relying as heavily as I have upon Richard Hoggart's *The Uses of Literacy* and Robert Roberts's *The Classic Slum*, I have tried to guard particularly against a willingness to trust too completely to the portraits which those two memories have evoked. Hoggart has been criticized – by Roberts, among others – for exaggerating the comfortable, homely virtues of the working-class world of his youth, the more justifiably to inveigh against the mass culture that threatens to destroy it. Yet his efforts to reach a new understanding of working-class community and of the psychology of working-class consciousness make his book one of the most creative and hence most useful on the subject. It is perhaps better read against the astringent directness of Roberts's sharply perceived analysis. Hoggart's virtue, however, is his ability not just to recall sights and sounds, attitudes and assumptions, but to connect them together so that readers can make further connections of their own.

The tricks of memory are an obvious hazard when analysing and evaluating the evidence of oral interviews. In granting me permission to make use of their remarkable archive of interviews with working-class men and women born before 1900, Paul Thompson and Thea Vigne have allowed me to give a dimension to this book it would not otherwise have had. They have discussed their methods at length (see particularly their article in *Oral History*, Number 4, 1972), acknowledging the dangers of trusting their respondents uncritically, yet arguing that the size and nature of their sample, the framework of their questionnaire, and their technique of administering it minimize the kind of gross distortions one would naturally hope to guard against. Having examined the results of their painstaking efforts at some length, I find the evidence they have amassed and their explanation of its usefulness fully convincing. Of course old men and women, recalling events of sixty years ago, will forget or confuse details. Just as naturally, they may decide to exaggerate the nature and extent of early sufferings, if they believe that is what their interviewers are hoping to hear recalled. Or they may minimize childhood deprivation if they have subsequently resolved to make their 'rough' past conform to their 'respectable' present. These dangers can, in part, be averted by a perceptive interviewer. And they will tend to diminish as the number of interviews increases, as a pattern emerges from individual instances. The question of particular reliability as well as that of more general application depends in the end on the historian's willingness to listen with thought and care, and to relate what he is hearing to what he has heard and read elsewhere. A housewife's proud, almost reverent, recollection of her skill as a step-scrubber helps confirm the nature of working-class respectability. The immediacy of a former housemaid's

9

memory of near-seduction mirrors attitudes discussed from across the boundaries of class by the author of *My Secret Life*.

In my survey I have attempted to allow for variations of time, location, occupation, and human nature. And I have excluded communities – mining villages, the Irish in Liverpool, the Jews of East London – 'particular' enough to require separate treatment. What emerge from the evidence are patterns of working-class consciousness and working-class life at the end of the Victorian era. Those patterns are shaped, however, not just by the facts, but by my particular perception of them. Others would have probably found other facts, and would certainly have arranged them in other ways. Walter Houghton, arguing for the existence of a Victorian 'frame of mind', quotes Leslie Stephen on the mysterious manner whereby the ideas of what Stephen calls 'intellectual leaders' are reflected in the 'darkened mirrors' of commonplace middle-class perception. The mirrors of working-class consciousness reflect a different set of images, imprinted less often by leaders, intellectual or otherwise, than by the shared experiences of fellow workers. The historian who stares at those reflected images in an effort to understand them will find it hard to avoid his own reflection as well. Whether he wishes to or not, he will become a part of what he sees, and hence of what he describes.

I am pleased to acknowledge my debt to Paul Thompson and Thea Vigne, not only for permission to quote from the archives of their 'Family Life and Work before 1918' project, but also for their willingness to further my education as to the nature of class consciousness and of working-class life. I am grateful for assistance, criticisms and suggestions received from the following: Carl Clark, Gail Clark, John Clive, Dave Davies, A. E. Green, T. W. Heyck, and David Unger. I am, as in the past, greatly indebted to my wife for her editorial assistance and for her sustained interest in the project.

Permission to quote from material in their possession has been gratefully received from the following: the BBC Sound Archives, Mr Henry Crapper and the Bradford Central Library, the Labour Party Library, the Library of Economic and Political Science, London School of Economics, Chatto and Windus and the Oxford University Press (for permission to quote from Richard Hoggart, *The Uses of Literacy*), and the Manchester University Press (for permission to quote from Robert Roberts, *The Classic Slum*).

Funds for research and for manuscript preparation were furnished by the John Simon Guggenheim Memorial Foundation and by the University Research Institute of the University of Texas at Austin.

S. M.

# 1 The working class

THIS BOOK IS about working-class life. It rests upon the assumption, articulated by E. P. Thompson in *The Making of the English Working Class*, that class is more than 'structure' or 'category', that it is 'something which in fact happens (and can be shown to have happened) in human relationships'. Existing as a part of historical experience, class is actuality, 'real people in a real context'. And because human nature is idiosyncratic and never totally predictable, class, which draws its own life from the lives of men and women, is not always easily discerned. To be understood intelligently, it must be studied over a period of time; otherwise it evaporates. 'If we stop history at a given point,' Thompson rightly argues, 'then there are no classes but simply a multitude of individuals with a multitude of experiences. But if we watch these men over an adequate period of social change, we observe patterns in their relationships, their ideas, and their institutions.'[1]

Taking as its period the twenty years or so before the First World War, this study attempts to define the pattern of working-class life as it was lived then. This was a time of social change, to say the very least. The era of cooperative political effort between labour 'aristocrats' and middle-class radicals was drawing to a close. That partnership had produced legislation to extend the franchise in 1867 and 1884–5, to remodel cities, to improve factory conditions, and to secure the legal status of trade unions. By encouraging self-confidence within the labour movement the alliance also induced workers to develop a set of institutions of their own: Friendly (insurance) Societies, Cooperatives, and the like.

Now, in the late 1880s, the mood altered for reasons – primarily economic – which we shall explore later. Turbulence succeeded cooperation; strife replaced harmony. Though the years from 1890 to 1914 did not witness violence on a scale to equal that which accompanied England's emergence as an industrial nation before 1850, the disturbances were of a magnitude to bring about what one historian has dramatically called 'the strange death of liberal England'.[2] The changes occurring after 1890 helped shape the pattern of working-class culture which we shall examine. By redefining the boundaries of class, change brought workers together – sometimes against their own will – as they had not been before, encouraging in them a fresh sense of their own common interests. Yet by bombarding them with the everlastingly new, circumstance often drove them to seek shelter in habit and tradition.

At the heart of the new consciousness lay a striving for order and predictability within a world that offered the working class very little in that line. Men and women struggled to come to terms with the constant threats of change and uncertainty. The period is witness to what Gareth Stedman Jones has termed 'a remaking of the English working class',[3] concerned with the refining of political consciousness, it is true, but even more with the definition of a reassuring – and particularly working-class – way of life. That concern, central to the general consciousness of the working class in the years before the First World War, is therefore central to this study.

Before we look at the life of the working class, we must at least attempt a definition of the class itself. Whom do we admit? Whom do we exclude? Marxists argue that it is a man's relationship to the means of production that determines his class. Is he himself an owner, or is he exploited by others who are? That is, for Marx, the ultimate question, and it is an ultimately material one. According to those criteria, we might simply say that we are talking of those ten million or so male manual workers and their wives and families who together comprised more than three-quarters of England's population in 1900.[4] But we can press beyond the statistics to ask, what of those people's consciousness of themselves? When manual workers nowadays are asked what class they belong to, some confound Marx by responding 'middle class'.[5] However surprising such a response, it cannot be set aside. Class is bound to class consciousness. And class consciousness is the subjective understanding, derived from human experience, of one's own position in relation to others. Inseparable from that understanding are its manifestations: attitudes towards family, neighbourhood, or job. This consciousness is what Thompson means by class as 'something which in fact happens'. It may be, in the eyes of a Marxist, 'false' consciousness, in that it fails, according to his terms, to identify itself with the material interests that define the proletariat. (Those manual workers who call themselves middle class are a case in point.) Class consciousness must presume some perception on an individual's part of his relationship to the means of production. But 'class consciousness' means as well a sense of one's relationship to other human beings, to those who appear alike, and to those who appear different.

In factory or workshop a sense of participating with many others, or with only a very few others, in some common enterprise might either strengthen or weaken that worker's sense of class. A set of company regulations, impersonally administered, would encourage him to think of himself and his mates as members together in a community; their experience in opposition to their masters would encourage a consciousness of that community as working class. Men at work under the direct supervision of an owner-manager, and hoping that they might some day rise themselves to manage the labour of others, would experience a sense of community as well. But community for them would not be bounded by class as it would for the factory hand. Even though they earned not a penny more in their workshop than a counterpart in the mill, their class consciousness would not in all probability be as highly sensitized as his.

The social experience of neighbourhood life contributed its share to the making of working-class consciousness. Richard Hoggart writes of the community in working-class neighbourhoods, 'not very self-conscious', drawing its strength

> ... chiefly from a knowledge, born of living close together, that one is inescapably part of a group, from the warmth and security that knowledge can give, from the lack of change in the group, and from the frequent need to turn to a neighbour since services cannot often be bought.[6]

Class consciousness, in neighbourhoods such as these, was fed by tradition. One was working class, whatever one's job, because one grew up in a neighbourhood that was working class: 'I was born in the slums of London of working-class parents and although I have attained a higher standard of living, I still maintain I am working class.'[7]

Hoggart adds that most people who feel themselves fixed tight within the life of a working-class neighbourhood, and who relish that feeling, stop short of attaching themselves, in any conscious way, to 'the working-class movement'. Yet some do just that, achieving class consciousness through political experience whose roots lie within neighbourhood life. John Foster has suggested that where working-class neighbourhoods housed skilled workers and labourers together and stood apart from the rest of the town, as they did in early nineteenth-century Oldham, class politics could flourish as they could not elsewhere.[8] Indigenous working-class leadership could direct the attack of the rank and file against an easily identifiable enemy. Economic circumstance pre-ordained class antagonisms between workers and masters; local geography unquestionably helped to articulate them.

13

Class consciousness cannot exist without some awareness of opposition. But opposition need not imply constant and volatile antagonism. To the Victorian working man it might mean a strike. Far more often it meant irony or disdain, privately nurtured and on occasion – at the music hall, for example – publicly expressed. 'I live in Trafalgar Square', the tramp sings, 'with four lions to guard me.' He asks his audience to join him in mocking overstuffed West End toffs:

> There's many a swell up in Park Lane tonight
> Who'd be glad if he only had my appetite.

He is not singing in order to raise a mob: let the swells stay where they are. He likes it where he is: 'If it's good enough for Nelson, it's quite good enough for me.'[9] As Colin MacInnes, the historian of the music halls, noted, songs of this sort bespeak an acceptance of the social order. They are assertive, but only as the expression of a distinct culture.[10]

Opposition was a consequence of economic fact. As long as men and women earned less than a pound a week, as long as even a skilled workman with a large family remained condemned to a graceless life of semi-poverty, there would be consciousness of 'them' and 'us'. A wage of twenty shillings a week meant that whatever one's 'social experiences', one could not simply think oneself out of the working class. No more did a packet of over twice that amount automatically place one somewhere among the ill-defined ranks of the lower middle class.[11] Here 'social experience', at home, in the shop, in the factory, did play its part in determining one's class consciousness, in locating a working man in his own eyes and in the eyes of his neighbours somewhere either firmly inside or apart on the upper fringes of the working class.

Vast numbers of men and women had no trouble in fixing themselves and their acquaintances in that way. The Salford factory operative, living in a two-up, two-down brick house, one of twelve in a drearily 'respectable' terrace; handing his wife the weekly pay packet and hoping she could make do with it; sending his children to a Board school until they came of age and took their place inside the mill; voting Lib-Lab or Labour, or not bothering to vote at all: that man was conscious of himself as working class. His friends, similarly circumstanced, thought of him, as they thought of themselves, as working class. And we need not hesitate to call him that as well. But what of the trade union functionary, once a mill hand but years away from the mill, and miles away in semi-detached comfort from the Salford of his youth, wearing his dark suit, his heavy watch chain, his high hat; apologizing, as often as not, on behalf of employers, and defending himself against attacks from his rank and file for doing so. Did he possess a working-class consciousness? And what of the Salford shopkeeper, living amidst her customers, extending them credit, as much a part of their neighbourhood and as poor as they were? Did her occupation separate her from the working class, no matter what her consciousness had taught her to assume?[12] In these instances the historian must try to understand where these people placed themselves, before attempting to attach his own labels to their consciousness.

Working-class consciousness, rooted, as Thompson insists, in pre-industrial images and impulses,[13] could not have flourished outside the urban culture produced by an industrial revolution. That social upheaval destroyed the web of an older social order. Though demanding much from the poor in return for very little, the network of responsibilities and obligations had provided the lower ranks with a sense of place. Industrialization forced the men and women of the new working class, and of the new middle class, to understand afresh their position within the social structure.

Capitalist expansion, which brought with it both enterprise on a larger and more impersonal scale, and periodic financial instability and depression, ensured increasing division along class lines in the years after 1870. Trade unions, 'new model' or otherwise, were the clearest expression of that division. Although still without a political party of its own, a segment of the working class had, in 1867, gained the vote and, with it, renewed political participation, if not political class consciousness. The debates on reform in the late 1860s had encouraged all elements of society openly to acknowledge class, as opposed to ranks or orders, as a fact of life. Political harangues led working-class listeners to a sense of their own identity; other, often subtler changes – a loss of faith, for example – might induce men and women to transform shared beliefs into a common battle against middle-class antagonists. George Sturt, the biographer of the rural working class, makes the point when chronicling 'the angriest recognition of class differences' he ever encountered. Two old women, returning from the county court, were castigating the magistrates who had fined a friend. ' "Ah!" one of them was saying with spiteful emphasis, "There'll come a great day for they to have *their* judge, same as we *poor* people." ' Sturt notes that the sentiment 'was too antiquated to mean much'.[14] Most working-class men and women, and certainly most of the urban working class, had ceased by 1880 to rely upon the Last Judgment for the retribution they believed was owed them. For years the middle class had attempted to persuade the poor to seek their reward in heaven, little thinking that the poor, if they thought of heaven at all, might pray not so much for their own salvation as for the damnation of their earthly tormentors. But now, as religion lost whatever slim hold it may have had upon the urban working class, men and women awakened to the thought that redress, if not vengeance, might be theirs, and not the Lord's.[15]

In no area did the divisions dictated by economic circumstance more clearly manifest themselves than in that of law and attitudes towards the law. Workers mistrusted it, were confused by it, and had as little to do with it as possible. Throughout the nineteenth century unions and workers struggled for security and recognition within a hostile legal environment. The Master and Servant Act, which sanctioned arrest and punishment by prison for the working man, while subjecting his employer to a civil action only, was a particular grievance until its repeal in 1875. The punishment of twenty-four London gas-stokers with prison sentences of six weeks' hard labour for having demanded the reinstatement of a fellow employee was but one of many instances during the early 1870s when the Act was put to use against workers. Trade unionists found themselves facing a new set of legal obstacles once employers awoke to the threat of renewed trade unions after 1889, and to their own increased power to combat that threat. The Taff Vale decision of 1901, which held unions liable for damages incurred by individual members during a strike, and the Osborne judgment of 1909, which declared that unions could not levy dues for political purposes, were only the two most severe in a long series of legal setbacks. *Temperton v. Russell* (1893) ruled against boycotts. *Trollope v. London Building Trades Federation* (1895) declared that union officers who published blacklists of non-union firms and free labourers were guilty of conspiracy. *Lyons v. Wilkens* (1899) pronounced against picketing, if it was determined to be 'picketing to persuade' – an interpretation which inclined one judge to remark that 'you cannot make a strike effective without doing more than what is lawful'.[16] *Charnock v. Court* (1899) found two union men guilty of 'watching and besetting' after attempting to persuade strike breakers in Halifax to return to Ireland and offering to pay their fare.[17] *Quinn v. Leathem* (1901) overturned an earlier decision favouring the Boilermakers' attempt to establish a closed shop. All the opinions showed the courts in a mood to do all they could to curb unions and prohibit strikes.

What workers found most repellent was the obvious double standard. The Law Lords condemned the unions' boycotts and black lists but sanctioned them when instigated by a shipowners' cartel.[18] The

Osborne judgment placed obstacles in the path of union officers, but not in the way of railway directors, who wished to sit in Parliament. Little wonder that the working class welcomed opportunities to clamour against such patent unfairness. 'Our courts are centres of corruption,' Ben Tillett thundered, 'and our judges are class creatures and instruments for the maladministration of the law. Our experience with solicitors has been but little better, for these have in notable cases been but blackmailers.'[19] Despite the rhetoric, the implied demands were by no means revolutionary. If they echoed class consciousness, in the sense of a class 'apart', they represented as well a desire on the part of the working class to be considered an equal partner in society as already constituted.

Hostile judgments were by no means the sole source of working-class disaffection for the law. In many areas – debt, divorce, compensation, the selection of juries – the law conspired in explicit ways against the wage earner and the propertyless.[20] The law on imprisonment for debt, though reformed in 1869, nevertheless contained a pitfall for the poor in the form of a provision that a debtor could be imprisoned if it could be proved that since the date of the order or judgment in his case 'he has or *has had*' the means to pay. 'Of course,' wrote a sympathetic commentator in 1914,

> . . . it is generally provable that, although he has no present means to pay a debt, he *has had* since the judgment, means to pay which he has spent on the maintenance of his family, or, if you will, on beer or tobacco, or picture palaces, or in a word, as good solvent middle-class people would say – improvidently.[21]

Insolvent middle-class people declared bankruptcy and avoided prison altogether.

Reforms in the laws regarding divorce and the rights of women were also of little practical value. Though acknowledging that a wife did possess nominal rights, they made it almost impossible for the working-class wife to enforce them. Should she wish to obtain a judicial separation, for example – the cost of divorce removing that remedy completely from her reach – 'her path towards it', observed the social worker Anna Martin, 'resembles an obstacle race which has been arranged with the express view of deterring all but the most reckless aspirants from the course'.[22] First, if charging mistreatment, she was called to produce two shillings for a summons, or visible evidence of injuries convincing enough to induce the magistrate to issue one free. Should she wish to obtain an order on the grounds of 'failure to maintain', she had first to leave her husband's roof, taking her children with her and, unless able to prevail upon a friend or relative for shelter, find and furnish a room before applying to the court. Meanwhile her furniture, by law the property of her husband, must remain with him. Even supposing a woman able to accomplish these necessary preliminaries, the chances of her receiving regular maintenance payments from her estranged husband were slim. Appeals to the court for help in obtaining the money met frequently with indifference. 'As far as the writer's experience goes,' Martin comments, 'the woman who worries the police-court officials concerning her husband's non-payment ... is soon made to feel she is a foolish and unpopular person.'[23] If, all else failing, the wife submitted her case to the Poor Law Guardians, the Guardians would, if they found the husband, first make him repay them their expenses for keeping his family. Then they might press him for further payments, but only if they could establish his ability to make them on a continuing basis, a situation so difficult to prove in the case of ordinary labourers, 'that nine out of ten men escape, and the tenth one would if he knew the law'.[24] Though in cases of this sort a woman's primary antagonist, her husband, was, like her, a member of the working class, her resentment extended to the middle-class institution which abetted him in his irresponsibility.

Police, executors of laws made by others, were the objects of general mistrust within working-class neighbourhoods. Few expected the police to do them any favours. Most memories are of the fear engendered by their presence. A lookout warned other children of their approach: 'He'd say, heads up, tails down and they'd fly for their life.' Often police 'took the cape' to children playing in the street. Exasperated working-class mothers tried to restore order by threatening 'to fetch a policeman on you'.[25] Because policemen were almost invariably from working-class backgrounds, their constant presence as an alien force within the working-class community smarted as a betrayal. Policemen clubbed strikers and sheltered blacklegs. Policemen worked while others went on the parish. 'Well there's one thing Ah'd like t'know,' snorts a character in Walter Greenwood's *Love on the Dole*, '... if tha knows all about it ... how thee and thy mates have the cheek to hold hand out for wages just f' walkin' about streets ... N' wonder folk call it a bobby's job.'[26]

As so often happened, a joke half dissolved the bitterness. Policemen were standard music hall fare:

> As I walks along my beat
> You can hear my 'plates of meat' [feet]
> And the girls all look enchanted.

> You can safely bet a pound
> I am always to be found,
> But never when I am wanted.[27]

Music hall songs helped workers come to terms with a middle-class world. Making it bearable, however, did not make it more understandable or any less threatening and distant.

No more did well-meaning middle-class patronage. Often intended as a device to bridge the social gulf, it generally failed in its attempt. The carefully planned parties of Canon Barnett and his wife at Toynbee Hall offered the poor not so much a bridge as a hurried flight into a foreign world and then back again to the reality of a dirty slum.[28] Middle-class philanthropists were loathe to believe the working class capable of managing its own life. Henry Solly, entrepreneur of the Workingmen's Club movement, insisted that 'gentlemen' sit on the governing committee to prevent 'jealousies' and 'dissension' from arising, as he believed they would, if working men took matters into their own hands.[29] Often patronage was so crude as to appear willfully demeaning. The headmaster of a Walworth School, 'noticing two brothers who seemed very weak and languid', asked if they were hungry:

> 'Yes, sir,' was the answer, 'we have had nothing to eat for two days.' To test the truth of this statement Mr Libby sent out for a pennyworth of the stalest bread that could be obtained; this he gave to the boys, and they devoured it ravenously. Believing this to be no isolated case, though perhaps a specially bad one, Mr Libby enlisted the sympathy and help of his fellow-teachers, and the Scholars' Free Meal Fund was started.[30]

Nor was it just the very poor or the very young who received this sort of treatment. A middle-class man or woman, speaking 'proper' English, addressed members of the working class much as many world tourists today address 'natives':

> As a whole, the middle and upper classes, self-confident to arrogance, kept two modes of address for use among the poor: the first was a kindly *de haut en bas* form in which each word, of usually one syllable, was clearly enunciated; the second had a loud, self-assured, hectoring note. Both seemed devised to ensure that though the hearer might be stupid he would know enough in general to defer at once to breeding and superiority. Hospital staff, doctors, judges, magistrates, officials and the clergy were experts at this kind of social intimidation; the trade unionist in his apron facing a well-

dressed employer knew it only too well. It was a tactic, conscious or not, that confused and 'overfaced' the simple and drove intelligent men and women in the working class to fury.[31]

Some chose to publicize their fury. A 'mill girl', writing from Lancashire to the *Daily Herald* in 1913, took out after the 'interfering busybodies' who, having seen the play *Hindle Wakes*, which dealt with the seduction of a young factory girl by her employer's son, began to lecture working girls on their morals:

> We are getting a trifle restive, we are feeling inclined to shove an oar in, if only to keep the boat rocking, and next time a play of this kind is produced, let it be looked upon as a play and an artistic achievement and not as a criterion of any particular section ... I can assure those persons who are trembling for our moral welfare that they can safely send their daughters to the Lancashire cotton mills without any fear that there would be a cotton-master's son in a five hundred guinea motor car waiting round the nearest corner to lure them off to Llandudno.[32]

Most members of the working class had neither time nor inclination for this sort of overt antagonism. Rather than chafe at their supposed 'betters', they turned their backs on them. To Paul Thompson's and Thea Vigne's question about 'people in other classes', a boilermaker's daughter who had grown up before the First World War replied: 'They seemed snobby to me. And when they were snobby, I hadn't time for them.'[33]

Aloofness could imply a determination to believe 'us' superior, in some general and usually hard to define sense, to 'them'. Most often superiority expressed itself not as hostility or 'active contempt', but as a kind of cheerful tolerance, which again was often heard in music hall songs. Aloofness might at the same time imply a willingness to let 'them' get on with their business, whatever it might be, and in that sense to defer to 'them' in matters that were considered their particular province. 'Passive acquiescence,' Gordon Allport has written, '... is sometimes the only way in which a seriously threatened [member of a] minority can survive ... By agreeing with his adversary he escapes being conspicuous, has no cause for fear, and quietly leads his life in two compartments: one (more active) among his own kind, one (more passive) in the outer world.'[34] Though not members of a minority, late Victorian working-class men and women might feel themselves 'seriously threatened' when standing alone against the authority of middle-class institutions and their representatives, and resort in defence to just the sort of game referred to by Allport. Hoggart describes what he calls 'the 'Orlick spirit': 'The "I ain't a gentleman, you see" attitude; a dull dog-in-the-manger refusal to accept anything higher than one's own level of response.'[35]

Consciously or unconsciously the players assumed their inherent superiority. Others deferred, however, not as part of a game, but out of habit and a belief in their own social inferiority. Local schoolteachers and clergymen were admired as often as despised.[36] Deference was for many a simple matter of financial necessity: 'We looked up to the people that was better off than us. Because a lot of them that we met . . . – mother and our family – were good to us. So we . . . looked to them really for help.'[37] For others, deference was a natural state of mind. A working-class school child, drilled to rise when visitors – invariably middle-class – entered the classroom, was astonished when the students rose for his own father: 'The afternoon master goes to the door, opens the door, and a little man comes behind him – and everybody stood up. It was my father. I felt about that size. I never thought . . . it'd apply to him.'[38]

Though distances and distinctions remained pronounced for most workers throughout the nineteenth century, a minority was able to live within a borderland between lower middle and working class. Eric Hobsbawm has described a 'composite stratum' of skilled craftsmen, small tradesmen and the like in his essay on the labour aristocracy. He draws evidence of its existence from reports of the Departmental Committee on Pupil Teachers, which list the backgrounds of the students at teacher training colleges: 'labourers, mechanics or small shopkeepers'; 'artisan class and tradesmen class'; 'clerks and a certain proportion of foremen or cashiers in shops'.[39] John Foster, in his study of Oldham, credits a threatened middle class with the creation of a tame 'aristocracy' in self-defence, and implies that the pattern he has defined may well have repeated itself in other industrial communities at mid-century. Proof of the continuing existence of some sort of socio-economic middle ground appears in a 1912 survey of the cotton trade, in which two statisticians reported that a number of current employers had originated from just such territory.[40] One must qualify their conclusions – query, for example, the number of former clerks as opposed to the number of former operatives questioned. Still, the evidence helps sustain the hypothesis of a 'composite stratum' and the notion that movement up within it or indeed up and out of it was by no means uncommon during much of the nineteenth century.

A well-paid 'aristocrat' might feel no compulsion to move in that way, particularly if he enjoyed the respect of his petty tradesman neighbour. Another worker, similarly skilled and paid, yet living with a sense of his own social disadvantages, might determine to use his wits and his privileged position to leave the working-class altogether – or to help his children do so. That decision was usually as difficult as it was personal. An Assistant Relieving Officer in London, interviewed by social workers in 1891, described for them his ascent into the lower middle class. His father, a warehouseman who had been apprenticed as a cabinet maker, died when his son was fourteen. The boy had already left school for a job as furniture porter, though a clerkship had been promised him. With his father dead, 'the struggle for existence began, but we never asked or received charity of any description, and always managed to dress well and live in respectable houses'. His mother worked, his sister worked, and he continued work until he was almost seventeen, when, 'owing to a quarrel with one of the men, a drunkard, I refused to work with him and was fined 2s 6d for insubordination, refused to pay it and left . . .' Applying for a clerkship with the railways, as he had several years before, he received an appointment at £35 per year. Four years later he competed successfully for his present position, at which point he felt himself at liberty to marry his sweetheart, a shop assistant.

Though marked by the death of their first child and the continued illness of his dependent mother, their marriage was a total success in terms of its lower middle-class propriety:

> My wife plays the piano and sings very well and I play the violin a little. I am also a member of the church choir. We have a good many friends to visit, who visit us, and we go to theatres and concerts as often as we can afford it, or get free passes, and when we are at home alone we amuse ourselves with music and reading . . .[41]

What was it that implanted the feet of that working-class child on the path to lower middle-class respectability? His mother, in all probability, who sent him to a Voluntary Church school, who encouraged him to sing in the choir, and who asked favours of no one. He rewarded her by leading the life she wanted him to lead and by supporting her in her declining years.

Women, according to Robert Roberts, could more easily move outside their class than men. He recounts how his own grandmother,

> . . . widowed early with four children, had had the foresight to bypass a mission hall near the alley where she lived and send her three good-looking daughters to a Wesleyan chapel on the edge of a middle-class suburb. Intelligent girls, they did their duty by God

and mother, all becoming Sunday school teachers and each in turn marrying well above her station, one a journalist, another a traveller in sugar, and a third a police inspector – an ill-favoured lot, the old lady grumbled, but 'you can't have everything'.[42]

Domestic service offered within its upper reaches an occasional opportunity for advancement to those intelligent enough to have progressed from scullery to parlour or boudoir, but without the inclination to work in a shop or the ambition to educate themselves to teach school. 'All my servants who have married,' wrote one woman in answer to an inquiry from the Women's Industrial Council, 'after being with me many years, have married tradesmen in good positions – some with property.'[43] Far more often, however, domestic service stigmatized a young woman in the eyes of her contemporaries. According to a London cook, aged thirty-one:

> I consider servants are a despised race. Not by the ladies, but by girls of their own class who are in business ... When I go to a seaside place and board where there are a number of business girls, I never enlighten them as to how I earn my living ... Of course there are exceptions. I have two very dear friends (of years standing), who are school teachers and several others who are in shops. They are, of course, made of the right stuff and if I ever say 'servant' to them, they invariably say – 'It is not what you do, it is what you are.'[44]

Those remarks illustrate how complex this whole business of class can become. The woman's occupation would, according to most sociologists' criteria, place her within the working class. Artisans, according to a social survey of the time, considered domestic service 'a calling much below themselves'.[45] And indeed, the cook's 'dear friends' demean her with their comforting remarks. Yet the cook, for reasons, perhaps, of psychic survival, ranks *herself* with 'business girls', shop assistants and school teachers. Where do *we* put her? Marriage to a London tradesman or to a mill hand from her native town would solve the problem for us. Until then, we shall be forced to leave her in limbo.

Although she was by no means alone there, economic and social facts of life were, by 1890, reducing the number of those living within the sociological spaces between lower middle and working class. External circumstance and an internalized consciousness of those circumstances operated to mark off clearer class boundary lines. Hobsbawm writes of a layer of 'white-collar workers, and, to a lesser extent, of technicians and independently recruited managers', wedged by the force of imperialist capitalism against skilled workers and artisans, '. . . reducing their relative social position, and limiting their chances of promotion, and creating an "alternative hierarchy" of civil and local government servants and teachers.'[46]

Booth noted that by 1890 artisans in London had ceased to push their children into clerical positions, realizing '. . . that an occupation [in the building trades] that secures 9½d an hour is not to be despised, and that a common, dusty coat may after all be better than the formal broadcloth of shop and counting-house.'[47] And clerks, though perhaps only a generation removed from the working class – perhaps because of that very proximity – held themselves apart. 'Numerous as clubs are in London', a working-class commentator noted wryly in the working men's *Club and Institute Journal*,

> . . . there are few where the average clerk can be found. Whether his small wages – I beg pardon, salary – will not allow him to indulge in club life I know not, but it is undeniably the fact that the clerk is conspicuous by his absence. Possibly his tastes bear no comparison with his pocket, and he scorns the idea of mixing with 'working men'. The clerk of 25s a week for monotonous work looks down on the plumber at £2 for 48 hours. The possessor of money generally obtains respect, but the fact of high wages obtained by workmen rarely leads the clerk to admire the working plumber. There is a great gulf between them and they are often as far apart as an aristocrat and a commoner.[48]

While this new white collar army stood guard against skilled workers on the boundary of the lower middle class, technological change was turning some of those 'aristocrats' back into the ranks of their less fortunate working-class comrades. In many trades, workers could no longer distinguish with any assurance between skilled and semi-skilled labour. Competition from new machines and the threat of consequent downgrading increased the working-class consciousness of those threatened by loss of either pay or status.[49]

Revelations at the turn of the century of conditions endured by the poorest members of the working class further served to heighten class differences. Though the surveyors themselves took care to draw distinctions between segments of the working class, their overall conclusions encouraged the sense of a straightforward division between 'us' and 'them'. 'In an average year,' L. G. Chiozza Money reported in his significantly titled *Riches and Poverty*, '27,500 persons die worth £257,000,000 while 686,500 persons die worth only £29,000,000.' Chiozza Money was but one of many to call attention to the contrast in infant mortality rates between rich and poor wards in England's cities: 331 per 1000 in the impoverished St Mary's ward, Birmingham; 133 per 1000 in suburban Edgbaston.[50] A working-class woman concerned enough to purchase *The Woman Worker* could feed her grievances on material such as this:

> An English millionaire has ordered an airship seven hundred feet long with all the luxuries of a hotel. A poor woman stated at a city inquest that she, her husband, and five children, had been trying to exist on sixpence a week.[51]

Freed from Victorian restraints and enjoying a resurgence of profits, the Edwardian rich were spending money freely and ostentatiously, in a manner which workers would both hear about and resent.

Though circumstances pushed labour aristocracy into closer communion with labour rank and file, tradition operated with equal force to keep them apart. For most of the nineteenth century the gulf between them had been wide. John Burns evoked the distinctions when he contrasted 'old' (skilled) and 'new' (unskilled) as they met together at the Conference of the Trades Union Congress in 1890:

> Physically the 'old' unionists were much bigger than the 'new'. And that, no doubt, is due to the greater intensity of toil during the last twenty or thirty years ... the 'old' delegates differed from the 'new' not only physically but in dress. A great number of them looked like respectable city gentlemen; wore very good coats, large watch chains and high hats – and in many cases were of such splendid build and proportions that they presented an aldermanic, not to say a magisterial dignity.
>
> Amongst the 'new' delegates not a single one wore a tall hat. They looked workmen. They were workmen. They were not such sticklers for formality or court procedures, but were guided more by common sense.[52]

Burns noted that both 'old' and 'new' recognized a need to cooperate:

> The 'old' see that labour-saving machinery is reducing the previously skilled to the level of unskilled labour ... the 'new' believe that ... class prejudices that have disintegrated the labour movement in the past must be abolished.

Yet the words Burns uses to contrast the two groups – 'workmen', as against 'craftsmen'; 'rough', as against 'respectable' – suggest, correctly, that the amalgamation of old and new would not be easily accomplished.

That 'old' unionist's skill had set him apart; the distinction he derived from his ability to accomplish a variety of technically difficult operations was as precious to him as the higher wage his ability could command:

> The craftsman always held himself aloof – sort of a little bit above the labourer. The labourer . . . can only do what he's told, but the craftsman, well he's responsible for it's being turned out . . . They looked . . . up to you as somebody responsible . . . they knew that you had the full authority . . .[53]

Often with the authority went money enough to lead a fairly decent life. Hobsbawm declares the level and regularity of a worker's earnings 'incomparably the most important factors' in determining a worker's membership in the nineteenth-century labour aristocracy.[54] If change now threatened to take from him both his skill and its tangible reward – a higher wage – even an orator of John Burns's abilities could hardly expect to persuade him that common cause with his less skilled and poorer fellow-workers would provide eventual compensation for his loss.[55]

Trapped as he was between circumstance and tradition, losing ground and afraid to lose it, Burns's 'old' unionist – and his family with him – would tend to cling the harder to the concrete and ready-to-hand distinction the working class had long ago made between 'rough' and 'respectable'. Respectability meant the effort to maintain certain standards and the determination not to let things slide. Prosperity did not, by itself, ordain respectability, any more than poverty proscribed it. But, naturally enough, it was harder to stay respectable on twenty shillings a week than on thirty-five or forty. Public worship, for example, might afford the chance to establish oneself in the sight of one's neighbours. Yet church for most was unthinkable without Sunday clothes, one fact why so few among the poor were seen in church on Sundays. Those who could not afford a Sunday suit, who, if they walked abroad in 'respectable' neighbourhoods were forced to do so in their work clothes, chose to remain inside.[56] In the words of a Keighley labourer, who claimed to belong to a 'poor, respectable family': 'It takes something to be poor and respectable.'[57]

Often, respectability meant little more than a mother's determination to isolate her children from 'roughs' in the next turning. 'Keep yourself to yourself', became the watchword. 'I think its the way we were brought up. It's just the same with my girls, with me. They keep themselves to themselves; they've got friends, naturally, but we never got in with . . . rough people.'[58] 'If I saw them outside I always spoke to them, just say hello . . . as I passed. But I never went down into the street and had any connection with them.'[59] That Darlington boiler-maker's daughter undoubtedly listened to more than one lecture from her mother on working-class politesse, on the way one might 'just say hello' and then hurry home, respectable both in the greeting and in the rebuff. 'There is no desire more firmly implanted in the mind of the respectable working woman', reported Parliamentary investigators in 1910,

> . . . than to keep her children from undesirable associates, and from hearing and seeing what goes on in a low class district. She knows better than anyone else the harm which such association can do. She will sacrifice, not only money, but health itself to this desire, by keeping her children within stuffy little rooms rather than let them play in the streets.[60]

When a rise in wages permitted, such a mother would encourage a move to a more respectable neighbourhood, since whole streets or blocks of streets bore labels known to those who lived within them. If an area was 'rough', everyone there was assumed to be rough as well. Those struggling to achieve respectability, if they could not move away, might begin to believe what others said of them.

'Respectable' meant attention to a strict but uncomplicated list of 'don'ts': swearing, except at work; drinking, in excess of an occasional weekend pint or two; gambling; persistent rowing; sexual promiscuity on the part of mother or daughters. These were social sins that, money or no money, would fasten a label to a family which only removal from the district could erase:

> I only swore once. I didn't swear again! That was when I was in the bath. I took a book up [off the floor] to read . . . and I let it drop. I said 'Oh, damn.' Oh, did I get it! No, you hadn't to swear.[61]

Respectability became a family enterprise; its achievement depended upon cooperation from the entire membership and an understanding that collective reputation took precedence over personal preference. Adolescent girls were warned away from jobs which, whatever the pay, had come to be considered 'low'. Spinning had a bad reputation, in part because of the loose smocks which girls donned in the heat of the sheds. Not unnaturally, the rougher the work, the less suitable it was deemed for the respectable girl. Only rough girls, for example, would work at tin plate pickling:

> No girl from a respectable family would do this sort of work. The girls who did work there were well known for their loose living and bad language. If a respectable family . . . heard that one of its boys

had an attachment for a girl who worked in the pickling section, they would be very worried indeed. On the other hand, the girls working on the plate-opening came from ordinary working-class families of course – but Chapel-going respectable families and certainly there was nothing against them.[62]

The evidence exudes respectability to the point that one is inclined to forget the 'roughs', until one encounters descriptions such as the following, an account from a story by Arthur Morrison of a Saturday night tram-car ride from Stratford to Bow in East London:

> From divers quarters of the roof came a bumping thunder as of cellar-flapping clogs. Profanity was sluiced down, as it were, by pailfuls from above, and was swilled back, as it were, in pailfuls from below. Blowsers in feathered bonnets bawled hilarious obscenity at the jiggers. A little maid with a market basket hustled and jostled and elbowed at the far end, listened eagerly, and laughed when she could understand; and the quiet mechanic, whose knees had been invaded by an unsteady young woman in a crushed hat, tried to look pleased.[63]

'Respectability' did not efface the pubs, the music halls, the tough humour, the street fights. The constant struggle of would-be 'respectables' – that quiet mechanic, for example – to rise above what was earthy and sometimes seamy is in itself testimony to the vitality of the 'rougher' strain.

A working-class wife without lace curtains had to prove her respectability with freshly whitened doorstep and freshly blackened grate. Often ferociously house-proud, she was the bane of middle-class social workers, who urged her to spend less time on her hands and knees and more time with her children or by herself. 'For God's sake, women,' trumpeted Ethel Carnie in *The Woman Worker*,

> ... go out and play. Instead of staring round to see what needs polishing and rubbing, go out into the open and draw the breath of the moors or the hills into your lungs. Get some of the starshine and sunlight into your souls, and do not forget that you are something more than a dishwasher . . .[64]

Easy enough to say, if you were yourself an 'emancipated' middle-class writer. But difficult to do, if you felt yourself burdened, not just with the chores of keeping a large family housed in four rooms and fed on ten or twelve shillings a week, but with the daily compulsion to prove your family respectable, to your neighbours and to yourself. We must avoid equating the compulsion with nothing more than excessive attention to the cleanliness of the grate. Respectability meant keeping one's self-respect, holding one's own against 'them'. Pursuit of respectability was not, for most, pursuit of the middle class.[65] Certainly some within the 'aristocratic' minority aspired to middle-class status. Others within that minority – trade union officials, for instance, carried off by the very success of their endeavours into a kind of bureaucratic class limbo – re-classed themselves without ever fully realizing the fact. The vast majority of workers, however, understood that the level of their wages would never permit them to 'get on' in the sense of moving up and out of the working class. Their struggle to attain respectability reflected nothing more than their desire, in the face of brutally disheartening economic facts, to lead an independent, orderly, and less than brutal existence.

# 2 House, neighbourhood and kin

LIFE IN A LATE Victorian working-class slum too often meant death. Population in the great industrial areas of central and northern England as much as doubled between 1870 and 1900. Workers bore the brunt of the resulting pressure. Railways and factories ringed their neighbourhoods, preventing any sort of orderly urban growth and dispersion. Overcrowding, by exacerbating wretched sanitary conditions, helped ensure that the working class suffered more than its statistical share of sickness and mortality. Manchester, in 1900, provided but one water tap for an entire street in many working-class districts.[1] Of 2,956 houses inspected in the poorer area of Bristol between 1910 and 1913, 2,276 proved defective; London inspectors served notices for repairs and sanitary defects on approximately 50,000 houses a year, the great majority inhabited by members of the lower middle or working class.[2] The existence of an inspectorate demonstrates growing official concern for conditions within the cities. The fact, however, that in Manchester each inspector was assigned responsibility for almost 3,900 houses argues that officialdom at best underestimated the magnitude of the problems it faced.

The less a neighbourhood's inhabitants could earn, the more derelict and deadly its environment grew. In London, a neighbourhood of peripatetic casual labourers resembled

> ... some article that has for long years been let out on hire to innumerable owners and now is past all repair. Each tenant patches the damage of his predecessor, adds his own contribution to the general dilapidation, and then hands it on to his successor, a flimsily adherent aggregation of cracks, holes, and yawning chasms.[3]

In neighbourhoods where men remained for any length of time unemployed, house fronts bore broad, dirty marks at hip level, testimony to the habit of men and boys 'standing, leaning a bit forward, as they smoke their pipes, and watching whatever may be going on in the street while above and below, the mortar is picked or kicked from between the bricks'.[4]

Respectability insisted upon neatness and cleanliness wherever possible. Windows and doorsteps in the neighbourhoods of steadily employed semi-skilled or skilled workers shone out in contrast to dingy brick or cobbles: 'Nowhere in London do streets exhibit a more precise uniformity, in every external attribute of the dwelling, than they do here.' Men and women seemed at least to one observer to submit themselves, along with their doorsteps, to a polishing process 'that removes and smooths down all knobs of individuality before they are permitted to occupy one of these spotless tenements'.[5]

Throughout England the sounds and smells in working-class neighbourhoods were much the same. In northern cities the knocker-up travelled the streets before daybreak, scratching at upstairs windows with his homemade device of stick and wires to waken factory workers too poor to own an alarm clock.[6] Next, the rasp of coal shovels across flags; then clogs scraping pavements, as men and women hurried to their factory shift, announced by the shrill summons of the hooter. All day long, machinery hummed in factories close at hand; trains whistled on embankments nearby; these sounds punctuated by those the children made as they trooped back and forth to school. Smells were as prevalent, and harder to ignore, than sounds. Outdoor closets, shared by more than one household and therefore the responsibility of none save, perhaps, a careless landlord, too often remained unemptied for too long. In many municipalities the Corporation assigned squads to clean out the tin receptacles, reached by a flap door at the back of each privy. Shovelled into open carts, the contents were eventually delivered to neighbouring farms. This activity occurred at night, sparing a neighbourhood an unpleasant sight, if not a more unpleasant stench. In poorer neighbourhoods a good deal of trash found its way, directly or indirectly, onto the street, where it mixed with horse dung to form piles that when frozen were unsightly and when not were a fetid menace. Middle-class visitors to these districts tried to accustom themselves not just to the trash or the night soil, but to what they came to recognize as the smell of poverty itself, the stench of 'grinding life, of shut windows and small inadequate washing basins, of last night's rain, of crowded homes and long working hours'.[7]

Yet no working-class district was quite like any other. Local geography and local industry lent each one distinction, sordid or otherwise. In York, the smell might be from the slaughterhouses; in South London, from the jam factories. In Bradford, the green of the not-too-distant moor might tempt a family for a walk on Sundays. In the potteries another landscape, less pleasing aesthetically, nonetheless invited children to enjoy themselves tobogganing down slag heaps.

31

Wherever the neighbourhood, and whoever its inhabitants, visual monotony was almost certain to be its most distinguishing characteristic. Whether houses were two-up, two-down or larger, back-to-back or open to a court, they stretched the same across the landscape, aligned together at the street's edge, built of a common stone or brick, furnished with but one pattern of cheap stock doors and windows, varying little if at all in general design for blocks on end, unrelieved by trees and only occasionally by flower boxes or by weedy grass plots. The eye searched in vain for something that had not been made by man, and made with a determination to cut costs: 'Grey streets of mean dwelling-houses'; 'nothing is old but everything is shabby'; dwellings, 'punctuated by struggling shops that display tinned foods and galvanized pails; even the few public houses show no sign of prosperity, and the church looks like the surrounding streets – at once new, poor and shabby.'[8]

The sameness could blunt, if it did not destroy, the sensitivities of the human beings within such a landscape. People lent it whatever vitality it possessed, singing and shouting a dingy pub to life, transforming a fourth-rate Saturday night market into a bazaar:

> You will see a pushing, swaying multitude of people, and an endless stream of traffic; hideous buildings that try to hide themselves in the shadows of night; flaring, hissing tongues of flame and glimmering feeble lamps that tear them from their hiding place, row after row of coster barrows weighed down with tempting and deceitful offerings; line upon line of shoddy shops where reeking masses of meat and vegetables and overripe fruit poison the air, and women struggle and fight for tomorrow's dinner.[9]

Walking the length of such a market, Booth remarks, with a fowl under each arm and 'perhaps a flower between their teeth', was for working-class men and women a kind of parade, a chance to move for a time outside the confinement in which their surroundings so often found them.[10]

What W. G. Hoskins has said about the dwellings of Preston factory workers can stand as an epitaph for working-class housing throughout nineteenth-century England: 'Neither good enough to promote happiness nor bad enough to produce hopelessness.'[11] Whatever the workers' mood, those who surveyed the housing situation in most industrial areas at the turn of the century found it difficult to hope for much marked improvement. The major problem was a shortage of houses. In 1891 over 11 per cent of the population of England and Wales lived more than two to a room. In Manchester a 1902 Diocesan survey, taking three to a room as its gauge for overcrowding, discovered that 120,256 people out of a total population of 546,000 lived under conditions that were as bad or worse. Eleven thousand men, women and children lived in 3,288 Liverpool cellars in 1908. Booth, at the time of his London survey, found 109,390 living three or more to a room.[12] Seebohm Rowntree and A. C. Pigou estimated in 1914 that from 65 to 80 per cent of the working class lived in overcrowded accommodation, both in terms of the interior space available and the number of inhabitants per acre. They insisted that the problem existed far beyond the worst slums, that it was just as prevalent in the 'monotonous rows' which marked every working-class district. 'At present,' Rowntree remarked, 'we are not even housing, but only warehousing them.'[13]

The effect in human terms is written into every report issued on working-class conditions before 1914:

> A two-storied house has four rooms and a scullery. Four families occupy it at present, each family consisting of two adults and a child. One water-tap and sink contained in the scullery (which measures 9 feet by 6 feet by 8 feet) serve all four families. The observer notes that the house is very dirty. One pail closet in the street serves for this house and the two neighbouring houses, which each contain two families.[14]

> Man, wife, and six children; four rooms; two beds, one sofa, one banana-crate cot. Wage 22s. One double bed for four people in very small room, crossing the window; cot in corner by bed. One single bed for two people (girls aged thirteen and ten years) in smaller room, 8 feet by 10 feet, with head under the window. One sofa for boy aged eleven years in front downstairs room, where police will not allow window to be open at night. The kitchen, which is at the back, has the copper in it, and is too small for a bed, or even a sofa to stand anywhere.[15]

Rowntree and Pigou attributed the shortage to the fact that potential builders no longer considered real estate a particularly attractive investment. Construction costs rose 10 to 12 per cent between 1904 and 1914, at a time when securities were paying higher dividends than they had in years. Investors saddled by long-term ground leases feared a decline in property values, and were uninterested in improving property they already owned. Land itself remained expensive, however, as industry, railways and various commercial enterprises continued to invade former working-class residential precincts.[16] In Newcastle, between 1891 and 1902, from five to seven thousand houses were converted to shops, almost all within working-class districts. Building costs were particularly high in Sheffield, where workers remained cooped up in overcrowded neighbourhoods while new houses, which they could not afford, stood empty. Industry expanded so rapidly in some areas – around Jarrow, for example – that construction could not keep pace with the continually increasing working-class population.[17] Often overcrowding occurred for the simple reason that landlords, or their agents, determined to squeeze as much money as they could from their properties. Houses divided so as to fetch rents of £40 per year when let to artisans, could be further divided when rented to a poorer clientele, and produce another £20 or so.[18]

As a general rule, the smaller a landlord's investment, the meaner and more overcrowded his properties.[19] With little in the way of funds to expand, the modest investor could be counted on to cut corners, to face his one or two houses with brick but construct the interior walls of rubble, to cement the bricks with mortar made with inferior lime, mixed not with sand but with ashes or road-scrapings; to frame the door and windows with cheap green wood which shrank and cracked and let in unpleasant and unhealthy draughts.

Into the poorest houses went the poorest families. Those who lived in back-to-backs, without windows on three sides and without a yard of any sort behind, dumped ashes in bins by their door and used privies opening directly on to the streets.[20] A through house in a very poor district promised little more comfort than a back-to-back. Two or three houses might give on to a common yard, containing at most two earth closets and an ash pit:

> Very often the flags are broken or loose, simply resting on a bed of filthy mud, and unless one steps about with care, the clothes become bespattered with sludge ejected from beneath the stone upon which the foot has been incautiously placed. The water necessary to keep up this condition is supplied partly by the housewife, who, to save herself trouble, throws her fluid refuse onto the yard floor instead of on the grid; partly from the rainfall, but chiefly from the pool of water which collects round a blocked grid on top.[21]

Inside, a four-roomed house might well contain two or more families. Rooms were tiny – working-class houses, good, bad, and indifferent seldom boasted rooms larger than 10 by 12 feet; ceilings were low. Children slept two and three to a bed. Window sashes which did not shrink to admit unwanted cold swelled shut to trap unwanted heat and smell. Water came from a tap outside, or at best on the ground floor. Cooking, where there was more than one family, meant sharing a tiny scullery and a kitchen range, or making do with a gas ring upstairs. From two to three million people lived in slums such as these in 1914.[22]

Elsewhere of course, other members of the working class lived far more decently. In many communities a small minority of the working class owned its own homes. Rowntree put the figure at 6 per cent for York.[23] Skilled workers, artisans – 'aristocrats' – could expect to live in modest comfort, if not luxury. Houses built for well-paid and steadily employed Birmingham workers in the years between 1878 and 1884 contained an average of from four to five rooms. Constructed in terraces, many featured an ample bay-windowed parlour and a tiny front garden. Behind the front room, the kitchen served as the family's living room, even in these 'superior' houses averaging no more than 100 square feet in area. Small sculleries and smaller pantries afforded a bit of further space indoors. Privies were exterior to the houses, some shared, some private. The two upstairs bedrooms were small – each one about 110 square feet. In some houses attics afforded extra, though unheated, sleeping space.[24] These were the houses of the ultra-respectable:

> Their streets are well-kept, their doorsteps are white, their windows are clean, there are things displayed in the front windows of their houses. Here you will see a big Bible, here a bird-cage with foreign birds – here a glass vase containing coral or Venus fingers from the Philippines, here something from India carved in fragrant wood, here a piece of brasswork from Benares.[25]

> Every house possesses a curtained bow-window, and every curtained bow-window a palm, and every palm emerges from the centre of a china pot. Each door glistens with varnish, at any rate for a time, and boasts an immaculate letter-box surmounted by an immaculate brass knocker.[26]

Between the extremes of the prototypically 'rough' and 'respectable' the vast majority of the working-class population managed to house itself, battling dirt and overcrowding in the struggle for respectability, improvising with an occasional plant or picture to keep deadly monotony at bay. Three, or, at the most, four rooms had to serve families of as many as ten. Often, in a house with four rooms, one was let to a relative or single lodger. Furniture, conspicuous by its absence in the houses of the very poor, so filled the house of an average working-class family as to make general movement difficult. A kitchen might well include a large table, chairs, a dresser, a mantle, and, of course, the range:

The most conspicuous object is the dresser, with its load of gaily coloured crockery; cups and jugs hang from hooks, while plates and saucers are artistically arranged on the shelves. The wall is hidden by a mosaic of garish oleographs, framed in heavy polished wood. Over the mantelpiece straggles a wilderness of quaint china ornaments, with a clock as centrepiece.[27]

With as many as five or six sleeping together, bedrooms were, not surprisingly, furnished with little else but beds:

In the back room which was a fairish size, there was room for two double beds and we had the four girls in the two ... And I think we had a little cot in that room for the smallest of the boys. Then we had another little cot in my mother and father's room for the other boy.[28]

Houses in London, where rents were particularly high, were almost always subdivided in some fashion or other. A respectable working man, earning a bit more or less than thirty shillings a week, could not afford to pay more than eight shillings for housing. And for eight shillings, unless he was very lucky, he could rent no more than three rooms and a scullery. Mrs Pember Reeves, in her 1913 survey of Kennington, discovered a family of ten lucky enough to have found a five-room house for ten shillings. By letting one of the small back bedrooms for two shillings, they could occupy the rest of the house and remain within their budget.[29]

The trick, of course, was to find a pleasant, cooperative lodger or lodgers. Should they be a newly married man and wife, negotiations concerning use of the range, for cooking, and the copper, for washing, had to be amicably concluded, or the ensuing friction might make the extra two shillings seem something less than a windfall. Feuding in such cases was not uncommon, particularly if the lodgers had to pass through the family's living quarters to reach the door to the street. To arrange matters to everyone's satisfaction called for a tact that the overcrowded working-class mother found hard to muster.

Little but the furnishings distinguished these houses from each other. Grime vanquished most attempts to vary them inside or outside with bright paint. Brown hid the dirt and therefore lasted longer; paint was expensive and nowhere to be found in most working-class budgets:

Everything is brown. The doors are painted chocolate brown, while the skirting boards, with their many dust-harbouring convolutions, are painted a more gingery brown; the wall paper in many years has lost most of its colour; it seems now to be a faded khaki with brown snakes and pineapples twining about it. There is no room for a hall stand of any sort; a drain pipe standing on end holds the umbrellas and much dust; a piece of painted belting with hooks holds hats and coats.[30]

Time and again middle-class observers came away from their surveys of working-class housing depressed above all else by the monotony of what they saw, and the hopelessness of doing much to change what they kept seeing. 'The house remains a mere receptacle for the family,' Reginald Bray observed, 'and when the father changes his place of employment he requires but little inducement to change one receptacle for another of precisely similar arrangement.'[31] 'When all is said and done,' Mrs Pember Reeves wrote,

> ... reformers could do very little as long as the present buildings exist at all, or as long as a family of eight persons can only afford two, or at most three, small rooms to live in. The rent is too dear, the houses are too old or too badly built, or both; the streets are too narrow; the rooms are too small; and there are far too many people to sleep in them.[32]

One must handle this evidence cautiously, seen as it is through middle-class eyes and smelled through a middle-class nose. The reports suggest a despair which, though it must have lurked at the fringes of working-class consciousness, most appear to have kept at bay. The Salford of Robert Roberts's working-class memory is grim, but it is not despairing. Toughness – not insensitivity – wins out. Inside their overcrowded, jerry-built houses, men and women pinned up the 'garish oleographs' which Bray appears to disparage, tried to ignore the smell from the privy, and went on with life.

For a time during the late nineteenth century, middle-class social reformers hoped that model tenements might prove a solution to the problems of working-class housing. Philanthropists attempted to prove that flats could be built which would provide a decent life for those who lived in them and, to those who invested in them, a dividend of 5 per cent. Municipal corporations followed suit, and in every large city undertook to build blocks of from four to six stories. By 1900, buildings of this sort were a fact of urban life throughout England.[33]

The middle class gave them a mixed press. Observers could hardly help but acknowledge that in terms of the facilities they afforded, they represented a marked improvement over many of the dwellings they replaced. Regulated in most instances so that occupancy did not exceed one person per room, they afforded tenants more breathing space than was the norm in single- or double-family housing. Yet critics complained that construction costs, and the demand on the part of investors for at least a modest return on their outlay, meant that rents would be high and that therefore tenements could not accommodate those who needed them most. In some localities the cost per room of tenement construction exceeded that of building workman's cottages – in Newcastle by more than twice as much.[34] The result was that most flats of more than two or three rooms were beyond the reach of un-skilled and semi-skilled workers – those who, in most cases, most desperately needed them. Rents appear to have averaged from 2s to 2s 6d per room in most cities; in London they were markedly higher.[35]

Most agreed that it was wrong to characterize tenements altogether as either a 'good' or a 'bad' thing. 'A lady resident' who lived for almost two years in two East London tenements provided Booth with a largely favourable account of life as it was lived there. She remarked, as did all observers, that much depended on the buildings' size and design. 'T Buildings', where she lived for a year – in the comparative comfort of two rooms to herself – consisted of two five-storey wings along a large asphalted court. Each tenement was self-contained, although tenants had to fetch water from a common tap on each balcony. Well cared for by the tenants in turn, the buildings were, according to Booth's informant, a cheery place in which to live. Window boxes and hanging baskets appeared in the summer time, neighbours gossiped and visited easily among themselves. 'S Build-ings', because they were much larger, made neighbourliness far more difficult. Their design – a completely enclosed central courtyard, dark and narrow passages and stairs – helped to produce a quality of life far less pleasant.[36]

Those middle-class reformers most concerned to improve conditions of sanitation and health welcomed tenements as an important step in that direction. Octavia Hill, in other respects a severe critic of tenement life, acknowledged that inspection and regulation, without which any marked improvement in sanitary conditions was impossible, were more easily accomplished in tenements than elsewhere. Yet it was just such regulation that the inhabitants of the tenements found most distasteful. One look at the rules 'to be observed by the tenants in order to secure their mutual comfort' – standard in general terms in cities throughout England – suggests the reasons why. By prohibiting tenants from letting rooms to lodgers, corporations hoped to prevent overcrowding, but often succeeded in dividing widowed parents from married children. By forbidding women to wash any but their family's clothes in the laundries, authorities reduced the level of communal confusion while denying housewives the chance to earn extra money. By ordering boys and girls off stairs and galleries and into courtyards, superintendents won the gratitude of those who craved a bit of peace and quiet and the enmity of 'respectable' mothers anxious to see to it that their children played as little as possible with the 'roughs' who might also inhabit the building.[37]

For those willing to submit to the regulations, life in a tenement could be not only a great deal cleaner than life in an urban cottage, but just as happy. Enough evidence exists, however, to suggest that many of the thousands who lived in 'model' buildings did so out of necessity and without enthusiasm.[38] In an ill-managed tenement a rough and disorderly few might set the tone for a respectable majority, both in terms of conduct and, as important, of reputation. 'No one', Octavia Hill reported in a survey for Booth,

> ... who does not watch the swift degradation of children belonging to tidy families, no one who does not know the terrorism exercised by the rough over the timid and industrious poor, no one who does not know the abuse of every appliance provided by the benevolent or speculative, but non-resident landlord, can tell what life in blocks is where the population is low-class.[39]

The result was that in many tenements residents tried as hard as they could to have almost nothing to do with each other: 'They avoid communication with their neighbours ... They pass each other in sombre silence on the common staircase, and neither brook nor offer interference. Compelled to herd together, they react by drawing apart "in sullen discontent and isolation".'[40]

Where conditions such as those described by Bray prevailed, one lived next door to others, but without neighbours and outside a neighbourhood. Life on a street of small dilapidated cottages could be hard and often depressing, yet it more readily offered families the chance to piece together the social fabric they needed in order to exist with some measure of security. About the working-class need for neighbourhood there can be no doubt. To understand the need we must understand how and why it was that urban workers came to live where they did.

Workers continued to migrate to the great cities of England during the period before the First World War, though not at as rapid a rate as they had in the middle years of the nineteenth century. In 1851, 50 per cent of the population of England lived in towns and cities. By 1911, the figure had risen to 78 per cent.[41] Evidence suggests that, as was the case in the years between 1800 and 1860, most migration was over short distances, from an outlying village into a city centre. Arthur Redford, in his book on early nineteenth-century labour migration, concludes that the increased availability of travel by rail might have encouraged more long-distance labour migration as the century progressed. He contrasts the population of Middlesbrough in 1861, when nearly three-quarters of the people were Yorkshire by birth, with the population just ten years later, when only half were native Yorkshiremen and women, and when 13·3 per cent came from Durham, 3·9 per cent from Wales, and 2·6 from Staffordshire. Numerous personal histories support Redford's contention, and lead one to agree with him that 'improved transport facilities had evidently strengthened industrial migration sufficiently to cause an appreciable (though slight) modification of the general [short-range] trend of movement'.[42]

Will Thorne, the trade union leader, left Birmingham in the 1880s for London, having heard from a friend of a job at the Old Kent Road gas works. After settling in London for less than a year, he lost his job and returned to Birmingham, where he lived with his wife's parents. A dispute with his foreman, however, forced him back again to London where, for the second time in as many years, he once more moved his family. Without the railway this sort of migration would have been unthinkable.[43] For every Will Thorne, however, there were hundreds of others who moved very short distances, and perhaps several times, before settling finally in a major city or industrial area. A survey of 479 Leeds women tailors in 1890 showed 330 born in Leeds. Of the remaining 149, 101 were born within Yorkshire. Examination of the birth place of the mothers and fathers suggests that migration was more common in the third than in the fourth quarter of the century. Over half the fathers and mothers were born outside Leeds; 103 fathers and 115 mothers outside Yorkshire.[44]

Whether they came from close at hand or far away, they came in the vast majority of cases in hopes of a job or of higher wages. Agricultural depression after 1870 drove labourers off the farm and into cities in search of work.[45] A growing demand for unskilled women, both in expanding service industries and as domestic servants, increased immigration as well.[46] A man's particular skill, and the general demand for it, determined the number and duration of the moves he might find himself compelled to make. Alfred Williams, the working-class author of *Life in a Railway Factory*, reported that boilermakers were, like smiths, forced constantly to move about in search of work: 'Very often they will have tramped the whole country, from end to

end, in search of employment, for though as a class they are indispensable their ranks are often over-crowded and when trade is slack the
services of many of them are dispensed with.'

Williams declared that in his experience the skilled boilermaker
preferred the thought of moving to abandoning his trade.[47] Naturally,
if married, he would in all likelihood bring his family with him as his
work took him from city to city. Sometimes a firm, moving to a new
location, brought along members of its skilled work force; a boilermaker, for example, more fortunate than those described by Williams:
'Me dad worked for a boilermaking firm, and this firm came to Bradford
to set up in business, and he brought father with him as his first man.'[48]

During the latter part of the nineteenth century, as industry within
various communities grew more specialized, workers whose skill was
in demand were drawn to the cities where they were needed. On the
other hand, those employed by firms compelled to move elsewhere
were often forced to move as well in order to keep the job. In the
northeast, specialization in iron and steel, ship-building and engineering
meant that 'many small firms decayed as production became centralized
elsewhere, the result being an exodus of skilled craftsmen looking for
work in other cities'.[49]

Although working-class men and women most often moved because
they needed a job, or hoped to find a better-paying one, they migrated
for other reasons as well. Some explained the compulsion to move to a
city in terms of the dullness of country life. 'Conceive, oh ye inhabiters
of towns,' wrote a school inspector, 'a condition of existence so devoid
of incident that the annual inspection of the village school is the event of
the year.'[50] More than the dullness, however, it was the long hours
demanded of agricultural labourers, the absence of holidays and, above
all, the oppressive atmosphere of subservience that, combined with
wretchedly low wages, encouraged men and women to try their luck
elsewhere.

One encounters the mood in books describing country life right
through to the end of the century: in Mabel Ashby's biography of her
father, *Joseph Ashby of Tysoe*; even, occasionally, in Flora Thompson's
benign *Lark Rise to Candleford*. Raymond Williams, in *The Country
and the City*, recalls his grandfather's eviction from his cottage. He
argues, rightly, against the notion of a totally subservient rural working class, citing the courage of men like Joseph Arch and Joseph Ashby,
and of their many hundreds of unrecorded sympathizers.[51] Yet courage
of a different sort impelled able men and their families toward the city,
which, if filled with uncertainties and anxieties, promised them a
greater measure of independence.

Young men, whether on farms or in cities, might move about for no other reason than to search for something new. 'I was restless, and wanted to see more of the world,' G. N. Barnes recalled in his autobiography. A young engineer, he left Barrow with a friend for London: 'We rambled around ... and took it into our heads that we would stay.' With twenty to thirty pounds between them, they threw their return tickets into the Thames, only to discover that in the depression year of 1879 jobs were hard to come by.[52] The temptation to move about was particularly strong in young men and women of seventeen or eighteen. They deemed the wages they had been earning as children no longer sufficient, and began the search for new jobs, the more adventurous of them willing to carry the search to a new city, and to risk changing occupations if necessary.[53]

London in particular continued to act as a magnet throughout the latter part of the century. Booth believed that the continuing influx of youthful labourers was due to the debilitating effect of urban life on second and third generation inhabitants. If great cities were to survive they would require constant replenishment, a steady flow of fresh, rural immigrants. Much town work, he believed, could not be accomplished by born townsmen: 'The great majority of brewers' men come from the provinces. "Countrymen," say their employers, "are steadier and healthier and not so well acquainted with the distractions and ideas of town life as cockneys".'[54] Gareth Stedman Jones has argued, however, that immigrants came, not to replace a degenerate labour force, but to enroll in newer industries not traditional to London – he mentions specifically gas works, breweries, the cab and omnibus trade, and railways. Builders were tempted to hire immigrants, Stedman Jones writes, because of the better training they were reported to undergo outside the metropolis. And if some masters hired men from the country because they considered them stronger and steadier, many more preferred them because they 'were thought to be less demanding and more adaptable'.[55]

Once working men and women had migrated from country to city, or from one city to another, circumstances would frequently force them to move again, from house to house and neighbourhood to neighbourhood. Sometimes the reason was no more complicated than a desire for additional space or a lower rent. The very poor moved most often:

We had so many addresses. We couldn't ... pay the rent. We had to keep moving. And we came home from school and find ... bits and pieces slung out on the road; or passed over ... the wall to the next bloke to look after, and while ... the landlord came in he found nothing there. And you was in the next garden, see. He looked after 'em until we found a place.[56]

That family – father unemployed, mother a cook – moved fifteen times between 1900 and 1918. The same phenomenon has been described as it occurred in West Ham, London: 'When the arrears of rent have become too heavy in one street, they move to the other; when the same happens there, they migrate to one of the worst streets in the New Town ward; then they come back to Broadway ward, and the cycle begins afresh.'[57]

Even when the poor could pay their rent, they continued to run the risk of eviction and an unwanted move. Programmes of rebuilding and redevelopment at the centre of late Victorian cities destroyed the most dilapidated and therefore the cheapest working-class housing. The pattern repeated itself across the country. The Deputy Corporation Surveyor of Liverpool reported to the Newcastle Town Improvement Committee in 1890

... that the poorest of the poor have been displaced by the pulling down of unsanitary dwellings, but these people do not form the class who have gone into the new dwellings erected by the Corporation. Notices were placarded in the districts where houses were pulled down informing persons of the rents of the model dwellings, but with no success in obtaining tenants from the very poorest class of the population. The houses – a little better than those pulled down – vacated by persons who have removed to the model dwellings, are now occupied by the former tenants of the houses pulled down . . .[58]

Mr Turton, the Surveyor, believed that these successive moves into housing of a better standard represented progress. Indeed, assuming that those displaced by the demolition all managed to find their way by some sort of socio-statistical magic into the houses of those who had themselves moved off to the model flats, one could perhaps agree with him. But of course all of them did not. By 1907, Liverpool had demolished 13,400 insanitary dwellings out of a total of 22,000 that had been condemned since 1864. In the process it left 3,000 people unprovided for, and uprooted – to their own advantage, it is probably true – those whom it had forced to move to new quarters.[59]

Casual labourers tried as best they could to stay close to the districts where they might most readily pick up a few days' work at a time. Moves for them were therefore particularly troublesome. Often a skilled worker would move his family in order to live near a new job. If he occupied cheap and comparatively comfortable quarters in an area where several firms hired men with his particular skill, he was in luck.[60]

If he lost work at one shop he could hope to find it at another nearby, and thus avoid either a move or a long journey to work and back every day. An increase in the availability of cheap urban transport at the end of the century altered this situation somewhat. Some workers now found it possible to remain where they had been living while travelling back and forth to new or frequently changing jobs far from home. The general effect of trains and electric tram cars on the working class was profound; Robert Roberts, writing of the electric tram cars in Manchester, declares that 'except for the war itself, this revolutionary new form of transport contributed more than anything else to breaking down that ingrained parochialism which had beset millions in the industrial slums of pre-1914 England'.[61]

Roberts's remark implies that before the trams, working-class families, when they had moved, had not often ventured out of the central urban districts to which their incomes had condemned them; that they had simply not moved very much at all, in terms of distance. With the exception of London, where the inner working-class district stretched from Bermondsey in the south to Shoreditch in the north, the implication holds true. With the coming of trams and trains, however, entire working-class suburbs sprang to life outside older decaying areas to accommodate the workers who were prepared, or were forced, to move into them. Life in the raw newness of a suburban development was not necessarily a congenial one. Houses remained terraced houses. A premium, the *Bradford Pioneer* complained in 1913, was placed on architectural sterility: 'Children with their innocent romps and harmless frolics would shake the lathe and plaster from the jerry-built structures that are the pride and glory of the speculative builder.'[62] Sterile or not, the suburbs attracted inhabitants as fast as they were built. In all the major cities in England, working-class migration outwards from city centres was perhaps the most noticeable demographic phenomenon at the end of the nineteenth century. John Burns's estimate, in 1907, that 13,000 families a year were leaving inner London for the suburbs, suggests the magnitude of the movement.[63]

Moving, whether from country to city, from city to city, or from city to suburb, could not help but further the sense of insecurity which economic circumstances forced upon the working class. Yet life within a neighbourhood could moderate the uncertainty that moving tended to foster. Families tried hard to establish themselves, wherever they lived, to fit themselves into some sort of network, the better to guarantee their physical, economic, and psychological survival. Without the sustaining services of a welfare state, men and women relied upon the neighbourhood for help when they or their children fell ill. The threat of unemployment and of consequent poverty produced a need to become known and trusted, so as to be able to call upon shopkeepers – and pawnbrokers – for credit or other financial aid.[64] Sickness, unemployment, poverty, removal: in the struggle to counter these unsettling conditions of its daily life, the working class looked to neighbourhoods for stability and connectedness. Neighbourhood meant more than houses and streets. It meant the mutually beneficial relationships one formed with others; a sort of social symbiosis. Industrial life called upon workers to move about whenever and wherever the labour market demanded. One middle-class observer warned the working class that it must 'morally despecialize itself', that a man who expected to earn a living in an industrialized society 'must not be bound by his habits of life to the factory in which he works' – and by extension, to the neighbourhood in which he lived.[65] The working class ignored the proferred advice and did its best to sink roots:

> A family who have lived for years on one street are recognized up and down the length of that street as people to be helped in time of trouble ... A family which moves two miles away is completely lost to view. They never write, there is no time and money for visiting. Neighbours forget them. It was not mere personal liking which united them; it was a kind of mutual respect in the face of trouble.[66]

If we follow Robert Roberts's lead and label as 'classic' the pattern of neighbourhood life that had emerged by 1900, we can better understand that pattern by viewing it in relation to those that came both before and after. The period Roberts describes – the period central to this study – succeeded one which can be characterized as 'heroic'. This was the era Michael Anderson analyses in his study, *Family Structure in Nineteenth Century Lancashire*. Using census data for the industrial city of Preston, in the years from 1841 to 1861, Anderson has drawn important conclusions about the manner in which working-class neighbourhoods took shape during the most intensive period of urbanization. His evidence allows him to conclude that individuals migrating into Preston from the surrounding countryside or from other industrial communities relied to a great extent upon kin to reduce the trauma of their move. Of his 1851 sample, 70 per cent was born outside Preston. Most of them probably made the move there as single teenagers or as young marrieds in their early twenties, at a time when they could more easily secure employment in the Preston mills.[67]

The tensions of life in a totally new environment were enormous. The threat of unemployment was increased by the fact that the law of settlement often meant migrants could not expect poor relief except in the community of their birth. If they returned temporarily to claim their benefit, as some did in times of trade depression, they faced the further problem of readjustment then and at the time they once more moved back to the city.[68]

In these circumstances, it is not surprising to find migrants relying upon kin for assistance during periods of sickness, unemployment and old age. Analysis of census material has produced evidence that far more than a 'randomly predictable' number lived with or close to relatives.[69] Their reasons for doing so were probably calculated in terms of personal and economic support:

> ... Migration in all societies presents special problems which must be met if the migrant is to adapt to a new life in his new community. He needs information about prospects and conditions to help him decide whether or not and where to go. If he goes, he is faced immediately with the problems of finding somewhere to live, of finding a job, and of adapting himself in the hundreds of other ways to the new community ... Kin were by far the most important source of assistance available to most migrants.[70]

Anderson argues convincingly that a migrant would form a lasting relationship with his kin only if it promised to be to his advantage, and documents 'a calculative, even to our eyes callous, attitude to kin'.[71] One expected to receive as much support as one offered in this 'heroic' age. The rugged conditions of life on the urban frontier demanded such a calculus.

For those who determined that their own best interests could better be served by a life apart from the demands of kin there were alternatives – lodging-houses, for example. Yet such an alternative demanded a good deal of self-reliance. Nor could the migrant depend to any great extent upon neighbours alone. Conditions remained, at this early stage, too unsettled. Kinfolk, whatever their shortcomings, could be trusted in a way that neighbours could not. And neighbourhoods, fostered by developing patterns of kinship, yet sustained by connections that lay beyond family, would await a less mobile population and the passage of time.

One hundred years later, in a post-war, 'post-classic' period, and in an era when the welfare state had abolished much of the uncertainty of mid-Victorian working-class life, families nevertheless continued to seek the security kinship provided. In Bethnal Green, as analysed by

Michael Young and Peter Willmott in their famous survey, *Family and Kinship in East London*, 'Mum' – the matriarch – stood at the centre of a network of family relationships that spread across the neighbourhood, giving shape and substance to its life. Others discovered much the same thing in their studies of working-class communities in cities as diverse as Liverpool, Swansea, and Oxford.[72] In one all-important respect, however, the situation which had dictated the tight kinship patterns of the 1850s had changed dramatically: by the 1950s migration had slowed in most communities to a trickle. That fact, and the fact of one hundred years of urban living, produced the quintessential working-class neighbourhood. Fifty-three per cent of Young and Willmott's sample was born in Bethnal Green.[73] In a working-class suburb of Birmingham, 24 per cent of those interviewed in the early 1950s had lived all their lives, or over 35 years, in the same house. Fifty-two per cent of the men and 63 per cent of the women had been born in the suburb.[74] On 'Ship Street', in a working-class Liverpool slum, 'the general picture is that each family has for two generations lived in this small cluster of streets', married daughter often succeeding mother as tenant. Here, as elsewhere, 'the tie to the locality' had become as binding as the tie to kin.[75] Once families could live for more than a few years, and then for more than one generation within the same area of streets and 'turnings', 'neighbourhood' became a web of assumptions and associations that Anderson's Preston immigrants had only begun to weave. Kinship now promoted the development of a sense of neighbourhood:

> When a person has relatives in the borough, as most people do, each of these relatives is a go-between with other people in the district. His brother's friends are his acquaintances, if not his friends; his grandmother's neighbours so well known as almost to be his own. The kindred are, if we understand their function aright, a bridge between the individual and the community.[76]

Despite the welfare state, working-class residents in the 1950s still relied upon their neighbourhoods to provide physical and economic security. 'The extent of neighbourliness, especially in times of adversity, cannot be overstressed,' Madeline Kerr reports of 'Ship Street', and then proceeds to catalogue the manner in which neighbours come to the rescue following illnesses, deaths, fires, and other disasters.[77] Gone are Anderson's unneighbourly transients, to be replaced by long-time acquaintances who, if they seldom spend much time in each other's kitchens, nevertheless come to each other's aid in emergencies.

'Mind you', reports a resident of the Oxford working-class parish of St. Ebbe's,

> ... we never go into each other's houses, because once you go inside, people begin to chatter. You can be just as friendly meeting in the road. Of course, if anyone wants help, I help. Like the man over the road when his wife was in hospital. I went over when he came back from work to ask if he had any lunch; he said not to bother; so he had a hot dinner every day for three weeks. And now, they sometimes give us things and only yesterday they left some strawberries here and some vegetables from their allotment, and that's more to me than money.[78]

More important than the physical and economic support they provide, however, is the psychological certainty which 'post-classic' working-class neighbourhoods can afford their residents. In 'Ship Street' there exists a 'vague, undifferentiated feeling of belonging, and the security of moving around in a well-known territory'.[79] For many people, familiarity bred content: 'Bethnal Greeners are not lonely people. Whenever they go for a walk in the street, for a drink in the pub, or for a row on the lake in Victoria Park, they know the faces in the crowd.'[80]

Somewhere beyond the Preston of 1850 and before the Bethnal Green of 1950 lay the myriad neighbourhoods in which the working class lived in the 'classic' period. Time had altered their initial character; families had in many cases been able to establish themselves for more than a generation. But time had not yet produced the tightly bound communities one now tends to think of as typical. Neighbourhoods could not yet offer the sort of shelter from uncertainty and confusion that they later did. The working man, C. F. G. Masterman wrote in 1904, '... has not yet clearly apprehended his position or appreciated its possibility. He has been "dumped" down in some casual street, unknown to his neighbours, unconnected with a corporate body or fellowship. He goes through his life in a kind of confused twilight, dimly wondering what it all means.'[81]

Evidence of that twilight – of the difficulty of establishing even the most fragile human connections within it – is nowhere clearer than in the testimony collected by the Women's Cooperative Guild in 1915 from its local officers, past and present, on the subject of maternity. Asked to describe their experiences in detail, the women replied with refreshing frankness. And one constantly reiterated complaint was of the isolation of urban life, adding to the always stressful, occasionally miserable task of childbearing in a working-class household:

My mother dying when I was three years old, I had no one to turn to for advice. I had spent all my youth in the country, and came as a stranger into a strange place, knowing no one but the man I married.

My mother is a qualified midwife, but was too far away at the time.

Now, in a strange town, and no particular friends and, shall I say, mock modest, I was almost afraid to go to a doctor for advice, in case he would think I was a coward, and did not try to bear what I thought was right.

We had removed to a strange place, and I happened to get a woman who did not know her work.

I went to live many miles away from my home and friends when I married, amongst strangers, and was too shy to ask anyone what I should or should not do (when I knew I should become a mother), and was so ill, tired, and depressed that I felt I did not want to do anything.

I had lived about eighty miles away from home for some years and was away from my mother at the time, also too shy and reticent to even mention my condition to neighbours.

I was very ignorant before marriage, and went away among strangers; and when I became pregnant I did not like to say anything to a strange doctor, and I had no lady friends whom I felt I could confide in.[82]

Some of these women do mention assistance received at the hands of relatives or, in a few cases, neighbours. But the constantly repeated refrain – 'away among strangers' – remains central to many of the letters. If such was the case for women whose education and general intelligence had led them to become officers in the Women's Cooperative Guild, what must it have been for their poorer and more ignorant sisters?[83]

Whether from the country, from another city, or from another neighbourhood, newcomers in the 'classic' period had a difficult time of it. Anderson has little to say about those from his earlier generation who arrived in Preston *without* the support of kin. Recent studies suggest that, if given the chance, they might well have surrendered their understandable defensiveness to an equally understandable desire to make common cause with other lonely newcomers. Ignoring the transitoriness, they might have joined other urban pioneers in battle together against the rawness of industrial life. Sociologists surveying post-war housing estates in England have reported this phenomenon. In the early years, as residents found themselves forced to adapt to a strange new environment, they were generally open with each other. 'It was a period of great mutual friendliness,' writes J. M. Mogey of the Burton estate outside Oxford.[84] With the passage of time, however, once the physical and emotional problems of newness had receded, openness gave way to 'a retreat from neighbourliness', a willingness to retire into 'the general ideal of "I keep myself to myself" '.[85] The consistency of that same refrain in the evidence from the neighbour-hoods of late Victorian England suggests that perhaps a similar transition was occurring then; that, for newcomers at any rate, being a neighbour was no less difficult a business by 1900 than it had been in 1850. The letters to the Women's Cooperative Guild are proof, at any rate, that it was for many a very trying task.[86]

Residents of ten or twenty years would, by this time, have put down their roots and established themselves. They would naturally resent the constant intrusion of arriving families and the consequent need to retrace patterns they had hoped had been defined once and for all. In defence they might do all they could to hold themselves aloof from their new neighbours, offering little assistance as the newcomers tried to understand the connections and connotations that the older residents had so painstakingly fashioned into a kind of locally oriented sixth sense. If the newcomers stayed, they would eventually acquire that sense as well, and come to be accepted. But for a time, their presence was resented. Arrivals and departures served as an unpleasant reminder, even to second generation residents, that economic circumstance might force them to move as well, requiring of them the same sort of struggle they were witnessing in the attempts of the new arrivals to fit into their own community.

Given these tensions, it is not surprising to find new families, despite their frequent need for advice and assistance, nevertheless tempted to isolate themselves as they struggled to comprehend their social situation. Aloofness, if it brought temporary loneliness, also reduced the chances of a gaffe that might permanently blight one's neighbourly relationships. One working-class woman, for example, a resident on a 'respectable' street, invited the dustman to step in for a cup of tea on a cold day, and thereby did considerable damage to her local reputation: 'It was not only that a newcomer had to observe the "village" standards ... he also had to make a point of showing that he observed them. Otherwise he was given a low ranking in the status order of "village" families and was treated as an outsider.'[87] The observation, though recent, could as easily have been made of the period before the First World War. Then, too, isolation – keeping onself to oneself – was the surest way to avoid trouble. Acquaintance was seldom allowed to lead to the kind of intimacy that bred quarrels. What neighbours learned of the circumstances of your daily life they might later use against you, when arguing publicly to determine the standing of various families on the street. Roberts describes the scene as it occurred on Saturday nights in Salford:

> One waved, for instance, a 'clean rent book' (that great status symbol of the times) in the air, knowing the indicted had fallen in arrears. Now manners and morals were arraigned before a massed public tribunal ... Purselipped and censorious, the matriarchs surveyed the scene, soaking it all in, shocked by the vulgarity of it all, unless, of course, their own family was engaged. Then later, heads together and from evidence submitted, they made grim readjustments on the social ladder.[88]

Little wonder that, as a London district nurse noted at the time, 'the chief virtue that can be shown by lads and lasses at school or in work-shops is not "they choose their friends well", but "they never pick up with no one".'[89]

Recent surveys suggest that in long established neighbourhoods time can induce a certain relaxation of the codes that led one to keep to oneself:

> In a community of long-standing [Bethnal Green] ... status, insofar as it is determined by job and income and education, is more or less irrelevant to a person's worth. He is judged instead, if he is judged at all, more in the round, as a person with the usual mixture of all kinds of qualities, some good, some bad, many undefinable. He is more of a life-portrait than figure on a scale.[90]

On Liverpool's 'Ship Street', although 'cruelty to children or stealing from your mother may be heartily disapproved of ... the people ... do not feel called upon to dictate to others what furniture they should have or what conduct they should pursue.'[91] The long established St Ebbe's community revealed a similar tolerance, expressed in terms of an understanding attitude towards neighbours' children.[92] Neighbourhoods of long standing – St Ebbe's, Bethnal Green, 'Ship Street' – can afford their residents a measure of mutual tolerance. Neighbourhoods in which almost everyone is a newcomer – the working-class slums of mid-century Preston – may compel their residents to connect, if only for mutual survival. Most neighbourhoods by 1900 had passed beyond that first 'heroic' stage in their development and had yet to reach the third. Connection was consequently a difficult if necessary business. Most men and women in 'classic' times could only hope to discover, and then subscribe to, the assumptions, the codes, the categories, that sustained common life on working-class streets. They hoped that their subscription would bring them closer to their neighbours and therefore to a sense of their own security. That it might, as easily, result in the further isolation of 'keeping yourself to yourself' was a paradox they had not learned to expect and found hard to comprehend.

Meanwhile poverty, because it so often forced families to move, because it allowed time for little more than the struggle to exist, continued to tear at whatever fabric there was in many of the poorer working-class neighbourhoods. Proud and embarrassed families refused to open themselves to others for fear of revealing their destitution. 'Hopelessness and fatalism in the face of desperate poverty', Suzanne Keller writes, '... may lead to that peculiar constriction of social ties characteristic of some backward villages or abandoned wastelands of cities. Under such conditions the concept of neighbour, not to speak of the good neighbour, is non-existent.'[93] The point was made compellingly by a London working man, raised before the First World War in an impoverished area of Paddington. Asked if neighbours ever helped look after his brothers and sisters: 'Christ no. They was all busy looking after theirselves.'[94]

And yet, despite poverty, despite migration, despite isolation, working-class neighbourhoods were an established fact of urban life by 1900. They were not large – often no more than several streets – separated not only from middle-class districts far beyond, but also by a factory, an embankment, or a tram line, from other seemingly identical working-class streets close by. Even a single street was not, by definition, a neighbourhood. That depended upon its inhabitants, their capability and determination to form the necessary networks and connections. The task was simpler when those who resided near at hand shared similar economic backgrounds and prospects. When they did not, when, for example, artisans and labourers happened to live near each other, or, worse, several working-class families moved on to a street which had until their arrival housed only members of the lower middle class, the prospects for neighbourliness lessened perceptibly. Such a street sheltered Frank Owen, the housepainter-hero of Robert Tressell's *The Ragged Trousered Philanthropists*:

> Lord Street ... like most other similar neighbourhoods – supplied a striking answer to those futile theorists who prate of the equality of mankind, for the inhabitants instinctively formed themselves into groups, the more superior types drawing together, separating themselves from the inferior, and rising naturally to the top while the others gathered themselves into distinct classes, grading downwards, or else isolated themselves altogether; being refused admission to

the circles they desired to enter, and in their turn refusing to associate with their inferiors.[95]

Tressell was writing of Hastings, where an absence of industry would naturally have held the working-class population to a low level and therefore operated against the establishment of closely integrated working-class neighbourhoods. In the north, in cities housing industrial armies, families were better able to live amongst their equals. In St Michael's Ward, Manchester, in 1904, for example, out of 102 families, 47 heads of households were labourers, 15 were porters, and 13 were hawkers.[96] Yet Roberts's Salford 'village', an area of 'some thirty streets and alleys locked along the north and south by two railway systems a furlong apart', and generally classified as poor, nevertheless contained enough diverse elements – 'tradesmen and artisans ... semi-skilled workers (still a small section) in regular employment, and then the various grades of unskilled labourers' – to require a sorting out and labelling of neighbourhoods in terms of every street.[97] Working-class Londoners, confronted by a constantly shifting population more socially amorphous by far than either that of Hastings or Salford, took particular pains in drawing their lines:

> [Poplar]: East India Rd was very nice. Commercial Road began to get poor and then up further along got more Jeweyfied. [West India Dock Road] you got the rough part – the Chinese and all that.[98]

> [Wapping]: Our part of Wapping, in our little sector was ... the more or less Church of England crowd, and as you got over the bridge you run into the St Patrick's crowd ... The only thing that separated them was a little small ground, small playground between the two of 'em.[99]

Poplar and Wapping were not alone, of course, in relying on race and religion, as well as pay packet or job, to determine neighbourhood boundaries.

As important as those criteria was the availability of contact points, common meeting places where familiarity could grow and information and gossip circulate freely. Women, encountering each other in the street just outside their own houses, might exchange a greeting and discuss a bit of local news. Neighbourhood shops afforded them an even more congenial atmosphere in which to become acquainted and to take each others' measure. The shops generally reflected the dinginess of their surroundings: 'The windows are rarely clean, and the goods they expose to view are arrayed as they have been for the last six months.'[100] Yet the customers, used to dinginess at home, paid it no heed abroad. They came to spend a little money and, on neutral

ground, to enjoy themselves for a few minutes of talk. Edwin Pugh, the author of stories of the working class in the 1890s, described one such 'Small Talk Exchange'. Frowsy though it was, its overcrowdedness, like the overcrowdedness of working-class kitchens, expressed a welcoming communal cosiness:

'The Provision Stores' was stuffed to repletion with every conceivable article of commerce that blows or grows or is produced by art or nature. If you were short of cash, Mrs Luzzell could supply you with seven pounds of coal or a peck of coke for a penny. If your collar-stud broke unexpectedly you could buy three bone ones on a card for a halfpenny, or a metal one for a farthing . . . Flanking the door were two large boxes. One contained Spanish onions at three a penny; the other, broken biscuits at twopence halfpenny per pound. Half of one of the windows was sacred to sweetstuff: the other half to toys: all at a penny each. Mrs Luzzell rarely sold more than a pennyworth of anything.

But, as Pugh's title suggests, it was neither dry goods nor provender, but talk that the customers came for:

They talked of the weather; of the price of coals; of their husbands; their children; their sicknesses; their quarrels with contumacious neighbours and relations; of School Boards; of marriages and births and deaths that had lately happened or were on the *tapis*; of funerals; of clothes and boots; of the dearness of provisions; of Mrs Nemo's new bonnet; of Mr Nemo's profligacy; of the decadence of filial love and duty; of Heaven and Hell; of the fine dinners they had eaten; of murders, suicides, fires, divorces, breaches of promise, wife-beating and husband-beating; the stupidity of country folk – a favourite theme; and their own sharpness and intelligence.[101]

Other meeting places – fish-and-chip shops, the pawnbroker's, very occasionally a church or chapel – offered women further chances to attach themselves to the life of a neighbourhood. And for men and women as well, there was the pub. As she travelled her daily rounds, the working-class wife and mother would try to weigh up the acquaintances she made, in order to pick from among them the one or two to whom she might entrust her confidences should the need arise. A 'good neighbour', a 'friendly neighbour', had to be ready to assist in an emergency, and be willing to keep to herself whatever she might learn of others' difficulties in the process. She came to wash dishes or clothes at a lying-in; she took children into her house of an afternoon if their mother was working; she was ready, if asked, with the spoonful of this

or cupful of that – relying on the history of past exchanges to insure their return. Money, because she would so seldom have a farthing herself to spare, she was almost never called upon to lend. Occasionally she might risk censure to repay a kindness, as in the case of a paralyzed mother who, in gratitude for visits from a neighbour who drank too much, sent her daughter to clean the woman's house 'rather than see her get into trouble with her husband'.[102] Neighbourliness implied reciprocity – looking out for one another. It was the stuff from which community was woven. Neighbours were intermediaries. Their encounters called upon them to pass messages and allowed them to exchange gossip. In their daily passings back and forth they sensed, before they saw, the still-closed curtain which signalled someone alone and sick:

> In Liverpool, as our mother said, if a neighbour missed another neighbour for two days they'd go and knock on the door. Well, see, the door was always open, they'd lift up the latch and they'd go in ... and see if that person was ill. Well then they'd turn to, and if the children were at school they'd get a meal ready and give it to the children, and do the place out and have it clean for the husband if he came home from work ...[103]

Unless properly attuned to neighbourhood customs, a woman might find her genuine concern resented as bothersome 'popping in', a habit which some neighbourhoods tolerated and others did not. Occasionally neighbours 'just came in to have a yarn and then off out'. 'It might be a cup of tea, but nothing more.' Generally, they crossed the threshold only if 'we wanted 'em for anything special' – to ask a favour, to diagnose a child's illness.[104]

Neighbourliness did not imply the intimacy of friendship. Indeed, working-class men and women did not 'make friends' as the middle class did, and still does.[105] They might become friends with someone as a result of acquaintanceship either inside or outside the neighbourhood. A neighbourhood, however, relieved them of the need to reach out in search of people with like attitudes and interests, and of the necessity for lengthy visits back and forth to confirm and strengthen an initial and tentative series of impressions. Once inhabitants accepted its ways and standards, the neighbourhood offered them a kind of communal insurance that made 'friendship' seem unnecessary, if not almost out of place.

The presence of kin provided insurance of an even more reliable kind. As in Anderson's Preston and Young and Willmott's Bethnal Green, men and women in the 'classic' period expected to assist their relations and to receive assistance from them whenever it was possible. One must balance the loneliness and helplessness reflected in the pages of *Maternity* with accounts such as these:

[A woman biscuit maker in Reading]: Her job is to feed the ovens, but she says she cannot stand it much longer; indeed, her husband is just beginning to work again and if her mother-in-law can get a job of charing she hopes to be able to leave it off. Meanwhile her one and only child (a year-old baby) is in the charge of her mother-in-law, and besides these two she has to help support her brother-in-law and sister-in-law, neither of whom is yet old enough to add to the family income.[106]

[A woman whose daughter's husband earns from 18 to 20 shillings a week]: She helps them, and the mother-in-law also gives help in the way of clogs, paying the rates, clothes, etc. The daughter came to her mother the other day, showing her two shillings in her hand, and said it was all she had over for groceries that week. The mother said, 'Ah, it larns 'em, they has to be careful. Of course I gave her some money; I allus do when she's short.'[107]

[A London plumber's family in the 1890s]: The family has no credit, nor can it count upon the aid of relatives, except that at rare intervals it gets a cast garment, which the wife makes up. When they lost their baby, the man's brother, though actually out of work, 'made' 30s (i.e., by pledging) and lent it to them to pay the funeral expenses. And the wife's mother, now dead, took in the man and his children when they were homeless.[108]

Families counted on what Elizabeth Bott has called 'connecting relatives', much as neighbourhoods relied upon intermediaries, to keep members informed of impending births, of sickness and death. Frequently those same relatives found themselves cast in the role of principal assistant at such times of family crisis. They helped channel useful information to those within the network who needed jobs: 'My step-sister's eldest son worked for the Mersey Docks and Harbour Board – he had a good job and of course . . . he spoke for [my husband] and got him there.'[109] In this case, perhaps it was the step-sister herself who served as the link. During the 'classical' period, the 'connecting relative' often appears to have been an aunt or unmarried sister, who could be counted upon to travel from house to house and lend a hand when needed: 'Their own particular lives, their own particular activities didn't permit of attendance on each other at times of sickness. No, they all had their own families to look after. The only aunty who was a

endurance – seeking stimulus in drinking, in betting, in any un-accustomed conflicts at home or abroad.'[119] The picture is of a multitude of individuals unsteady and apart from each other, of lives more often coinciding than touching.

But the picture is a false one. The pressures were real; the response far less passive than Masterman's dirge would suggest. City life did tear at past patterns of social organization. The working class fought back, determined to reshape those patterns to accord with its new experiences, just as it was determined not to discard them completely. By 1900 the battle was by no means over. Its tensions produced the uneasiness and uncertainty that the evidence reflects. But the working man was, in the words of yet another middle-class observer, 'developing, under the stress of city life, a new type of humanity, which may, in spite of its present glaring defects, eventually lead to something more perfectly adjusted to the demands of town existence and to mod-ern industrial requirements.'[120]

Far from individualistic, in the manner described by Wirth and Parsons, the 'new humanity' was communal – though, at this stage, often cautiously so. Class consciousness, shaped by economic cir-cumstance, compelled community: 'Neighbours used to stick together and help each other, because they knew they'd be in the same boat anytime.'[121] The urban working-class village shared with the rural communities of the past a foundation built of mutual responsibilities and obligations. Unlike those earlier communities, however, there was to be no resident governing class, imposing its own will – philan-thropic, condescending, authoritarian – upon the rest. Urban manor houses such as Toynbee Hall, however well meant, would have no lasting place in this new environment. Instead the working class under-took to look after itself, relying when necessary on families and neighbourhoods for physical support and psychological sustenance. In ordering its own life, it often imposed standards as harsh in their way as any prescribed by a rural squirearchy. If one was prepared to live to those standards, one could be certain of eventual acceptance and therefore of survival. Arthur Morrison tells the short, sad tale of one who could not. Her failure speaks of both the realities and the needs in working-class neighbourhoods before the First World War:

There was once a woman who sang – a young wife from the country. But she bore children and her voice cracked. Then her man died, and she sang no more. They took away her home, and with her children about her skirts she left this street forever. The other women did not think much of her. She was 'helpless'.[122]

# 3 Women at home

WOMEN OCCUPY a central position in working-class family and neigh-bourhood networks. What Young and Willmott discovered in Bethnal Green, others have found in post-war housing communities elsewhere. Peter Townsend, in his study of the family life of old people, remarks on the matriarchal connection, 'the special unity between grandmother, daughter, and daughter's child'.[1] Community life is lived along that line. The sixty-one families on 'Ship Street' included forty-four in which married daughters had resided or were still residing with their mothers. In thirty-two cases, the mother and daughter lived or had lived within five minutes' walk from each other.[2] 'Home', for the working-class wife, may thus mean the home she left when she was married, as well as the home she is now making as wife and mother. 'Yes, we still say we're going "over home" when we go there, even though Mum's been dead for years.'[3] The remark implies a continuity in the matrilinear structure of family life that even death cannot impair. Occasionally one encounters remarks such as: 'When the mother dies the family goes to pieces and it is never the same again.'[4] Far more often, however, daughter replaces mother as the pivot 'around which the extended family revolves, managing the family affairs, criticizing or approving behaviour, exacting affection and loyalty and demanding family cohesion, "holding the family together", with her home serving as a nodal point and junction box for relationships.'[5]

The ability of a later Victorian working-class mother to sustain this sort of network depended to a great extent, of course, on the proximity of her own mother or her married daughters. Frequent moves, a fact of life for large numbers of working-class families, would inhibit the development of tight matriarchal systems. Yet evidence suggests that wherever circumstance permitted mothers and daughters naturally sought each other's company and support, and that those networks that did exist relied upon a matriarchy to sustain them. A Durham mother, whose own mother lived nearby, 'used to go down every morning with the pram, yes, it wasn't far, and ... have a coffee with her. I used to ask her sometimes if she wan't very

well, what I had to do, and she used to tell me what she did.'[6] Roberts describes the Salford matriarchy, an 'inner ring' of grandmothers,

> ... marked enough to be known among our irreverent youth as the 'old queens'. Wielding great influence behind the scene, they of course represented an ultra-conservative bloc in the community. As long as a grandmother kept up her home to which children and grandchildren could regularly go for material help and counsel she reigned supreme. But as soon as illness or need forced her to give up house and live with son or daughter her influence in both clan and street generally diminished, though affection remained.[7]

Whether or not proximity afforded women the chance to establish themselves within some sort of matriarchal connection, their constant presence in the household, throughout the day, day after day, for years on end, unquestionably made them the central figures there: 'She is the constant factor of the home. Others come and go, but she never disappears ... Any week will find her at home in a long stretch of forty years.'[8] Oral and written evidence sustains the assertion, confirming that in the eyes of the family members, it was she who 'held things together'. 'She managed to find us all enough to eat.' 'Somehow mother managed.' 'She kept a lot from us, she didn't tell us anything ... She bore it, most of it, herself.' 'As the family got larger, then of course mother moved about.' (Father, in this case, was a navvy, living at home. But the assumption is clear: mother was expected to manage the moves.) When death, an accident, or a long spell of unemployment brought in train the inevitable financial crisis, mother coped, as she was expected to. Jack Jones's widowed mother put herself to work, and 'by dint of hard scraping and economies that would terrify a church mouse, we did what we set out to do: we kept our little home over our heads'. Will Crooks's father lost his arm in an accident: 'I don't know what we should have done but for Mother. She used to toil with the needle far into the night and often all night long, slaving as hard as any poor sweated woman I have ever known.'[9]

Some of this may be apocryphal, memory's distillations, all impurities filtered away. Townsend describes this literature of hagiography, which appears in death notices and on burial cards. Almost always a mother's labours are exalted in a way that a father's are not:

> Rest on dear Mother, thy labours o'er,
> Thy willing hand will toil no more:
> A faithful Mother, true and kind,
> No friend on earth like thee we find.

Thus an old widow's card celebrates the life and works of her late sister. Her brother's card, Townsend notes wryly, 'merely asked the Lord to forgive him for all his sins. There was no reference to his labours, nor to his toiling hand.'[10] Ramsay MacDonald, in a foreword to Robert Smillie's autobiography, went so far as to credit the spirit of the labour movement to the guiding counsel of uncounted working-class mothers:

> Most of our faithful men owe to mothers or grandmothers the spirit which protects and maintains them. A poverty-stricken woman, harrassed with family cares, but with 'a heart abuve them a',' a woman who can sing old songs, tell fairy tales, enliven the imagination, and impart the colour and the movement of romance is, as a rule, the creator of the character of uprightness, loyalty and stead-fastness which men like Keir Hardie and Robert Smillie have possessed. Their oppositions not being based on hatreds but on visions, not upon pockets but on conscience, are always tempered by charity, and for that very reason can neither be drugged nor bought off.[11]

The literature, whatever it may tell us about a working-class mother, undoubtedly confirms her central position within the household. It may also have played a role in persuading young women to forsake the independence and pleasures of life as an unmarried working girl – money at hand for cheap finery and a good time, responsibilities at bay – for a life of unremitting drudgery. For an exchange such as this, a woman would ask something in return. She could believe herself justified in expecting psychological cosseting, if physical comforts were to be denied her. An objective analysis, however, could not but reveal that, in most cases, she nevertheless got the worst of the bargain.

Of course, she did not see it that way – she was conscious of marriage not as a bargain, whatever its terms, but as a matter of course. What one sociologist has discovered to be true for modern working-class girls was true generally for their grandmothers: 'She does not choose [whether or not to marry]. She does what appears to her to be natural. It is difficult to envisage what she might do otherwise.'[12] Many marriages were, in part, the result of the discomforts of living at home, or of the not always pleasant experience of living in lodgings. Faced with a house overfilled with younger brothers and sisters, a woman of seventeen or eighteen would not look amiss at the chance to set up housekeeping with the young man who had been her steady companion over the past months. She 'walked out' with him because there was no room to sit down: 'If you lived with your father and mother, and

many brothers and sisters, in one common feeding room, perhaps you would not be bold enough to present your fiancé.'[13] And so you courted in the streets or in whatever seclusion the inhospitable urban landscape could provide. An Essex iron moulder, himself a self-professed failure, descibes the ritual's first steps:

> I just couldn't run a conversation on the silly little backchat that I've heard these other people do, you know. I was frightened off. The locals would go to White Colne, or something, Sunday evening and talk with a group of girls, just silly talk and . . . well, vulgar almost, not that I claim to be much different, but I just could not join that, or stand by shop doors and trip girls up as they come by, I just couldn't possibly.[14]

In this case, respectability was the inevitable consequence of shyness. More often it had to be preached by anxious mothers: 'When I was going out with my husband, you know, courting, and I came back a bit late and she was behind the door. I needn't tell you what happened. She wasn't having me a little stop-out. That's what she said . . . Now I laugh but then I thought she was terrible.'[15]

'Little stop outs' got themselves pregnant. So long as they married before the baby came, in most cases they did their reputations no permanent damage. But they would be looked upon by some, at least, as being 'no better than they should be'. Pregnancy, along with convenience and convention, was simply another reason for marriage. Timing might depend on the availability of a house. Or simply the realization that nothing really stood in the way of a pleasanter, less overcrowded way of life. 'Funny, ain't it, Helen,' remarks the hero of Walter Greenwood's *Love on the Dole*. 'Ah mean it's funny we ain't never thought of getting married afore . . . Fancy, though, us livin' in different houses when there's nowt t' stop us from gettin' a home of our own.'[16] A wedding was seldom the great occasion that a funeral was. There was little fuss as a rule, and few presents. A Saturday wedding meant a celebration at a pub near the church, where friends not invited to the ceremony would drop in to wish the couple well. In most cases the groom would be back to work the following Monday, the bride as well if she was employed.

Straightforward economic common sense resulted in second marriages: 'He wanted someone to look after his girls and mother wanted a few more bob – sort of financial agreement, I should imagine.'[17] Some of these marriages were without benefit of clergy, often because one of the partners to an earlier union was guilty of desertion, not in itself grounds for divorce. Even supposing the grounds sufficient, the cost, on the average about £100, was an expense almost no one in the working class could bear.[18]

The nature of the tie between a working-class woman and her husband would depend, in great measure, upon the extent to which she remained bound to her own kin or to a network of nearby acquaintances. On unfamiliar ground in a neighbourhood new to her, and denied the sociability available to her husband at his place of work, she would rely on him for companionship and, in all likelihood, generally subordinate her life to his. If, on the other hand, she lived close by female relatives, if she could call in frequently at her mother's house, her marriage would probably develop a double focus.

The shift from domestic to industrial production in the nineteenth century increased women's dependence on men, 'not only in economic terms, but in the psychological subtleties of their relationships. Authoritarian patterns of behaviour, sanctioned by the factory, were carried into the home.' More than ever, survival depended on the husband and father, 'the one who "earned life" for the whole unit'.[19] A marriage in which both partners led socially 'segregated' lives was not, on that account, a marriage in which the husband was in any sense subordinate to his wife. Families could be both dominated by the father and centred about the mother; such appears to have been the case in the majority of working-class families at the turn of the century.[20]

However bound to each other, both husband and wife regarded their lives together without much illusion. Marriage brought heavy responsibility, and only a very temporary sense of independence. One catches the ambivalence acutely in a passage from Alfred Williams's *Life in a Railway Factory*, describing the manner in which rites of passage were performed upon working-class husbands-to-be:

> As soon as it is known that the banns are published – and this is certain to leak out and news of it be brought into the shed – he becomes the object of very special attention. The men come to him from all quarters and offer him their congratulations, sincere and otherwise, very often accompanying them with advice of different kinds, sometimes of a highly sarcastic nature. Many insist upon shaking hands with him, and with mock ceremony, compliment him on his decision to join the 'Big Firm', as they call it, assuring him, at the same time, that they shall expect him to 'stand his footing'. Occasionally, if their mate is poor, the men of a gang will make a small collection and buy him a present – a pair of pictures, a piece of furniture, or a set of ornaments. Perhaps this may be carried out ridiculously, and the whole thing turned into a joke, whereupon

the prospective bridegroom loses his temper and soundly lashes his mates for their unsolicited patronage.

If the workman divulges the time and place of the wedding there will certainly be a few to witness it, in order to see how he behaves during the ceremony. Very often they wait outside the church with missiles of several kinds, such as old shoes and slippers, rice, barley, Indian corn, and even potatoes, ready to pelt him. Occasionally, however, it happens that the wily mate has deceived them with regard either to the time or the place, and if they turn up at the church they will have to wait in vain, the laughing-stock of all passers-by. When the newly married man recommences work he is received with a loud uproar. This is called 'ringing him in'. A crowd of men and boys beat upon any loose plate of metal that will return a loud clang – such as lids of tool-chests, steel bars, anvils, and sides of coke bunks – and make as much noise as possible. This is all over by the time the hooter sounds. With the starting of the shop engine the men fall in to work, and the marriage is forgotten by the crowd.[21]

Economic uncertainty, the final arbiter of working-class existence, meant that a 'successful' marriage depended first and foremost on simple survival. Poverty brought quarrels, desertions and death. To have made it beyond those pitfalls was cause enough for celebration:

> We've been together now for forty years,
> And it don't seem a day too much.
> There ain't a lady livin' in the land
> As I'd swap fer me dear old dutch.[22]

So sang the aged common-law husband in what was probably the most popular working-class tribute to marriage. He hymned the comradeship that was the reality of most married lives. The matter-of-fact air with which the working class went about courtship and marriage does not imply a lack of genuine and lasting fondness between husband and wife. Working-class men and women were as capable of affection as their middle-class counterparts. Their proximity to the facts of life, however – whether an empty food cupboard or an overfull bedroom – led them to expect little romance in life and left them even less time to look for it. The very modesty of their expectations could impart to them a simple, honest dignity: 'I think all the pleasure that a woman got was living with this man . . . And I think they had to love one another and that was the pleasure that they got out of life . . . was loving one another and living with one another.'[23]

The assessment tallies with conclusions Geoffrey Gorer reached in his study of English character: 'What English men most value in their wives is the possession of appropriate feminine skills, whereas what English women most value in their husbands is an agreeable character.'[24] The ability to endure crises together with common sense and without panic, an understanding of one's predetermined role and a willingness to assume it – these were the commonplace qualities which sustained a successful marriage as perceived by the working class.

An 'agreeable' husband might be one who could, in addition, offer his wife the pleasure of sexual fulfillment. Yet if we can believe the admittedly scanty evidence, few women expected that satisfaction or considered it important to their marriage. More frequently, 'agree-ability' meant a husband's willingness to spare his wife as much as possible from the trials of a sex life which she conceived of as a duty but could not enjoy. Her attitude was determined in part by her ignorance. One might expect that the crowded conditions of working-class existence would have made sexuality an unavoidable fact of everyday life. Baths before the kitchen fire; beds and bedrooms shared not just by brothers and sisters, but by parents and children; adolescent gossip at the mill; evening walks unchaperoned into country lanes – surely all this might lead to sexual precociousness. The evidence is by no means clear cut. The anonymity of urban life might facilitate sexual adventuring for the curious young man; the connectedness within a working-class neighbourhood might as easily thwart it. Roberts writes of incest as a fact of working-class life; but he is quick to note that it was regarded as 'the ultimate disgrace'.[25] Hoggart concludes that although 'sexual matters are nearer the surface, and sexual experience in the working classes is probably more easily and earlier acquired than in other social groups', the proximity of it all leads to its being locked up, or at least held at bay. There is, he points out, 'a great shyness about some aspects of sex – about discussing it "sensibly", about being seen naked, or even about undressing for the act of sex, or about sophistications in sexual behaviour.'[26]

Evidence from the late Victorian period bears Hoggart out. A girl of fifteen hits a boy in the groin for saying 'fuck', but will tell her father of the incident only when the house has been cleared of her brothers and sisters. A mother keeps her boys outside on Friday nights until the girls have had their bath. Parents are loathe to discuss sexual matters with their children: 'Everything was kept hidden from us. We couldn't talk like the ... mothers and daughters today ... Everything was hushed up. You didn't know life as we ... know it now.'[27] Reticence induced a remarkable degree of ignorance in young, unmarried working-class women. Nor did marriage itself necessarily enlighten them.

I had a stepmother who had had no children of her own, so I was not able to get any knowledge from her; and even if she had known anything I don't suppose she would have dreamt of telling me about these things which were supposed to exist, but must not be talked about. About a month before the baby was born I remember asking my aunt where the baby would come from. She was astounded, and did not make me much wiser.

[I asked the midwife] where will it come from? Mrs Morris answered back and said, well, where it went in, that's where your baby will come out. And you can tell how – how I was.

In fact, when the midwife came to me when I was in such pain, I had not the slightest idea where or how the child would come into the world. And another thing, I was not even told what to expect when I was leaving girlhood – I mean the monthly courses. I often wonder I got along as well as I have.[28]

How common was such ignorance? In reading evidence such as this from the Women's Cooperative Guild survey, one should remember that it comes from literate, educated working-class women who may have been reared in severely 'respectable' households. Even among the raffish, however, the same reticence could prevail. A woman whose mother deserted her husband and took her daughter with her to live with another man recalled the mother's unwillingness to discuss menstruation: 'I remember once when I had the first period I'd ever had and – I said something to her about it. "Oh," she said, "that's nothing." See, that's all I got to know.' Later, the mother, discovering the girl flirting with soldiers, laughingly remarked that 'you don't know what you do to those boys'.[29] Ignorance certainly made it no easier for a working-class wife to enjoy sexual relations with her husband. And, if we are to believe Roberts, most husbands assumed that the experience would be little more than routine for either partner:

I remember the savage disatisfaction with his spouse of a young brass moulder. 'Last night,' he said (during what was made plain had been the 'very lists of love'), 'she goes an' ask me not to forget to leave twopence for the gas!' The wife of a fettler in the same group was prone, it turned out, to reach her *crise d'extase* whilst eating an apple. A third, swathed in clothes, permitted her husband only the act *per se* and, on her mother's advice, allowed no 'dirty' manual contact whatever. 'It's about as exciting', he said, 'as posting a letter!' This was a common inhibition.[30]

Any excitement the woman experienced was generally tempered by a fear of pregnancy. The 386 women who answered the Women's Cooperative Guild inquiry had given birth to 1,396 live children and had experienced a total of 218 miscarriages and 83 still-births – a pre-natal death rate of 21·3 per 100 live births compared to a national average of 10·9.[31] Some of the women reported with pride the fact that they used a birth control device, though in most cases only after several pregnancies:

> When at the end of ten years [at the age of thirty-two] I was almost a mental and physical wreck, I determined that this state of things should not go on any longer, and if there was no natural means of prevention, then, of course, artificial means must be employed, which were successful, and I am happy to say that from that time I have been able to take pretty good care of myself, but I shudder to think what might have been the result if things had been allowed to go on as they were.[32]

Reliable preventatives were an added expense and, particularly in the case of female devices, not that readily obtainable. The result was a reliance on coitus interruptus or, on the part of the wife, on various homemade devices – oiled sponges, or pessaries compounded of lard and flour. Attempts to abort unwanted children were common, according to all accounts. Women would try pennyroyal syrup, turpentine or soda douches, or one of a variety of patent medicines guaranteed to remove 'obstructions', in order to relieve themselves of the trials of an unwanted and debilitating pregnancy.

> There's Alice Radcliffe I've just left. Like a bear with a sore head 'cause there's another on the way. Bottle after bottle of pennyroyal she's supped but it hasn't worked. By God! I thought things were bad enough for me, but her . . . Eleven of 'em, and now another, and him only bringing home eighteen shillings a week when he can get it.[33]

Pregnancy, for a working-class mother, brought with it a portion of discomforts and complications unfamiliar to women of the middle and upper classes. Her generally debilitated physical condition increased the odds for further trouble. The Fabian Women's Group, inquiring into the nutritional needs of expectant mothers in South London, had to abandon its scheme to include only healthy women in its experiments. So many suffered from pulmonary and respiratory ailments that to have excluded them would have reduced their sample by about 50 per cent.[34] The letters to the Women's Cooperative Guild catalogue an enormous volume of medical problems: fallen wombs, varicose veins, urinary and kidney infections. In most cases the victims assumed that their difficulties were an unavoidable consequence of their condition: 'It was sheer *ignorance, and the idea that we must put up with it till the nine months were over.*'[35]

And when the nine months came to an end, there remained the ordeal of the lying-in. Whenever possible, a relative or, in less economically straitened families, a hired girl, would be engaged to help manage. Older children were alloted more than their usual number of tasks. In many instances, the husband would undertake a portion of the household chores.[36] Yet in most cases, the mother would be expected to remain at the helm. 'There is no peace for the wife at home,' one such woman complained. 'She is still the head and chancellor of the exchequer. If she were confined on Friday, she would still have to plan and lay out the Saturday money, and if it did not stretch far enough, she would be the one to go short or do the worrying.'[37]

Whether she employed a doctor or a midwife – the fee in either case generally varied from ten shillings to a guinea – the working-class mother could not expect the degree of expertise available to the middle class. When the birth presented complications, the risks ran high:

> My first child was a boy, and I nearly lost my life because the doctor did not bring his bag containing the necessary instruments for use at these times, and his home was five miles away. So I can assure you I was nearly gone when the child was born. Then when I had the second one – which was a girl – the very same doctor (there was only one doctor within miles then) came nearly drunk, and I had a frightful time. What is called the after-birth had grown to my side and he never got it all away. I had milk fever first, and then childbed fever.

> The last miscarriage I had I lost that much blood it completely drained me. I was three whole months and was unable to sleep; I could not even sleep one half-hour. I had lost my sleep completely; my hair came off and left bald patches about my head.

> Alas! The doctor who attended me suffered from eczema of a very bad type in his hands. The disease attacked me and in twenty-four hours I was covered from head to foot ... finally leaving me partially and sometimes totally crippled in my hands.

> [The Doctor] had just left the infirmary, and we had heard he was very clever in maternity. When he saw me and questioned me, he sent for the nurse. The rest of that night is too terrible to go through even now after twenty-eight years. Suffice it to say that very next morning there was a poor little baby boy with a very large swollen head dreadfully cut, and a young mother dreadfully cut also.[38]

Even without medical complications, childbirth was recalled by most mothers as an unpleasant and messy experience. Brown paper was laid down upon the bed to prevent staining. Many midwives disapproved of washing anything but their patients' faces and hands after delivery:

> Never once can I remember having anything but face, neck and hands washed until I could do things for myself, and it was thought certain death to change underclothes under a week. For a whole week we were obliged to be on clothes stiff and stained, and the stench under the clothes was abominable, and added to this we were commanded to keep the babies under the clothes.[39]

One of this woman's four children had been born in this way in damp rooms 'nearly underground', so crowded that two beds had been set up in the living room. Her husband's wages ranged from ten shillings to one pound a week.

These letters illuminate Bott's conclusion that working-class wives regarded physical sexuality as 'violent and disruptive', and as 'an intrusion on a peaceful domestic relationship'.[40] As one woman wrote: 'Very much injury and suffering comes to the mother and child through the father's ignorance and interference. Pain of body and mind, which leaves its mark in many ways on the child. No animal will submit to this. Why should the woman?'[41]

Militancy is not a hallmark of most responses to the Guild's inquiry. Far more typical are remarks suggesting that duty compels a wife to submit with a good grace to the demands of her husband, whatever the consequences in terms of her own health and the well-being of the family. Much the same attitude was still prevalent a few years later: 'He said it was his rights, and he'd have consumption if we took any precautions. He said that's what always gives men consumption. And now I'm like this!'[42] Sex, tied as it was to the dreary routines of childbirth that often marked more than a third of a woman's life could, with a particularly demanding or unthoughtful husband, become a hell. But, if the Guild's letters are to be believed, most husbands tempered their insistence upon 'rights' with enough consideration to make sex, if not a pleasure, a kind of compromise, arrived at after an initial period of some tension, and not so intolerable as to jeopardize a generally happy marriage.[43]

Happiness on 25 shillings a week[44] represented a considerable achievement, for which the working-class wife could usually take much of the credit. Upon the housewife's ability to manage with very little – no less than upon the husband's success in bringing home as much as he could – depended the family's very survival. 'If she be a tidy woman and a good manager,' Beatrice Webb wrote in her report for Booth on the London Docks,

> decently versed in the rare arts of cooking and sewing, the family life is independent, even comfortable, and the children may follow in the father's footsteps or rise to better things. If she be a gossip and a bungler – worse still, a drunkard – the family sink to the low level of the East London street; and the children are probably added to the number of those who gain their livelihood by irregular work and by irregular means.[45]

Rowntree describes the lengths to which a 'good manager' had to go in order to sustain herself and her family on 17 shillings a week, never buying a joint of meat, occasionally indulging in a sheep's head or 'meat pieces' for sixpence, saving a penny at a time to pay for a nurse to care for her and her family during a confinement.[46] These women could never afford even the slightest miscalculation; the cost of food and shelter did not rise and fall along with wages. One London docker, whom statisticians would have regarded as fully employed, in fact brought home, in the summer of 1913, the following wage packets over a period of eleven weeks: £1 3s 6d; 18s 8d; 7s 8d; £1 3s 2d; £2 7s 4d; nil; £2 1s 4d; £1 0s 10d; 19s 2d; 18s 2d; 14s 4d.[47] The average of a little more than 21 shillings a week would have placed the family on the poverty line in any case. But how was a wife to manage week by week on a budget determined, as was this and countless others, by the capriciousness of the labour market?

In most cases the answer was by mounting indebtedness. Robert Tressell records the frightening tangle of debts into which even the most prudent households might fall, in the chapter entitled 'The Financiers' from *The Ragged Trousered Philanthropists*. The victims are the house painter Easton, his wife Ruth, and their infant son. Their income for the past week totalled £1 4s 9½d. Their debts, as they commenced their calculations, amounted to £4 10s 11d.

> 'If we pay the two week's rent that'll leave us twelve shillings to live on.'
>
> 'But we won't be able to keep all that,' said Ruth, 'because there's other things to pay.'
>
> 'What other things?'
>
> 'We owe the baker eight shillings for the bread he let us have while you were not working, and there's about twelve shillings owing for groceries. We'll have to pay them something on account. Then we want some more coal; there's only about a shovelful left . . .'
>
> 'It seems to me,' said he, as, after having cleared a space on the table and arranged the paper, he began to sharpen his pencil with a

table-knife, 'that you don't manage things as well as you might. If you was to make out a list of just the things you *must* have before you went out of a Saturday, you'd find the money would go much farther. Instead of doing that you just take the money in your hand without knowing exactly what you're going to do with it, and when you come back it's all gone and next to nothing to show for it.'

His wife made no reply: her head was bent down over the child.

After again charging his wife with neglecting her duties as household manager, Easton is astonished to discover her in tears:

'I always do the best I can with the money,' Ruth sobbed. 'I never spend a farthing on myself, but you don't seem to understand how hard it is. I don't care nothing about having to go without things myself, but I can't bear it when you speak to me like you do lately. You seem to blame me for everything . . . Oh, I am so tired, I wish I could lie down somewhere and sleep and never wake up any more.'[48]

Most working-class couples were often confronted with the same sort of grim figures. In an article written for the *Trade Unionist* in 1892, Tom Mann confirmed Tressell's account in language equally impassioned. Arguing on behalf of communal kitchens, as a way of reducing working-class expenses, Mann depicted the average housewife's existence as comprised of 'scarcely anything but difficulties'. 'Many women,' he declared, 'are literally driven mad by the mental anxiety caused by the effort to procure the household necessities with the money alloted them; hundreds of thousands are in a continual state of dread for fear of being overtaken by adversity which they would not be able to surmount.'[49]

A woman's problems increased in those households where the husband, even if earning a steady wage, refused to surrender an agreed sum each week to his wife. Custom varied considerably in this regard. In some cases a husband would hand over his entire packet to his wife and receive spending money back from her. Far more often, the husband withheld a set sum sufficient for his own personal needs – mostly beer and tobacco – and gave his wife what remained. When this was the case and when the man's total wage was itself irregular, his wife was forced to adjust her own budget accordingly. 'He just left it as it was and . . . if I hadn't enough – well I just had to go without.'[50] Nothing suggests that the women particularly resented this practice; they accepted it where it occurred as a given fact, and planned to accommodate to it. Seldom, however, except at times of extreme crisis, did husband and wife sit down together to discuss the week's expenses as Tressell shows the Eastons doing. The husband expected his wife to manage as best she could; the wife acknowledged the responsibility and tried to exercise it so as not to burden her husband with further worries unless absolutely forced to do so. Their roles were distinct: his to provide as steady an income as his abilities and his good fortune would permit; hers to spend it as carefully as her stock of common sense would let her.

Matters were complicated by the growth cycle through which most families passed. When first married, a man and wife could live in relative prosperity, always assuming the husband was regularly employed. If his wife worked as well, so much the better. They might have initial expenses for furniture and other household goods; but they could manage well enough. Indeed, it was often the simple realization that they could get by very nicely on their combined wages that induced a courting couple to go ahead and marry. Once children began to come the picture changed: more mouths to feed, pressure for roomier accommodation and, if the wife gave up her work, a sharp reduction in family income. According to statistics compiled from the 1911 census, expenses weighed most heavily against wages when the father was somewhere between thirty-five and forty years of age.[51] Pressure grew less severe as older children left school for work, contributing a share of their weekly wages to the family's general income. They increased again, once old age or sickness threatened further unemployment, or death deprived the family altogether of its major source of income. Analysing that period in a family's life when finances were at their tightest, Seebohm Rowntree, in his study, *The Human Needs of Labour*, concluded that 46 per cent of married working-class men had a wife and three or more children dependent upon them for a period of five years or more, and that a wage which provided support for only three children would have been inadequate in a third of the households he surveyed.[52]

Against the pattern of this cycle, the working-class wife struggled to keep the family afloat. Almost inevitably a time came when her money ran out; then she would resort to the neighbourhood store for credit, or to the pawnshop for a loan. Roberts, whose mother was the proprietor of a Salford shop, describes the process she employed to decide who was to receive credit and who was not:

A wife (never a husband) would apply humbly for tick on behalf of her family. Then, in our shop, my mother would make an anxious appraisal, economic and social – how many mouths had the woman to feed? Was the husband ailing? Tuberculosis in the house, perhaps? If TB took one it always claimed others; the breadwinner next time, maybe. Did the male partner drink heavily? Was he a bad time keeper at work? Did they patronise the pawnshop? If so, how far were they committed? Were their relations known good payers? And last, had they already 'blued' some other shop in the district, and for how much? After assessment, credit would be granted and a credit limit fixed, at not more than five shillings' worth of food stuffs in any one week, with all 'fancy' provisions such as biscuits and boiled ham proscribed.

Roberts adds that for many women, a tick book became a symbol of respectability, acknowledging the fact that they could be trusted and had therefore been accepted in the neighbourhood.[53]

A pawn ticket, though not a talisman of the same sort, by no means implied disgrace. The pawnshop was simply another source of immediate credit. Families – almost always represented by the wife – would pawn their best clothes on a Monday, redeem them on pay day, sport them on Sunday, and return them once more to the shop the next day. Here again, a reputation for reliability stood one in good stead. 'If the tradesman knows his customer, and knows that the things pledged are almost sure to be taken out again on Saturday for Sunday's use, he can afford to advance an extra sixpence.'[54] Brokers normally charged customers 5d per week interest on the loan of a pound. Able, in this way, to live a week in advance of wages, women found it hard to break their reliance on the pawnshop. The broker did a lively business and was a generally respected member of the community. One recalled lending £450 a week, on as many as 900 items: 'All those things had to be packed away and the ticket put on them . . . it was hard going.'[55] A sharp customer appeared at his shop each Monday to pawn clothes in return for £1. With the money, she then proceeded to the local Co-op where she purchased her week's groceries. For spending a pound at the Co-op, she received 3 shillings interest; for borrowing on a pound's worth of clothing, she paid 5d interest. The pawnbroker considered himself taken. In circumstances such as these, pawning was for the housewife nothing more or less than a device to make budgeting easier, a necessity in times of real hardship, a convenience otherwise.

Hardship or habit drove some women with nothing left to pawn into the hands of local loan sharks, men and women who lent a shilling a week for a penny interest. It took financial sophistication of a kind most poor women did not possess to recognize that if the debt remained unpaid for six months – and a bout of sickness or unemployment might well mean that it would – she would end by paying interest at a rate of over 200 per cent.[56]

Rent comprised a major portion of every week's budget. And rents varied to a considerable degree throughout England. All those who studied the matter agreed that generally the working class paid more than it should have for housing that was at best adequate, and too often far less than that. Experts estimated that families ought to spend somewhere between one-tenth and one-seventh of their combined earnings on rent. The sum was often closer to one-fourth or one-third. The percentage increased in inverse ratio to income. Pember Reeves pointed out that in London, where rents were at their highest, a working-class husband and wife with four children might pay as much as 8s from a total of 24 for two rooms – one-third of their income – whereas a middle-class man earning £500 a year would pay £85 for his house, or only one-sixth of his. The middle-class renter was also able to avail himself of water and waste pipes to which his working-class fellow citizen might not have access, despite the fact that both paid taxes proportionate to their rents.[57] Rowntree and A. C. Pigou, in their survey of housing conditions in 1914, support Pember Reeves's estimate, adding that elsewhere in England it was not uncommon to find at least one-sixth of the weekly income devoted to rent; A. L. Bowley and A. R. Burnett-Hurst, using 1911 census figures, declared that the figure of one-sixth was probably too low, especially since it assumed what could not be assumed: a steady income throughout the entire year.[58]

If we assume a weekly income of from 18 to 35 shillings, and measure it against rents demanded, the percentages take on additional meaning. Rents for corporation houses in Sheffield were 5s 6d per week in the early 1900s, for similar accommodation in Birmingham, 5s to 6s 3d. Two-room houses in Manchester cost an average of 3s 5d; four-room houses, 4s 10d. Bowley and Burnett-Hurst discovered that, in the industrial towns they surveyed, the largest percentage of rental housing available to the working class fell in the 5 to 8 shillings range. In Reading, 67 per cent of the houses rented for more than 6 shillings; in Northampton, 54 per cent; in Stanley (a mining community), 33 per cent; in Warrington, 18 per cent.[59] Rents in London decreased the farther one travelled from the centre of the city. A labour aristocrat earning good wages could afford a house of four and five rooms in working-class suburbs for a sum that would pay for but two rooms in central London. There, rents averaged 5s for a single room, 6s 6d for two rooms, 8s 6d for three, and 10s 6d for four. Philanthropic trusts charged rents for tenement flats that generally prohibited poorly paid labourers – those most in need of accommodation – from living in them. Three-room flats in one such estate rented for from 7s 6d to 8s 6d per week. The fact that the trust in this case put an upper limit of 30 shillings a week on the wages of those to whom it would rent flats of that size, demonstrates the readiness of even a philanthropic enterprise to assume, contrary to expert opinion, that the working class could afford to spend from one-fourth to one-third of its income on housing.[60]

You paid your money; but seldom, unless your ear was to the ground, did you have much chance to take your choice. A husband's nearby place of work, a wife's relations a block away – habits and connections meant that there was more to moving than carting off one's bits and pieces, and that bargain-hunting for shelter was a complicated business.

With rent depleting the weekly wage packet as it did, the housewife found herself forced to exercise both frugality and ingenuity if she was to feed her family on what was left to her. Rowntree estimated that in 1914 food enough to keep a manual worker at anything like the peak of his proficiency cost 4s 4d per week; food for his wife, 3s 6d per week; for each of his children, 2s 5d.[61] Assume a family of father, mother and three children: applying Rowntree's standards, their weekly food budget totalled 15s 1d. Add to this 5 or 6 shillings a week rent, and the total already exceeds the 21 shillings which Rowntree and Booth declared to be the line below which approximately one-third of the working class was living. Add, again, the 2 or 3 shillings per week that families had to spend for fuel, clothes, and cleaning materials – to say nothing of the shilling or two they would want to spend on their own entertainment – and one can readily understand why families often went short of the food they needed.

The London County Council sponsored programmes in its schools' domestic science classes to acquaint pupils with a 'proper' breakfast menu and its cost, for a family of six:

|  | d. |
|---|---|
| $\frac{3}{4}$ teasp. tea | $0\frac{3}{4}$ |
| $\frac{1}{4}$ lb. sugar | $0\frac{1}{2}$ |
| milk | $0\frac{3}{4}$ |
| one loaf of bread | $2\frac{1}{2}$ |
| $\frac{1}{4}$ lb. dripping, margarine, jam, or treacle | 1 |
| $\frac{1}{4}$ lb. oatmeal | $0\frac{1}{2}$ |
| Rashers or kipper (for the father) | 2 |
|  | 8d |

The total cost per week, 4s 8d, was beyond the means of most working-class families.[62] Pember Reeves estimated that the families with an average of a pound a week in wages could afford no more than 7 or 8 shillings for food, contrasting this figure with the 4 shillings a week per head the London Board of Guardians allotted for food to parents of foster-children. 'Assuming that there are four children, and that it costs 4 shillings a week to feed a child, there would be but 4 shillings left on which to feed both parents, and nothing at all for coal, gas, clothes, insurance, soap, or rent.'[63] Unemployment brought further reductions, further debts, or both:

> Mrs H's family numbers twelve, and ranges from a son of twenty-five to a baby of twenty-four months. The husband has had no regular work for five years, but does what he can. Four of the children are at work. This family takes much pride in itself, and the standard of life insisted upon has nearly worried the mother into her grave. One day she bewailed herself as follows: 'My dinners come to 2 shillings a day, and I can't do them under, and the children eat a loaf every day in addition to their meat and vegetables. The grocer's book is never under eleven or twelve shillings.' A careful investigation into the accounts of the family showed that the absolutely necessary expenses, including rent, mounted up to £2 a week, and, as the income seldom reached that sum, the mother was never out of debt. 'I can't help it!' she exclaimed desperately; 'if I don't keep their bellies full now, what will happen to them when they are older?'[64]

Keeping bellies full asked of the mother a degree of skill in domestic science which she often did not possess, and of her husband and children a tolerance for plainness and sameness which it would have been almost heartless to expect. 'For 1s 2d I myself can get a good dinner for three adults and four children,' one working-class matron claimed. 'I get one and a half pounds of pieces [meat scraps] for 7d, four pounds of potatoes for 2½d, a cabbage for 1d, and a halfpenny worth of onions. Then I get a half-quartern of flour and a pennyworth of suet or dripping for a pudding. The children don't get much meat, but they have plenty of vegetables and pudding with gravy.'[65] The meal sounds less nourishing broken down into its components per person: 3⅕ ounces of meat, 1 medium-sized potato, ⅐ of a cabbage head, and 5⅓ ounces of pudding. Lady Bell analysed the 7s 6d spent in one week by a Middlesbrough family of three in terms of the quantities that actually ended up on the table. What she discovered was a total amount that, excepting tea and sugar, 'would last about two days for a family of the same size in better circumstances': one ten-inch-long dish of meat, 'tolerably full, not piled up'; seven and a half quartern loaves, 15 inches long, 8 inches high, 6 inches wide; two wedges of butter, 5 inches long; one similar wedge of lard; bacon 'about half the size lengthwise of a large octavo volume'; four tumblers of milk; a bag of potatoes 16 inches high and half as wide; ten teacups full of sugar; two breakfast-cups full of tea leaves.[66]

Meat was a gauge by which working-class families measured their prosperity. Its consumption increased markedly in the period between 1875 and 1914. Prosperous working-class households could expect to dine on meat as often as four or five times a week. The son of a Bradford boilermaker, whose mother worked part-time as a fancy laundress, recalled weekly menus of Sunday roast joint and Yorkshire pudding, liver and onions, meat and potato pies, and stews with left-over scraps from the joint. 'We always had good meals.'[67] In Ben Turner's house there was usually some sort of meat for the noontime meal, 'always providing the funds ran to it'.[68] Left-over meat became part of what were called 'resurrection meals'; 'scouse', a stew of meat scraps and vegetables, appeared as a staple in working-class diets. When scraps were scarce, barley was added, and the mixture dubbed 'blind' scouse.[69] The price of meat depended, naturally, on its quality. 'Pieces' were sold for anything from 6d to 3d a pound, though in the latter case, the meat was bound to consist mostly of sinew and gristle. Entrails of various sorts – hearts, lights, tripe – were favoured by those women who knew how to stew them up in a tasty fashion. Pork rinds, stewing bones, and faggots, made of pig entrails, could be combined with rice or potatoes into a satisfying meal: 'I've often made a good supper for my man and myself for three halfpence. When faggots are cold you can get one for three farthings. I boil a pennyworth of rice till it is quite soft, and then cut the faggot through it and boil up together. The faggot makes the rice so savoury that anyone could eat it.'[70] The fact that quantities are measured, not by their bulk, but by their cost, documents the attention housewives were constantly forced to pay to their budgets.

Tinned and imported frozen meats, substantially cheaper than the fresh domestic, did not find universal favour among working-class wives, despite their price. Beef in tins did not appear to resemble meat at all: 'I have a vivid recollection of the unappetizing look of the contents – a large lump of coarse-grained meat inclined to separate into coarse fibres, a large lump of unpleasant-looking fat on one side of it – and an irregular hollow partly filled with watery fluid.'[71] 'Chilled' meats from abroad were assumed, on very little basis, to be of a generally inferior quality. Roberts discloses that no respectable artisan's wife before 1914 would deal with a butcher who sold only imported, frozen beef and mutton.[72]

The fact that meat became a mark of respectability was a measure of its cost. Families that upon occasion enjoyed meat in some form or other, nevertheless lived on bread. Potatoes were a staple as well, and in the north, porridge. Those lucky enough to rent an allotment supplemented their diet with vegetables. But week in, week out, bread furnished the working class with the bulk of its nourishment. In some houses baking was a part of the weekly ritual; housewives prided themselves on their ability to turn out a variety of loaves – white and brown, tea cakes, ginger snaps, and the like. More relied upon local bakeries, where two two-pound loaves – a quartern – could be purchased for from 4d to 6d. Bread was what has now come to be called 'convenience food'. It was cheap, it came ready cooked; one could eat it any time and anywhere.

The less the housewife cooked, the less fuel she had to buy. Most working-class families spent from one to two shillings a week on coal or gas, or a combination.[73] The working class could not purchase coal by the ton: there was seldom enough money for such a large investment. Even if there had been, there would have been no room in most working-class houses to store a ton of coal. The housewife bought instead by the hundredweight, paying up to ten shillings more per ton for that privilege. If she could save a bit by cutting bread for a meal, instead of cooking a stew, she would be sorely tempted to do so.

The sameness of daily fare led to a craving for something 'a bit tasty'. Three halfpence would purchase a generous portion of fish and chips; 3d or 4d would buy a whole dinner from the shop in a basin. The latter was a tempting bargain, especially to the wife who worked all day: 'It saves trouble to get the food ready cooked, especially where, perhaps, the frying pan is nearly the only utensil in use. The children's dinner is bought for 1d; and 2d and 3d worth of potato pie, boiled ham, trotters, or roast pork form the usual dinners.'[74] Social workers might lament the fact that cheap fried fish made up the 'marrow and muscle' of much of England's working-class population,[75] overlooking the monotony that persuaded working-class wives to enliven their menus with food deplored by middle-class dieticians.

Even when willing to spend the time and money to put wholesome meals on the table, a woman's efforts were thwarted by the generally inferior quality of the food available in local shops. Once again, as with housing, her chances of receiving value for money were far less than those of her middle-class counterpart. She paid more, proportionately, in return for adulterated or tainted food that merchants would not have dared sell outside a slum. A description of the wares of a typical working-class provisioner testified that

> his sugar is grey and gritty, and does not sweeten well; his margarine is strong, he very rarely seems to stock the well-known labelled brands, but some species that he manipulates with butter pats behind a marble screen, so that no one can see what he is doing. His bacon is always rancid, and his cheese second-rate; his cocoa is adulterated with corn flour, his jam is that brand made by famous firms under another name; it consists of the refuse from the good, well-advertised jams that have made the firm deservedly famous.[76]

Roberts confirms the report with recollections from his mother's shop, of milk doctored by the dairies with formaldehyde to prevent souring, of maggotty ham and bacon washed in charcoal water to prevent putrefaction, of eggs broken and in dirty crates selling nevertheless for sixteen a shilling.[77]

Budgetary restraints and the quality of food available conspired to produce a poorly nourished working class. The practice of ensuring that at least the father was well fed, so that he might sustain himself at work, too often resulted in the underfeeding of wife and children: 'In the households of well-to-do people, two kinds of diet can be used – one for adults, the other for children. In the household which spends 10 shillings or less on food, only one kind of diet is possible, and that is the man's diet. The children have what is left over.'[78] Babies were not put on solid food until about five or six months old; they were not weaned, as a rule, until they were a year. Milk, adulterated or not, was expensive – as much as 4d a quart in London. A pint of milk per day – by no means a generous portion – would bring the weekly milk bill to 1s 2d, too much for most budgets to accommodate.[79] Prepared baby foods came on the market at the end of the nineteenth century, but their cost prohibited their use by the poor. As a result, when mothers began to feed their babies solid food, it was the food from the family table, indigestible and therefore unsuited for infants. Tressell describes the results in his chapter on the Eastons:

> [The parents] walked softly over and stood by the cradle side looking at the child; as they looked the baby kept moving uneasily in its sleep. His face was very flushed and its eyes were moving under the half-closed lids. Every now and again its lips were drawn back slightly, showing part of the gums; presently it began to whimper, drawing up its knees as if in pain.
> 'He seems to have something wrong with him,' said Easton.

'I think it's his teeth,' replied the mother. 'He's been very restless all day and he was awake nearly all last night.'

'P'raps he's hungry.'

'No, it can't be that. He had the best part of an egg this morning, and I've nursed him several times today. And then at dinner-time he had a whole saucer full of fried potatoes with little bits of bacon in it.'[80]

Children of the very poorest families were spared the indignities of bacon and potatoes; for them, a diet of 'sugar butties' – pieces of bread with a scrape of dripping or lard, dipped first in tea, then in sugar.

By the time a boy or girl left school for work, the chances were that his diet consisted in the main of bread and tea. A Manchester working-class boy in 1904 subsisted on the following diet:

*Breakfast* (carried to work). One-half pound of bread and butter, a little cheese as relish, a can of very strong tea.

*Dinner* (eaten at home). Bread, at the beginning of the week supplemented with meat, tea, and pastry.

*Tea*. Bread, strong tea, butter or jam.

*Supper*. A slice or two of bread and tea.[81]

Mothers, who in many households made a practice of serving themselves last, ate no better very often than their children. D. J. Oddy, in a recent investigation of working-class diets, declares that 'essentially the women's diet was one of bread and tea, while almost all men consumed a main meal of meat or bacon or fish and potatoes'.[82] Unless a working-class family enjoyed an income of over 30 shillings a week, they were forced by their inability to purchase enough food to exist on a diet that kept them undernourished. Despite a rise in real wages over much of the period under survey, and a fall in food prices, Oddy concludes that 'on the whole, what they ate was very similar to the diet of the worst group (needlewomen in London) examined by Dr Edward Smith in 1863, except that sugar consumption was double that of the 1860s'.[83] These conclusions confirm those reached by investigators who surveyed the working class at the beginning of the twentieth century. Rowntree exposed the fact that the diets of those in York living on weekly earnings of 26 shillings lacked an average of 17 per cent of the standard requirements of 3,500 daily calories. A team of experts found that the average working-class diet in Edinburgh fell below the 3,500 mark. W. A. Mackenzie, surveying the standard of living in the period 1860–1914, discovered that families earning wages which placed them in the lowest decile of the population lived on fewer calories in 1914 than in 1880.[84] All of which statistical data is embodied in the cry of one York housewife: 'I'm dead sick of bread and butter – nothing but bread and butter until I hate the sight of it.'[85]

Once the housewife had paid the rent and bought the food and fuel her family required, she might turn, with what little she had left her, to examine the family's wardrobe. Rowntree printed yearly clothing budgets, devised by members of the working class, which averaged 27 shillings for men, 26 shillings for women, 27 shillings for a boy of twelve, and 17 shillings for a child of two.[86] Given a family of five, with one child of twelve, one of two, and one somewhere between, the annual clothing budget would amount to something between £5 and £6, or over 2 shillings a week. These estimates were minimal. In a later study Rowntree established that a similar family would have needed to budget 5 shillings a week for adequate clothing.[87] Further evidence that Rowntree's York figures had been pared to the bone appears in budgets printed in a 1911 Board of Trade study of wage-earning women and girls. There, in cases where unmarried women were living at home or in lodgings and were spared the full expenses of household management, their expenditure on clothing, while hardly extravagant, nevertheless far exceeded Rowntree's average of 26 shillings. A comparison of the detailed budgets shows why. A Lancashire cotton winder, at home with her mother, and earning an average of 12s 7½d per week, spent the following on clothes in the course of a year:[88]

| | Total for 52 weeks | | | Average per week | |
|---|---|---|---|---|---|
| | £ | s. | d. | s. | d. |
| Dresses, blouses and skirts | 3 | 15 | 7 | 1 | 5½ |
| Coats and waterproofs | 1 | 9 | 6 | 0 | 6¾ |
| Hats | 1 | 6 | 5 | 0 | 6 |
| Underclothing, handkerchiefs and aprons | 1 | 17 | 4 | 0 | 8¾ |
| Scarves, ties, collars and gloves | 0 | 11 | 10 | 0 | 2¾ |
| Boots, shoes, etc., and repairs | 1 | 10 | 6 | 0 | 7 |
| Miscellaneous | 0 | 1 | 0 | 0 | 0¼ |
| Total dress | £10 | 12 | 2 | 4 | 1 |

The highest estimate in the York budgets for women reads in dreary contrast:[89]

|  |  | s. | d. |
|---|---|---|---|
| Shoes | 1 pair 5s 6d; repairs 3s 6d | 9 | 0 |
| Slippers | Wear old boots | | |
| Dress | Ready-made skirt 8s; | | |
| | blouse 2s | 10 | 0 |
| Aprons | 4 at 6d each | 2 | 0 |
| Skirt | Go without | | |
| Stockings | 2 pairs at 9d | 1 | 6 |
| Underclothing | 1 of each article | 2 | 10 |
| Stays | 1 pair | 2 | 6 |
| Hat | New one would cost 4s 6d, | | |
| | but would last several years | 1 | 6 |
| Jacket | Do. | 1 | 6 |
| Shawl | Do. | 1 | 0 |
| | | 31 | 10 |

The Lancashire cotton winder dressed herself warmly and with a certain style. She had clothes enough to allow her always to appear neat and clean. The York housewife had clothes enough to cover her body, and precious little more. To maintain even that scanty wardrobe, along with an equally spare one for her husband and children, might have cost her more than she was able to afford.

Boots were a particular expense. Workmen's boots cost 9 shillings a pair; ironworkers wore through three pairs in a year. Most working men could effect a rough re-soling when necessary. Pember Reeves reported a printer's handyman who spent part of each day repairing his children's shoes: 'As soon as he has gone round the family the first pair is ready again.'[90] Families with daughters in service could often count on cast-offs from benevolent employers. Neighbours might exchange outgrown children's garments, though anything worth saving was usually handed down within the family until it was worn through. Many women made at least some of their family's clothes themselves; there was debate, however, whether ready-mades — particularly secondhand — were not cheaper. A sewing machine cost £8 or more, an expense well beyond the reach of the average budget. With shopping to attend to, a house to clean, and meals to cook, most working-class mothers had time and inclination for little more than mending.[91] Women who could afford to put aside a regular sum each week for clothes preferred to join a clothing club, managed by a local tradesman, rather than to save for a sewing machine.

Frugality resulted in monotony. To live within one of Rowntree's budgets, man, woman, and child would have to wear the same clothes for months on end. Men wore heavy jackets and trousers to work, an overcoat if lucky, and on Sundays a 'best' suit with a scarf. Roberts recalls that bowlers were 'compulsory wear' in Salford: 'Only the lower types wore caps.' On the other hand, a Yorkshire contemporary maintains that in Bradford the respectable working class wore flat caps of wool.[92] Whenever possible, children were treated to new outfits for the Whit Sunday Walk, an excuse in the north of England for a public fashion show. Patent leather shoes were the favourite indulgence for this occasion. But 'when they were done, they were done.' The rest of the year, the children made do with polished clogs.[93]

If money ran short, most often the wife did without new clothes for herself. Here, as so often, respectability played a part in her decision. Her husband went from the neighbourhood to work, and her children to school. They appeared in public more regularly than did she, and therefore had the greater need for decent-looking clothing. A woman could make do at home with a blouse, a patched skirt and an apron, with a shawl to wear out for a trip to the local store. When she put on her 'best', it was usually a jacket and skirt or dress, and a hat. Loane wrote approvingly in 1907 of the fact that the dress of London working-class women was plainer and less tawdry than it had been twenty to thirty years before.[94] Too often, plainness was not a matter of taste but of necessity. The constant strain of budgeting taught the housewife that monotony was to be the norm, and she ceased to hope that she might appear in something that was more than merely clean and decent. She almost never had clothing that was 'pretty and fresh and right *at the same time*; if she buys a new coat and skirt, she has to have a much washed blouse and trimmed up last year's hat; she never experiences the delicious thrill of looking at herself in the mirror and feeling how nice she looks.'[95]

Furniture was a major expense for most working-class families only when husband and wife were first married. Suites for parlour or bedroom cost from £5 to £7; secondhand furniture a good deal less. Ben Turner, in his autobiography, recalled having saved £4 7s 6d to spend on furnishings.[96] Couples without the opportunity or inclination to save could buy on time. As a result, many working-class homes were comfortably if not elegantly furnished. As children came, families made do in rather less style. Even the cost of a baby's cot of the cheapest kind – a banana crate with a sacking bottom, a bag filled with chaff for mattress, cotton blankets – was beyond the reach of women trying to get by on a pound a week.[97]

Two other items figured prominently in most budgets. Joseph Rowntree estimated that working-class families spent an average of as well as store-bought, remedies: treacle and sulphur; senna, raisins and boiling water; rue and wormwood – all cleared the system and were administered routinely as a spring tonic. Coughs were dosed with sugar and butter; sore throats with sulphur.[117] When it came to their own health, women expected complications from child-bearing and from menopause. Often they would assume one or the other of those causes to lie at the root of whatever bothered them – a backache, a headache, ill temper. They could postpone a visit to the doctor on the grounds that their illness was only natural, given their condition; they could excuse their short tempers and frayed nerves for the same reason. Lady Bell found working-class women almost eager for menopause: 'They encourge themselves to look for it; they make no attempt at self-control, they eagerly watch for symptoms; they are ready to refer any and every passing disturbance to that crisis, either impending or actually arrived.'[118]

Ailments of one sort or another, their own or their family's, meant that for most housewives nursing was part of the normal routine. Real illness – a debilitating accident at work, cancer, or consumption – shattered that routine with upsetting force. Chronic asthma and rheumatism, easily contracted when working in the damp or out of doors, could force a man to bed. Once there, he made family life more complicated, overcrowding the house still further, and perhaps requiring special treatment both day and night. His successful convalescence might depend on a fuller diet than the family budget could stand, so that he would have to return to work only half well, a prey to further sickness.

With so much to attend to, the housewife's leisure was apportioned to her much as her tea and her sugar was, in small daily amounts: a chat at the door with tallyman or bookmaker;[119] a gossip at the shop with neighbours. Shopping might include visits to relatives or to the pub. The middle class attempted to arrange diversions for her. Booth extolled the programmes of church-sponsored mothers' meetings, at which thrift and savings were fostered by coal and clothing clubs, 'while tea parties and excursions pleasantly bind the whole together'. Most parishes in working-class neighbourhoods at one time or another initiated such efforts; though seldom effective in propagating the gospel, they did afford entertainment of a sort, at the risk of well meant but annoying patronage.[120]

The working-class wife read less frequently than her husband, her schedule seldom allowing her a chance to sit down for any period of time with a book. In a survey of 200 working-class couples, Lady Bell discovered that 17 women could not read (compared with eight men);

that only three women owned to disliking reading, that in 28 of the households no one cared to read, in 58 only newspapers were read, and in 37 either husband or wife was genuinely fond of reading.[121] Weekly newspapers catered to women with a mixture of household hints, romantic fiction, and scandal in high places. The *Home Companion*, a penny weekly, laced its novelettes with characters such as 'The Honourable Mrs Latimer, of Curzon St, Mayfair', and its column *Pictures and Paragraphs* contained trivia of the following nature:

> Princess Charles of Denmark is a very enthusiastic gardener.

> The Grand Duchess Olga, of Russia, the Czar's eldest daughter, who is now in her eighth year, is probably the wealthiest little lady in the universe.[122]

*Reynolds's*, one of the most popular weeklies, allowed itself more licence, offering its readers, for example, a breathless account of the storming of Sultan Abdul Hamid's seraglio calculated to draw all but the most steadfast from an adjacent report of Lloyd George's budget battles:

> The eunuchs made no show of resistance and were at once seized and placed under a strong guard. Then their captors turned their attention to the women, whose terrifying screams woke the echoes of the great palace. Pale and trembling they shrank into the corners of the rooms and tried to hide behind curtain hangings. But there was nowhere that could afford them more than temporary conceal-ment. The correspondents refrain from details of the plight of these poor creatures, but there seems, unhappily, no room for doubt that the officers failed to exercise any proper restraints over the brutal natures of many of their men.[123]

Hoggart, in discussing popular working-class papers and magazines, writes in praise of their 'nearness to the detail of the lives of their readers', citing stories like 'Mother's Night Out', full of the actualities of working-class life, as examples to prove an unsuspected genuineness in this literature.[124] The quality appears far less in the papers of the early twentieth century. The *Cotton Factory Times*, filled with house-hold hints and with news from factories, 'Voices from the Spindle and the Loom', nevertheless ran as its 1905 serial a novelette whose title betrays its nature: 'Sir Anthony's Secret: or a False Position'.[125] *Reynolds's, Home Companion, Lloyds, News of the World*, these and other papers were undoubtedly designed to appeal to lower middle-class as well as to working-class tastes. To what extent Lady Bell was correct in asserting that the working-class woman, if she read much at that only three women owned to disliking reading, that in 28 of the households no one cared to read, in 58 only newspapers were read, and in 37 either husband or wife was genuinely fond of reading.[121] Weekly newspapers catered to women with a mixture of household hints, romantic fiction, and scandal in high places. The *Home Companion*, a penny weekly, laced its novelettes with characters such as 'The Honourable Mrs Latimer, of Curzon St, Mayfair', and its column *Pictures and Paragraphs* contained trivia of the following nature:

> Princess Charles of Denmark is a very enthusiastic gardener.

> The Grand Duchess Olga, of Russia, the Czar's eldest daughter, who is now in her eighth year, is probably the wealthiest little lady in the universe.[122]

*Reynolds's*, one of the most popular weeklies, allowed itself more licence, offering its readers, for example, a breathless account of the storming of Sultan Abdul Hamid's seraglio calculated to draw all but the most steadfast from an adjacent report of Lloyd George's budget battles:

> The eunuchs made no show of resistance and were at once seized and placed under a strong guard. Then their captors turned their attention to the women, whose terrifying screams woke the echoes of the great palace. Pale and trembling they shrank into the corners of the rooms and tried to hide behind curtain hangings. But there was nowhere that could afford them more than temporary concealment. The correspondents refrain from details of the plight of these poor creatures, but there seems, unhappily, no room for doubt that the officers failed to exercise any proper restraints over the brutal natures of many of their men.[123]

Hoggart, in discussing popular working-class papers and magazines, writes in praise of their 'nearness to the detail of the lives of their readers', citing stories like 'Mother's Night Out', full of the actualities of working-class life, as examples to prove an unsuspected genuineness in this literature.[124] The quality appears far less in the papers of the early twentieth century. The *Cotton Factory Times*, filled with household hints and with news from factories, 'Voices from the Spindle and the Loom', nevertheless ran as its 1905 serial a novelette whose title betrays its nature: 'Sir Anthony's Secret: or a False Position'.[125] *Reynolds's, Home Companion, Lloyds, News of the World*, these and other papers were undoubtedly designed to appeal to lower middle-class as well as to working-class tastes. To what extent Lady Bell was correct in asserting that the working-class woman, if she read much at as well as store-bought, remedies: treacle and sulphur; senna, raisins and boiling water; rue and wormwood – all cleared the system and were administered routinely as a spring tonic. Coughs were dosed with sugar and butter; sore throats with sulphur.[117] When it came to their own health, women expected complications from child-bearing and from menopause. Often they would assume one or the other of those causes to lie at the root of whatever bothered them – a backache, a headache, ill temper. They could postpone a visit to the doctor on the grounds that their illness was only natural, given their condition; they could excuse their short tempers and frayed nerves for the same reason. Lady Bell found working-class women almost eager for menopause: 'They encourge themselves to look for it; they make no attempt at self-control, they eagerly watch for symptoms; they are ready to refer any and every passing disturbance to that crisis, either impending or actually arrived.'[118]

Ailments of one sort or another, their own or their family's, meant that for most housewives nursing was part of the normal routine. Real illness – a debilitating accident at work, cancer, or consumption – shattered that routine with upsetting force. Chronic asthma and rheumatism, easily contracted when working in the damp or out of doors, could force a man to bed. Once there, he made family life more complicated, overcrowding the house still further, and perhaps requiring special treatment both day and night. His successful con-valescence might depend on a fuller diet than the family budget could stand, so that he would have to return to work only half well, a prey to further sickness.

With so much to attend to, the housewife's leisure was apportioned to her much as her tea and her sugar was, in small daily amounts: a chat at the door with tallyman or bookmaker;[119] a gossip at the shop with neighbours. Shopping might include visits to relatives or to the pub. The middle class attempted to arrange diversions for her. Booth extolled the programmes of church-sponsored mothers' meetings, at which thrift and savings were fostered by coal and clothing clubs, 'while tea parties and excursions pleasantly bind the whole together'. Most parishes in working-class neighbourhoods at one time or another initiated such efforts; though seldom effective in propagating the gospel, they did afford entertainment of a sort, at the risk of well meant but annoying patronage.[120]

The working-class wife read less frequently than her husband, her schedule seldom allowing her a chance to sit down for any period of time with a book. In a survey of 200 working-class couples, Lady Bell discovered that 17 women could not read (compared with eight men);

all, preferred 'something about love, with a dash of religion in it' one cannot say with any certainty.[126] Those who printed her papers appear to have assumed that she did; most women were offered the choice of that or nothing.

The cinema, in the years just before the First World War, began to offer another kind of escape. A Darlington woman recalls her futile attempt to persuade her husband to escape with her: 'There was once or twice he went with me and he was in misery 'cos he didn't like them. ... So he used to give me the money and I used to go with a friend.'[127] Further evidence, perhaps, of the fact that working-class husbands and wives enjoyed their leisure more often in company with their own sex than with each other.

The place where working-class men and women were most likely to enjoy each other's company was the pub. It was generally agreed that drinking was on the increase among working-class women. Booth credited the change to a general emancipation which led them to understand that their appearance in a public house would not forever disgrace them. An East End woman confided to one of Booth's informants that 'when she was young no one would have dreamt of going inside a public-house. But things have altered. Her son is engaged, and the girl goes with him there sometimes. In earlier years you would have put her down as not respectable, but not so now.'[128] How frequently the drinking led to drunkenness was not clear. Booth implied that in general women were social drinkers: 'A woman is so often talking with her neighbours; if she drinks, they go with her.'[129] Joseph Rowntree, a temperance reformer, cited statistics to prove the percentage of women among all those arrested for drunkenness was on the increase, 28 to 30 per cent nationally, and as high as 36 and 38 per cent in Manchester and London.[130] Drinking was the custom among all sorts of women: factory women because they could afford to; housewives, again according to Booth's informant, because of 'their slavery at the wash tub'.[131]

Not all working-class women drank, or drank too much. Respectability kept as many from the pub as monotony or sociability drove there. Determined though she might be to avoid the stigma supposedly attached to her public appearance as a drinker, what were the alternatives open to her? A visit with friends, or a trip to a tea shop, where her determination not to disgrace herself amidst alien teacups and tablecloths might put a swift end to her enjoyment:

> Watching a working-class woman in even so undissipated a place as one of Lyon's tea-shops, one is struck with her nervousness, her

suspicion; she fingers her fork as if afraid of it; she pours tea as though she has never done so in her life; she eats so solemnly that one is reminded of a murderer's last breakfast.[132]

Respectability wasn't worth that sort of self-imposed torture. How tempting by contrast, the familiarity of the local; how comfortable the predictability of neighbourhood acquaintances, before whom she could not help but move beyond pretension. She could drink with her husband, knowing him thankful that she was not waiting at home to throw up a double standard in his face. Or she could drink without him, thereby, in a small but important way, 'making some sort of personal claim on life',[133] which made so many constant claims on her.

# 4 Working wives and mothers

IN 1901, OVER FOUR million women were at work in England and Wales, all but 300,000 or so in 'working-class' jobs.[1] In many parts of the country a sizable proportion of the employed force of working-class women was married. A. L. Bowley, surveying women workers in twelve urban centres, discovered 'few who have no children under 14 and who are unoccupied'. B. L. Hutchins estimated that of all occupied women in 1911, approximately one-fifth were married.[2] Figures varied widely according to locale and the predominance of certain industries. Mining communities, in most cases, afforded women little opportunity for employment, textile towns the reverse. Cotton mills demanded that women work in factories; the clothing industry, that they labour either in workshops or at home. Using the 1911 census, William Beveridge determined that the percentages of married women in occupations ranged from 13·2 in London, to 10·72 in the West Riding, to 17·54 in Lancashire, to 3·37 in Durham. Within the county boroughs he found the same disparity: 19·46 in Bradford, 4·11 in St Helens, 21·98 in Stoke-on-Trent, 44·46 in Blackburn.[3] His inclusion of these statistics in his book, *Changes in Family Life*, suggests that whatever the percentages, working wives and mothers existed in numbers sufficiently large to warrant the attention of social observers.

Married women worked while others argued about whether or not they should. A formidable company spoke out against the practice. Employers complained of their irregularity.[4] Social workers elaborated on the theme, declaring that working mothers neglected their children: 'In the poorer parts of the towns, much harm results from the women going out to work. Not only do they themselves often suffer from exhaustion, but their families lack the care which is necessary if they are to grow up as good citizens.'[5]

Particular concern was expressed that employment might contribute to a rise in infant mortality. Medical officers of health reported that employment which drew mothers back to the factory before their newborn babies were completely weaned increased the likelihood of a variety of childhood diseases.[6] Those who had spent any time at all with the poor could not help but despair at the double life a working mother was forced to lead. B. L. Hutchins, in a survey of married women's work, reported from Yorkshire of 'Mrs A.', 'who has stayed up all night to get her washing, cleaning and baking done'; 'Mrs E.', who 'thinks that industrial work alone, or housework alone would not be too much, it is the combined strain that is "wearing her out" '; 'Mrs D.', who 'owns to having sat up all night to make or mend children's clothes, and says she gets "run down with overwork".'[7]

Most trade unionists joined those social workers who deplored the practice of married women's work. In this case concern for the health and well-being of the wife and mother combined with a fear that married women, whose interest lay primarily in supplementing their husbands' incomes, would be willing to work for less than they should and thereby depress the wage scale for women workers generally. Arguing in favour of legislation that would prohibit married women from working, the *Women's Trade Union Review* declared that 'the loss to the household's earnings occasioned by the withdrawal of the mother as wage-earner will be compensated by the fact that her competition in the labour market is also withdrawn, and by the additional thought which she will be able to give to the ordering and management of the household when she shall be permanently at its head'.[8]

Those who supported the claims of the married workers countered that orderly household management depended more upon adequate household budgets than upon time devoted to dusting or shopping. A social investigator for Clementina Black's survey on married working women reported that, of 114 houses inspected, only 16 were 'not very clean or actually dirty'. In some of those cases, the wives were the sole support of the family, their husbands suffering from temporary unemployment, and their wages ranging from nine to fourteen shillings a week. 'It is perhaps not astonishing under the circumstances,' the investigator concluded, 'that the homes were not immaculate.'[9] Proponents countered the statistics of the Medical Officer of Health with figures of their own. A Birmingham sample of 1908 was offered in evidence, showing that the infant mortality rates in two working-class wards were higher among those families in which the mother remained at home than in those where she went to work.[10] Investigators declared that factory work served to develop a woman's sense of independence. Women now operated machinery which they had been told no woman could ever learn to work:

In some cases women who take pride in this work, and have achieved their measure of skill and efficiency, will wish to continue at it after marriage, and will prefer to pay someone else to perform nursery work for their children. Has society any right to penalize these women, unless neglect or ill-treatment of the children be discovered?[11]

Much of this rhetoric reflected a middle-class feminist bias. From arguing that married working women were not, as a class, less concerned for their families than their unemployed sisters, some turned to arguing that they were more concerned. The authors of the Birmingham survey contended that perhaps 'a natural selection may have operated' in separating out those who worked from those who did not, 'many women who go to work being thrifty and energetic, and determined not to get below the poverty line, nor yet neglect their home duties'.[12]

The conclusions of most social observers tallied generally: the employment of married women was 'not so much . . . an evil *per se*, as the effect or result of evil circumstances.'[13] It was the effect of widowhood or desertion, or of an income reduced by the conditions of a husband's employment or lack of it to the point where the wife was driven to work to keep the family from debt or destitution. Figures would appear to support those conclusions. Of the working wives Hutchins questioned in Yorkshire, 63·3 per cent cited the insufficiency of their husband's wages as the reason for their own employment.[14] The Birmingham sample – 657 married working women – revealed that 556 had taken a job to supplement an otherwise insufficient family income. In 15 per cent of the cases, the husband was unemployed. Average wages in those families surveyed where wives did not work were 23s 1d, in those families where wives *did* work, 20s 1d. Even with the extra money a working wife brought in, her family lived at the edge of the poverty line.[15] Conditions in Manchester, though superior to those in Birmingham, nevertheless pointed to the same conclusion. Husbands' wages in the families of married women workers amounted to between 21 and 22 shillings. With an average addition of 10s 8d per week from the wife, they rose to a point where their insufficiency at least no longer directly threatened the family's physical well-being.[16]

Undoubtedly some married women worked because they wished to retain the independence they had tasted as working girls. A short article in the *Cotton Factory Times* in 1905 proposed that a young woman who married after having held a job 'has her future in her own hands . . . The working woman has an alternative. Matrimony is not her only means of support. She can wait to marry until she is sure she is acting in her own best interest.' And, the article implies, once married her proven ability to work at a responsible job will make her relationship with her husband a more satisfactory one, whether or not she continues a wage earner.[17] Black found the same sense of self-respect in women workers to whom she talked: 'By degrees the pleasure of having money of her very own comes to be dearly prized, and the woman who said: "A shilling of your own is worth two that *he* gives you" spoke the mind of many of her sisters. It is not, I believe, merely the command of the tiny sum to which their earnings amount, but the sense of partial freedom and independence by which their hearts are thus warmed.'[18] The observation must be balanced against that of a Londoner who recalled that, in her experience, women who went out to work ran the risk of losing caste in the eyes of their neighbours: 'They used to feel that the husband . . . wasn't providing her with what she was entitled to, presumably.'[19] Independence in Yorkshire; servitude in London: local traditions and particular circumstances would determine the way in which families and neighbourhoods absorbed the not uncommon occurrence of married women's employment.

Tradition was among those factors which helped a woman decide what job to take. Some, as we have seen, were respectable; others were not. And the distinctions remained by no means constant; they changed along with the technology of a particular trade. In printing, folders took advantage of machinery to hoist themselves up the ladder of propriety: 'Folding and sewing girls look down on the machine girls tremendously, and would not sit at the same table with them for anything.'[20] Low class jobs were messy jobs. Menders at a Keighley textile mill were a cut above weavers because weavers had to clean their own looms: 'We hadn't men to come and clean them like they have now . . . We had to do it ourselves and we used to get ever so dirty. And . . . that'd be why, you see, that they thought they was a bit . . . better.'[21] Japanning and blacking, a process which required women to immerse their arms in paint, was considered 'so dirty that it is mostly undertaken by a very rough class of women'. Lacquering, on the other hand, won for its practitioners a high degree of social prestige. 'Lacquer girls are ladies,' a press girl declared, in response to one survey of women workers. Investigators reported a case in which management had abandoned plans for an employees' dining room, since lacquerers refused to eat together with dippers. Lacquerers received a wage commensurate with their skill – as much as 18 to 20 shillings a week. Other socially prestigious jobs, warehouse work, for example, paid depressed wages for the very reason that women would willingly sacrifice money for a more subtle form of social security.[22]

Only a minority of the employed women worked at skilled trades; the percentage of married women workers who held such jobs was even smaller. The fact that their lives were tied to their families meant they had less chance to develop a skill, unless they had done so before marriage. Even then, a move necessitated by her husband's search for work could place the working wife beyond the reach of a job that would allow her to practice whatever skills she might possess. If her desire was to supplement the family's income, she might be tempted or forced to seek only temporary employment, the need to care for children, or to await the arrival of yet another one, thwarting her ability to hold a job for any sustained length of time. Irregular employment shut women off from highly skilled and highly paid work. Even semi-skilled work with machinery demanded regularity and a certain amount of practice.[23] Skilled work required a commitment, often in terms of a low-paying apprenticeship or training course, that most married women were either unwilling or unable to make. They wanted work that promised immediate and tangible financial return, even if that work condemned them to the depressed wage scales prevailing in unskilled occupations.

The temptation was therefore great to forsake the search for employment in factory or workshop altogether, and hire oneself out as charwoman or laundress. The work was hard and the hours long, but jobs were not hard to come by. Women could pick up a day or two with one or more families, at an average wage of 1s 6d to 2s 6d a day. Often this was the only recourse open to them. As in the case of married women factory workers, the major reason women took to charing was the irregularity or insufficiency of their husband's wages. One such, who described the dangers of 'laying out what you are not sure of getting', went to work to supplement the 20s to 24s weekly wage of her mail-driver husband. She was employed for a time as a confectioner, earning as much as 12s a week, but 'you could not get that now'. Her regular job at a boarding house four days a week from 9.00 a.m. until 6.00 p.m. added 8s to her family's weekly income. On Mondays she earned her two shillings doing laundry for the 25 residents of the house, 'and it is heavy work, as they all wear flannels'. An old woman upstairs looked after her three children for 6d a day, their father coming home at meal times to supervise in his wife's absence.[24]

The need to fit employment into domestic routines demanding an irregular schedule led many married women to work at home. A skill once learned could, in theory at any rate, be practiced at odd hours sandwiched between the chores of housekeeping and child-rearing. Though undertaken in the hope that it might allow for the setting of her own pace, work at home could disrupt a woman's routine even more than factory work. Seasonal demands, particularly in luxury trades, required women to work through the night at one time of the year, while ensuring that at others they would remain virtually idle.[25] Women took home an extraordinary variety of work: packeting, paper-box making, leather work, brush-making, varieties of sewing and machining, all for the same reason that most others went out to work – to supplement their family's income.[26]

Widowed mothers with children were naturally the most precariously placed of any women within the working class. Figures from a Board of Trade census in 1906 showed that full-time women factory workers in the textile industry averaged 15s 5d per week; in the clothing industry, 13s 6d; in paper and printing 12s 2d; in pottery, glass, and chemicals, 11s 10d; in food, drink, and tobacco, 11s 5d.[27] Local and occupational surveys made at roughly the same time confirmed these statistics; in the brass trade, women's wages ranged from 9s 0d to 14s 9d; in West Ham in 1907 the median wage among women chemical workers was 12s 0d, as was that for women in the confectionery trade.[28] Statistics such as these are accurate only up to a point. Those in the 1906 survey assume full-time employment, and take no account of seasonal or other lay-offs. Nor was it really possible to calculate realistic figures for a trade like confectionery, which paid its workers according to complex schedules of piece rates. Clementina Black discovered that though it was theoretically possible for women to earn as much as 24 shillings a week in a large London factory, by far the greatest number of those whose pay sheets she examined during a two-week period earned only from five to ten shillings, the majority, indeed, earning less than eight.[29]

Women in workshops – 'sweated workers' – could expect even less in return for their labour. Skilled London dressmakers, if lucky, might average 14s a week throughout the year: a pound a week in the peak of the season – Easter–July, October–November – far less in other months.[30] Homeworkers probably fared worst of all. Piece wages were the rule, and condemned women and children to long and continuous hours of labour before even the tiniest margin of profit appeared. A widow with five children 'employed on combinations', whose case history appeared in the *Daily News* Exhibition of Sweated Industries in 1906, showed a wages book in which she recorded fortnightly earnings of 6s 8¾d, 9s 2¼d, 3s 7½d, 5s 2d, 8s 1d, 3s 11½d. 'She said she sat up all night when she could get work to do, but there was a great deal of "idle set".'[31] As they grew older, women found themselves less capable of maintaining the required pace. The widow recalled a time when she could count on 17 to 18 shillings fortnightly. A dress-maker could expect to find herself making from one to two shillings less per week by the time she reached 45 or 50: 'From fifty onward, her foothold becomes excessively precarious; if she loses her place she has no hope of getting another, though she will probably be still a good worker.'[32]

Apologists and critics alike advanced a number of reasons for the disparity between men's and women's wages. Most agreed that the major cause stemmed from an assumption – valid or not according to one's point of view – that women considered their work as temporary or their wages as supplementary, or both: 'Few women expect to be life-workers. Practically all look forward to marriage as an escape from work.'[33] Hence their willingness to work for less, and the futility of any attempt on their part to raise wages to a man's level. Too many remained prepared to work for 10 to 12 shillings to make agitation worthwhile. The fact that they were driven to work for low wages did not necessarily imply, as Cadbury appears to suggest, that they would not have welcomed more. Married women workers, whose particular needs might be far more pressing than those of generally younger unmarried co-workers, nevertheless found themselves tied to a wage scale that the majority, because they continued to live at home or in shared lodgings, did not find unduly oppressive. Booth declared that not until more women were dependent upon wages for their livelihood, rather than for pocket money, would wages improve to any extent. The same point was echoed by Ramsay MacDonald in his survey of women in the printing trade: 'Although the women spasmodically interest themselves in their conditions, they feel so little dependence on wages that they can never be taught to make that steady upward pressure which would improve the organization of these trades and yield more return for labour.'[34]

If comparative affluence could persuade a woman to work for less than she might otherwise have asked, so could destitution. Women who worked for 'a little extra' would not consider it worthwhile, if their pay did not appear to compensate them for their time and trouble. But in cases of great need, women might be prepared 'to take anything, however badly paid, rather than refuse and run the risk of a long delay before anything can be found'.[35]

Destitute or affluent, married or not, the woman worker was in all likelihood paid as she was because of her sex. Employers listed various reasons for the fact that women so often received so much less than men. B. L. Hutchins recorded the following rationalizations in her report on Yorkshire for the Black survey:

(1) The women's wage would not attract men to the industry, and the manufacturer must have men for overtime and night work.
(2) Men can earn more per unit of time; that is, the productivity of the machine is greater with men weavers.
(3) The men require less help from tuners. Men usually tune their own looms.[36]

Ramsay MacDonald's study of women in the printing trades uncovered the same sort of reasoning: women have less technical skill than men; women are more prone to leave work for reasons of marriage and pregnancy.[37]

Working men themselves feared what working women might – and often did – do to their wage scales. In some divisions of the textile industry, men and women worked for the same rates at the same jobs. Hutchins discovered this to be the case among warpers: 'The best women will earn the same as the best men, but the average woman will earn less than the average man.'[38] Women worried that as soon as they began to offer themselves to employers at wages equal to those men were getting, employers would inevitably hire men instead of women. 'As to the statement of the Trade Unions', complained a Miss Whyte of the London bookbinders in 1900, 'that they were willing to admit women so long as they received equal pay with men, the women knew that such a rule would operate to the entire exclusion of women, for if a woman offered herself in competition with a man for the same work, the latter would be accepted'.[39] Competition with men could result in the sort of convoluted situation recalled by Margaret Bond-field. In the course of an investigation of married women workers in 1910 she encountered a situation in Leeds where male twisters-in had struck for an improved price list and against the employment of women. At the same time, women weavers, without warps as a result of the men's strike, had struck themselves, 'to get the men back in the twisting-in process, without which their own work could not proceed'. The striking women, in this case, were protesting the blacklegging of other women in jobs which had, until then, been the province of the men.[40]

To many men, the simplest solution to complications of this sort, or to the more common threats of replacement and wage reduction, was to insure that certain jobs remained in their hands alone. In a woolcombing mill, Hutchins found that men sorted and tended the washing machinery; women handled the 'back-washing', 'punch-balling' (mechanical combing) and 'boxing' processes.[41] Women, for reasons of respectability, or because of tradition, or both, appeared generally content with this sexual subdivision of labour. MacDonald's investigators were met with the remark that certain jobs – varnishing, for example, 'were man's work, and we shouldn't think of doing it'.[42]

So sharp did the division appear in some trades that Cadbury was led to generalize that men and women were not in competition with each other for jobs. 'As a rule', he wrote, 'men and women do different work and the relation between men and women workers is, on the whole, that of two non-competing groups.'[43] Working men in many industries would have scoffed at the analysis. Testifying in 1908 before the Poor Law Commission, a trade union official declared that

> ... the women are ousting the men in most trades, including the iron trades. Many women are doing the light kind of drilling, etc., which used to be done by men. We have hundreds of them in Manchester now doing work that was formerly done by men on drilling machines. Women in the iron works were unknown a few years ago, but there are hundreds of thousands of them now.[44]

More than twice as many women as men entered the engineering trade in the two decades from 1891 to 1911. Cadbury himself lists nineteen trades in Birmingham in which women had begun to replace men, including such apparently masculine occupations as brass lathe burnishing, tin plating, press stamping, cycle work, and bookbinding.[45] Nor did women represent merely an intramural threat – entering a particular trade only to drive men already employed there out of work. The presence of women workers in large numbers and in various unskilled or semi-skilled trades across a community could lead to a general casualization of labour among men. This was the case in Norwich, where over 65 per cent of the employees in the town's major industries – food and drink – were women, girls and boys:

> The social importance of such a fact can hardly be exaggerated. Where there is good employment for wives and sons and daughters families will come into a town and stay in a town, however little work there may be for adult males. The family as a whole can be certain of a regular though possibly insufficient income, even if the proper breadwinner is dependent on casual work. This will make the chance of a casual job even more attractive than it otherwise would be. There are many men in Norwich who would not be content to stay for five or six days' work a month, who do, in fact, stay now because they can add to their own highly speculative earnings the more regular wages of their wives and children.[46]

Content they may have been, but that contentment must in many cases have exacted some sort of psychological toll, increasing, in the process of its extraction, the already existing tensions in an ill-paid working man's family. In Newcastle the men resented their working wives, the result being a willingness on the women's part to 'keep their work as secret as possible'.[47] The working man assumed, because custom and tradition had taught him to do so, that his was the bread-winner's responsibility, and that he had first claim on the wage fund. The facts of his present economic plight might argue that he would himself be better off if his wife, along with him, could earn according to a more equitable scale. In the case of a Norwich casual labourer, economic facts might even argue that he was better off with a few days' work a month, so long as both wife and children could together earn what he should be earning on his own. But facts, whether Norwich facts or Newcastle facts, could make little headway against the psychological certainty that he should be doing what they were compelled to do.

One avenue open to women anxious to raise their wages was trade unionism. Relatively few chose to follow it. In 1912, only 318,358 women were members of trade unions, the large majority of them in the textile industry.[48] The temporary nature of most female employment was blamed for low membership, as it was for low wages. Margaret Bondfield regretted, in the *Women's Trade Union Review*, that unmarried working girls would not interest themselves in the movement, and that habits of indifference, once learned, were difficult to overcome: 'They look upon [their work] as a temporary occupation, to be superseded by marriage. They fail to see any need for bothering themselves about the wages and general conditions obtaining in their trade.'[49] MacDonald found women in the printing trades 'had no incentive to aspire to high standards of wages'; the president of the Birmingham Pen-Workers' Union deplored the fact that women had little faith in their ability to help themselves: 'Their mistrust of each other is constitutional. Their hopelessness is pathetic, and forms one of the greatest barriers to their complete organization.'[50]

Leaders in the fight to organize women – Margaret Bondfield, Mary Macarthur, Margaret MacDonald and the like – battled against working-class apathy and prejudice. Macarthur described the process, illustrating from her experiences among Ipswich corset workers: 'It is no good talking about human welfare or the future of the race. They will not understand. You have got to talk about why they should be fined twopence or threepence a week, or why the employer does not pay for thread.' The result, in the case of the corset workers, was a meeting of 1,500, with two more scheduled to handle the overflow.

Yet Macarthur complained that there was nothing so 'slick' as the way women came into a union 'except the way they got out'.[51] Successes, when they occurred, were usually modest. Few equalled that of the fiery Lizzie Willson of the Leicester women's section of the Boot and Shoe Operatives, whose anger at male unionists' contempt and condescension led her to form a breakaway union in 1911 which lasted into the 1930s.[52] More often, annual reports read like that of the Manchester, Salford, and District Women's Trade Union Council for 1911, recording the formation of new unions among flax workers and rag sorters, and an increase in wages for the former of one shilling a week.[53] Or the histories detailed the minutiae of union negotiations that never made headlines, but represented substantial progress to the women whose livelihood was at issue:

> The Penmakers' Union at Birmingham has been struggling with very serious difficulties, though it has, in spite of this, scored several successes ... A number of instances in which bonuses had been withheld from the workers owing to their membership with the Union, were brought into Court, and, in the majority of instances, these were rescinded. The extension of the Particulars Clause to the pen trade has been obtained by the Union, and the lists enabling workers to calculate the rate at which they will be paid are being brought into use in all the firms ... Further steps by which the application of the clause may be rendered more satisfactory are contemplated.[54]

Because of the casual nature of their employment, women feared using the strike as a weapon to raise their wages. Reprisals, often in the straightforward form of outright dismissal, discouraged militancy. And when organization did result in an increase, the women found it hard to understand why they should then persevere. The attitude is reflected in material on women's trade unions amassed by the Webbs before the First World War. Some women, reported the secretary of the Liverpool Anti-Sweating League, 'expect everything to be improved at once, and if not, fall out again, or perhaps they obtain some benefits and think everything is coming and it is not worth remaining in.'[55]

Women frequently expressed a reluctance to take union matters into their own hands. The problem was addressed in a report to the Webbs from a representative of the Bolton Weavers, Winders and Warpers Association, whose membership included the healthy total of 11,400 women: 'Women will come to meetings if a specific grievance is to be aired, or if the men go round to ask them to turn up and vote for them, but will not turn up to vote for each other.'[56] Apparently the men seldom did much to encourage women to act independently. The secretary of the all-female Manchester Trades and Labour Council, when interviewed by the Webbs, told them that the women's branch of the Amalgamated Society of Weavers had a male secretary, and that the post of collector was open to men only. 'The secretary showed no bitterness about this attitude,' the Webbs recorded. 'Seemed to regard it as a law of nature.' An official of the Weavers' Institute attempted to explain the acquiescence in terms of 'modesty' or 'the way they've been brought up'.[57] Sexual stereotypes were as common to the thinking of working wives as to their husbands.

Men remained ambivalent about women trade unionists, for much the same reasons that they remained chary of women workers generally. Experience suggested that trade union enthusiasms were, for most women, a short-lived matter; until they came to be more than that, they were to be mistrusted. George Shipton's remarks, as president of the London Trades Council, to the Women's Trade Union League in 1892, echoed the sentiments of many of his brethren then and later. Men wished to see women organize, he declared, but

> ... they cannot aid you until you show a dogged determination to combine and form unions which shall not only last a year or two, but remain for others who will come after you and will require the aid of those unions. Unless you are in that position you cannot help acting prejudicially to the interests of the men engaged in the same occupations as yourselves.[58]

Twenty-two years later Will Thorne, whose general union numbered over 5,000 women workers – mostly in textiles – wrote that 'women do not make good trade unionists and for this reason we believe that our energies are better used towards the organization of male workers'.[59] The trade union banner, apotheosis of the movement, echoed Thorne's sentiments as symbol. Real women were seldom emblazoned there. As angels or as disembodied virtues, yes; but as labourers, almost never.

Women who went to work in factories encountered conditions less dangerous and unpleasant than those endured by their mothers or grandmothers in the first raw days of England's industrialization. Legislation amending the Factory Act of 1878, passed by Parliament in 1883, 1895, and 1901, had provided a means which, in theory, was to lead to the correction of some of the worst abuses of the mid-Victorian system. Public health authorities assumed control of sanitary standards; special provisions governed the conduct of various dangerous trades; new standards of ventilation, temperature, and humidity were imposed in the textile industry; and a beginning was made in the regulation of laundries and home-work. But, as Clementina Black noted in *Makers of Our Clothes*, 'in no two factories is there any identity of conditions'. It remained a case of 'individualism run wild'. Some factories conformed to standards; many did not. Their condition depended upon the determination of their owners to obey both the spirit and the letter of the law, upon the presence or absence of an inspectorate, or upon both.[60]

Improvement tended to come about piecemeal and, in particularly dangerous industries, far too slowly to suit those who pressed for reform. Conditions under which women worked in the potteries remained stubbornly grim throughout the years before the First World War. Reports in the *Women's Trade Union Review* read as pessimistically in 1912 as they had in 1894. Long hours and the resulting increased threat of lead poisoning from glazes had bred into employees, 'as in the times of sudden pestilence, a reckless gambling spirit', which grew 'naturally out of the circumstances of their lot. Instances of colic, succeeded by paralysis, which the presence of lead in the system causes, might be given by hundreds.' In 1899, the *Review* reported that in the three years since notification had been required by legislation, over one thousand cases of plumbism had been reported, the majority of them among females. A government circular, issued the following year, led to some improvement, but a decision in 1904 to permit the use of lead in amounts up to 5 per cent, rather than the 2 per cent recommended by employees and experts, dampened an otherwise optimistic report in that year. In 1912 the *Review* noted that factory and workshop inspectors had discovered an increase in the number of cases and lamented delays in the implementation of government safety regulations: 'All the dangers we reported two years ago are still there.'[61]

Few industries were as hazardous as the potteries. Far more women contended with general physical discomfort than with the threat of a debilitating or fatal disease. In textile mills temperatures were kept very high, and women suffered as a result from various pulmonary disorders. A factory inspector for the North West Division in 1911 reported 42 instances of temperatures exceeding 90°, and four cases of over 100°.[62] One former employee, interviewed by Thompson and Vigne, recalled that her sister would go barefoot in the cotton spinning mill where she worked, so warm was the floor: 'But even if you was going on the stairs, as I did one day to go to the cotton mills and take my sister's dinner, and I was nearly overpowered, fainting, with the heat.'[63] Sanitary conditions represented an extreme case of Clementina Black's managerial 'individualism run wild'. Employers often complained to factory inspectors that the amenities they did provide were seldom used by the workers for whom they had been installed. In one case, the *Women's Trade Union Review* quoted an inspector's published response:

> The fact is ignored that the water to fill [the basins] has to be carried from the other side of the factory; that if the washing is to be of any use each basin has to be carried away to be emptied and again refilled five times; that towels either do not form a part of the 'washing conveniences' or are provided at the rate of three a week, and that this washing has to be done during the time when the workers are naturally eager to rush off to their mid-day meal, or, tired out, are anxious to get home to rest and supper; finally, that these elementary arrangements are not put under the control or care of any one responsible person.[64]

Official and unofficial reports from the period describe a wide range of conditions: from the gleaming tile of the Cadburys' Bourneville to the squalid horror of the sweaters' East London. Safest to say that while the majority of work places were better than unbearable, they were not places in which a person, unless compelled to do so, would willingly spend ten hours a day.

Interest in what she was doing might compensate a woman for the conditions under which she was forced to work. The most wretched-looking girl Clementina Black could recall was not a chain-maker, a laundress, or a rag-sorter, but

> . . . was engaged upon no harder task than the packing of cocoa. My attention was called to her, in a room full of girls, by her ghastly appearance. She may have been eighteen or nineteen; she was absolutely colourless, and although there was no sign about her of any specific illness, seemed exhausted utterly almost to death. She sat day after day pouring powdered cocoa into ready-made square paper packets, of which she then folded down the tops and pasted on the wrappers. She received a halfpenny for every gross. In the week previous to that in which I saw her she had earned 7s.[65]

Women found it easier to contend with dirt and monotony if they could count on sympathetic and humane treatment from their supervisors. More upsetting to most than a degree of physical unpleasantness was the constant financial uncertainty that accompanied the fining system. The Truck Act of 1897 outlawed all but 'fair and reasonable' fines; in practice they continued to be levied in amounts and for offences that led employees to believe the law was there to be ignored. Gertrude Tuckwell complained on behalf of women clothing workers that, between charges for materials, and fines and deductions for less than perfect workmanship, even the upper grades of women's labour were sweated.[66]

The Women's Trade Union League campaigned strenuously and continuously against fines, reporting, as a typical case, one in which a woman had knitted ties with a faulty needle in her machine, a fact which she did not discover until she had made a dozen. Instead of receiving 1s 6d for her work, she was instead fined the retail cost of all the ties; at the end of the week she took home only 4½d, and remained in debt to her employers.[67] A woman weaver in Bolton recalled what was perhaps a more common experience. Her supervisor, when examining the vests she had made, 'used to go through every one and she always threw one or two out. If you couldn't find anything wrong with them those were supposed to be seconds, you see, and you didn't get paid for them.'[68] Walter Greenwood's memory of 'Mr Wheelam', overlooker at the big weaving shed where his mother had worked before her marriage, tallies with other reports and recollections. Each piece came under his scrutiny as it passed from the looms:

> One end of it was thrown over a head-high roller placed against the light while Mr Wheelam stood, as in a tent, pulling the piece down yard by yard on the look-out for defects in weaving. Each one detected meant a money fine against the weaver with no allowance made for poor warp or weft over which the weaver hadn't any control.

When Wheelam stopped to offer Mrs Greenwood a job after her marriage, she would have none of it: 'I have seen all that I wish to see of weaving sheds ... Eight and sixpence after your fines, that's all I've brought home many a time for a full week's work. No thank you, Mr Wheelam, I would rather pick oakum.'[69]

Employers believed that financial rewards and punishments could be used with effect to increase the quantity as well as to improve the quality of their products. The system of 'driving' employees by offering overseers a commission on their own wages to speed the productivity of workers under them drew the ire of industrial reformers. The Women's Trade Union League in 1901 protested the case of a Manchester pieceworker, Eliza McCartney, whose 'tackler' or overseer had pushed her to work beyond her capacity. The tackler was to receive a commission if the girl earned at least 24 shillings in piecework wages. She was able to earn all but the last two, was discharged as a result, and committed suicide. 'The Coroner', the *Review* reported, 'said he thought that was the worst case of "driving" in cotton mills he had ever come across – and he came across a great many . . . Morally, though not legally,' he declared, 'that girl's death rested upon John West, the tackler, and the manager and master of Olive Mill.'[70] If women worked especially hard, they won a bonus for their tackler; if they were believed to be slacking, they were themselves fined. They might earn at a rate of only 3d an hour; they were fined at the rate of 1s an hour if unpunctual. Employees continued to be punished monetarily for looking out windows, laughing, or leaving their work station for the toilet. At a factory employing more than 500 women, an inspector discovered a system whereby employees were made to hand a tally to a male overseer as they entered the lavatory. He recorded their time inside, forwarding his report to the manager, who fined them at the end of the month if their total exceeded four minutes.[71]

Booth reported that in factories where women were prepared to admit the necessity of fines, 'because some of the girls would otherwise be so careless', they nevertheless condemned their thoughtless treatment by foremen. Booth particularly criticized the system whereby managers paid foremen by the piece and left them free to hire and dismiss the employees in their department. That such an arrangement might lead to bribery or to other forms of indulgence at the expense of the girls and women, was but a reflection of the 'darker side of life in the East End'.[72] The extent to which women found themselves at the mercy of overseers was a matter of some debate. Cadbury concluded that there was more than myth in the general assumption that foremen took sexual advantage of factory hands. He had interviewed women who complained of the 'forwardness' of their supervisors, who 'spoke as they didn't ought'. Yet the majority of inspectors and observers appear to have agreed that if there was immorality on the factory floor, it was the fault not just of foremen but of older men and married women. An article in the 1909 *Woman Worker* mentioned the dangers of exposure to an overlooker's advances; it dwelt at greater length, though, on the tendency of older women, especially in weaving sheds, to corrupt the younger. Margaret Bondfield in her autobiography recalled a visit to a Bradford home for unwed mothers, during which the matron inveighed against 'the influence of married women in the mills'. And Cadbury himself reported the feeling on the part of some girls that 'married women and men working together tend to say and talk of things unfit for the unmarried'.[73] An observer's impression was shaped in great measure by the department he visited and by the type of work carried out there. If rough work, then the chance of encountering rough women, rough language and rough conduct increased; if respectable, then, whether or not older and younger women mixed

together, the chance was small. In any event, their reputation as cor-
rupters of the young did nothing to assist married women, whether
rough or respectable, in attaining employment for themselves.

Overseers, if they felt it necessary, could without much trouble
prevail on women to remain silent about unsatisfactory working
conditions. The Webbs reported a conversation with a senior factory
inspector in Manchester who informed them that it was very dangerous
for workers to complain. She described one instance in which fellow
workers, at the behest of their foreman, had persecuted a woman
employee of nineteen years with 'the silent treatment' because she was
supposed, in this case incorrectly, to have lodged a complaint.[74] Women,
even if undeterred by pressures from their supervisors, were not
wholeheartedly cordial to the practice of inspection. Their ambivalence
was particularly apparent in those trades where overtime work was
often the rule. Women complained that well-meant legislation designed
to curtail the number of permitted hours had the unfortunate result of
severely limiting their power as wage earners. They found it difficult
to welcome inspectors whose task, so it seemed to them, was to thwart
their chances of making as much money as possible.

Legislation effective in 1896 had limited women to only thirty days
of overtime per year in most trades and to a maximum of three days in
any one week. The issue was a particularly heated one in the dress-
making trade, where many workshops, dependent on seasonal business,
claimed the need to adjust their overtime accordingly. But women
working at other jobs as well considered themselves the victims of
unnecessary parliamentary solicitude. Two investigators reported the
unintended results of the legislation as it affected the mineral water
bottling trade. Because of the increased demand for charged water in
the summer, women had been used to, and depended on, seasonal
overtime. To conform to the new legislation, manufacturers had
attempted to spread the work throughout the year, only to discover
that the charged water began to burst its bottles with every change in
the weather. The result was a decision to replace women workers with
men, whose overtime hours were not restricted.[75]

Many articulate working women argued against any sort of special
legislation on their behalf. A Leeds worsted worker wrote to Ramsay
MacDonald to protest against the infant Labour Party's espousal of an
eight-hour day for women. She put the case directly: 'Less hours mean
less wages.' She argued that chances for compensation in the form of a
higher rate of standard wage were nil. Indeed, she reported, the two-
loom system was threatening a further decrease. If the Labour Party
wished to do women workers a service, she declared, it would abandon

its campaign for an eight-hour day and urge instead a ban on all married women workers.[76] Advocates of women's legislation countered that much women's work was by nature casual and unsettled, that regulation would work to steady it and thereby make it more rewarding. 'True freedom for a woman', the Independent Labour Party argued in a 1900 pamphlet, 'is not freedom to earn *any* wage under *any* conditions. It is freedom to live a life worth living, and to develop her powers to the full; and this she cannot have while she is practically a slave to the caprice of her employer and the pressure of unrestricted competition.'[77]

The debate passed above the heads of most women workers. Undoubtedly, they would have welcomed an opportunity to work shorter hours for the same amount of money. Common sense, however, told them that was an opportunity they would not soon enjoy. Meanwhile the economic compulsion that drove women, and particularly married women, from house to factory or workshop could not allow them to focus on more than immediate gains to satisfy immediate necessities. True freedom may have meant a life worth living. The married woman worker could reasonably retort that life worth living meant, first of all, a house and food for her family. If providing those necessities meant industrial bondage, then one could do little more than receive the yoke and leave freedom to those who had the time and money for it.

Perhaps the most severe bondage to which a married woman might subject herself was home-work. Few factories were as squalid as the houses of those women who were forced to turn their kitchens into work rooms, few overseers as demanding as was the routine for those mothers whose livelihood depended on their ability to work at a trade at the same time and in the same place that they were working to sustain some sort of family life. The work demanded was often exacting, as in the case of artificial flower-making:

> Drawing and cutting the wire is not altogether pleasant, for the thin wire is liable to cut the hand, unless the worker is well protected. But shaping the petals is really hard work. Sitting hour after hour at a table, a stiff rubber pad in front of her, a small gas stove beside her, in which she warms her steel tool, the worker proceeds to separate the cakes of petals, and subject them all to the pressure of the warm tool upon the rubber pad until they assume the necessary contour. This work makes a great strain on the wrist, the arm, and the chest. Having her stems ready to hand, her thousands of petals are pressed, her paste pot handy, the worker now proceeds to flower-making.[78]

Flower-making was a notch or two removed from matchbox-making which, as described by Clementina Black in her study of sweated industries, evokes, as nothing else, the deadliness and dreariness to which home-work sentenced the married woman:

The women fetch out from the factory or the middle-woman's, strips of notched wood, packets of coloured paper and sandpaper, and printed wrappers; they carry back large but light bundles of boxes, tied up in packets of two dozen. Inside their rooms the boxes, made and unmade and half-made, cover the floor and fill up the lack of furniture. I have seen a room containing only an old bedstead in the very last stage of dirt and dilapidation, a table, and two deal boxes for seats. The floor and the window-sill were rosy with magenta match-boxes, while everything else, including the boards of the floor, the woodwork of the room and the coverings of the bed, was of the dark grey of ingrained dust and dirt. At first sight it is a pretty enough spectacle to see a match-box made; one motion of the hands bends into shape the notched frame of the case, another surrounds it with the ready-pasted strip of printed wrapper, which, by long practice, is fitted instantly without a wrinkle, then the sand-paper or the phosphorus-paper, pasted ready beforehand, is applied and pressed on so that it sticks fast. A pretty high average of neatness and finish is demanded by most employers, and readers who will pass their match-boxes in review will seldom find a wrinkle or a loose corner of paper. The finished case is thrown upon the floor; the long narrow strip which is to form the frame of the drawer is laid upon the bright strip of ready-pasted paper, then bent together and joined by an overlapping bit of the paper; the edges of paper below are bent flat, the ready-cut bottom is dropped in and pressed down, and before the fingers are withdrawn they fold over the upper edges of the paper inside the top. Now the drawer, too, is cast on the floor to dry. All this, besides the preliminary pasting of wrapper, coloured paper and sandpaper, has to be done 144 times for 2¼d; and even this is not all, for every drawer and case have to be fitted together and the packets tied up with hemp.

The conditions of life secured in return for this continuous and monotonous toil are such as might well make death appear preferable. The poor dwelling – already probably overcrowded – is yet further crowded with match-boxes, a couple of gross of which, in separated pieces, occupy a considerable space. If the weather be at all damp, as English weather often is, even in summer, there must be a fire kept up, or the paste will not dry; and fire, paste, and hemp must all be paid for out of the worker's pocket. From her working

113

time, too, or from that of her child messenger, must be deducted the time lost in fetching and carrying back work, and, too often, in being kept waiting for it before it is given out.[79]

The rhythm imposed upon the life of a working wife and mother could often be both frantic and irregular: up at 5.00 to 5.30; to bed at 11.00 or midnight, snatching at spare minutes throughout the day or night to clean, to cook, and to care for her children. Seldom was she able to enjoy even those meagre satisfactions that an established routine afforded to women who were not trying to earn a livelihood as well. Ten hours in a factory, half an hour for lunch, half an hour travelling to and from work, eleven hours away from her house and family: 'We had to be at work by 7.00 a.m., and you could see the day break over the hills, and they are always such a comfort and help.'[80] Few managed to extract that sort of consolation from their morning journey to the mill. Women with young babies would either try to get home to nurse them at noon, or arrange for their transportation to the factory. Walter Greenwood recalled the confused lunch hour in the textile mills of his youth:

A white jet of vapour under pressure plumed forth and another shrill note was added to the general discord. Weavers threw the driving belts on to the idler pulleys; the deafening clatter stopped abruptly though its echoes still pounded in my ears. A burst of chatter, a clattering of clogs as weavers lined up with pint mugs at a gas geyser and brewed tea. The mothers claimed their screaming off-spring, sat on the floor by the looms and began to suckle their infants while friends put steaming pints of tea at their sides and whatever it was had been brought to eat.[81]

Working to supplement their minimal family incomes, married women would be understandably anxious to return to the factory or workshop as soon as possible after the birth of another child had made that income all the more inadequate. If their family or neighbourhood afforded them the chance, they would deposit their babies with relatives or friends. Older women might charge two or three pence a day to mind children younger than school age. If they took in more than one or two, the conditions under which their charges were cared for tended to deteriorate considerably. One woman, 'rather feeble-minded', who took five or six children of laundresses and charwomen by the day in a working-class London suburb, '. . . does keep them clean, but they are tied up in chairs all day long, which must be bad for their backs'.[82] Some cities made an effort to establish crèches, 'schools for mothers', and 'infant consultation centres' in the hope of making the task of child-rearing an easier and more rational one for both working and non-working mothers. In some cases, however, crèches would accept only babies young enough to be fed from bottles; older children continued to be farmed out elsewhere. If at school, children might nevertheless return home for lunch. Black reported the routine of an eiderdown quilt maker, with five children between the ages of five months and eight years. The two youngest she left at a crèche; for the others, she returned at noon every day to prepare a lunch: 'She managed to keep the children clean and tidy, but it is not surprising to hear that she herself was "very tired looking".'[83]

'How do you manage about the housework if you are out all day?' Anna Martin asked a woman in her 1911 survey of married women workers:

> I rise at 4.45, sweep the place a bit, and get my husband his breakfast. He must be off before six. Then I wake and wash the children, give them each a slice of bread and butter and the remains of the tea, and leave out the oats and sugar for Harry to prepare for the rest later on. [Harry is ten years old.] Then I open up the beds and take the baby to Mrs T. My own work begins at 7 a.m. At 8.30 the firm sends us round a mug of tea and I eat the bread and butter I have brought with me. I used to come home in the dinner hour, but my feet are now so bad that I get a halfpenny cup of coffee in a shop and eat the rest of what I have brought. At 4.30 I have another cup of tea and get home a little before 7 p.m. I do the hearth up, get my husband his supper, and make the beds. Then I get out the mending and am usually in bed by 11. On Saturday I leave work at noon so as to take the washing to the baths.[84]

The strain was not merely physical. The psychological pressures resulting from a woman's knowledge that the very survival of her family depended upon her employment were intense. Pulling against that understanding would be the sense, perhaps, that her husband, because he must depend on her, resented that dependence; or that her neighbours understood her work, and the untidy house that was its result, as no more than a sign of her declining respectability; or that her children, alone or with strangers most of the day, would fail to realize that her sharp tongue and raw temper were the price they must pay for food that they would otherwise not eat, or shelter that they would otherwise not enjoy. Employment was a burden to be shouldered along with other burdens.

# 5 Husbands and fathers

WOMEN LIVED AT the centre of the working-class family; men stood at its head, their place sustained in the vast majority of working-class households by their role as principal breadwinner. Even in those cases where wives or children contributed to increase the family's total weekly earnings, habit of mind helped persuade them that their contribution was no more than a supplement to what their husbands or their fathers brought home. When he could find no work at all, he and his family responded by assuming he would find it soon again. To have reacted otherwise might have denied him the 'dependents' upon which his authority rested. Families preferred fiction to fact, if it took fiction to preserve what custom prescribed. A wife, when she served her husband first at table, did so because she understood that he, before all others, needed nourishment to sustain him in his work. At the same time, she unconsciously celebrated his traditional role and the subordination of herself and her children to it. In fact, she might be earning as much as he was. But fact retreated before symbol, as she paid him his ritual due:

> She'd see to him first; he'd got to have, yes, and he used to love a sheep's head, and she used to make the broth and we kids used to have the broth ... But Dad would eat all the meat out of it, and she used to press the tongue, and he'd have the tongue out of it as well ...[1]

Custom afforded welcome reassurance. Contending with economic uncertainties, striving to establish and maintain connections within a neighbourhood, neither husband nor wife were anxious to further complicate their lives by questioning the roles that tradition had assigned them. The clearer the lines of definition, the easier the task of remaining within them. Husband: 'to go to work, to keep the family and get the family'. Wife: 'only washing and baking and looking after the children, having another child ...'[2] The very starkness of those remembered definitions promised security. They might, on occasion, be made light of; they were seldom questioned. The saying that 'one lump o' sugar's worth nine fathom o' whipcord' was employed to suggest that a wife could very well manage her husband if she went at it right.[3] In Jarrow working-class streets, yearly carnival processions concluded with the figure of a man in a nightshirt and bare feet, carrying a baby and labelled 'Sleepless Nights'. 'His humour', a resident recalls 'was very popular with the women who revelled in any man's discomfiture. So often in those days where a different domestic tradition obtained, men had much the best of it, and to see a man made to look ridiculous, even in mime, gave the women great and unaffected pleasure.'[4] But it was the pleasure of make-believe. Few women, no matter how much they resented the presumptions explicit in the role of 'husband' and 'wife', were ready to sacrifice the psychological comfort they nevertheless derived from playing their role as it had always been played.

Thompson and Vigne's interviews have shown that, despite the stereotypes, some husbands were willing to lend a hand with chores about the house. Many of them mended shoes; some filled coal buckets, though this was frequently the task of older children, not of the wife. In emergencies, particularly during a lying-in, husbands would assist with the dishes and with the dressing and undressing of young children. On Sundays, they might lead a procession to the park while mother remained at home to prepare the dinner. Further and more unusual examples of the helpful husband included a breadmaker, a bedmaker, a picklemaker.[5] A man's principal domestic charge, however, was the administration of discipline. He would expect his wife to deal with petty crises during the day; he would equally expect her to defer to him when it came to setting standards and enforcing their acceptance: ' "To tell the truth, or else!" Yes, we used to have thrashings from Father if we just didn't do what we were told.' 'What we call a deliberate punishment would be Father. Mother would punish on impulse, you know, smacks . . .'[6] The general pattern tallies with that remembered by Young and Willmott's Bethnal Greeners: 'When I was a boy most of us feared our fathers more than we liked them. I know I feared mine and I had plenty of reason to.'[7] Perhaps children were less conscious of fear than of distance, the natural result of a father's absence from home and of his traditional role as head of household. He was a person at one remove from the clatter of daily life. He and the members of his family cooperated in dignifying his apartness as authority.

Nevertheless, there were many variations on this theme: musical evenings, for instance, in which fathers played a light-hearted, if not frivolous, central role: 'Father [a Liverpool bootmaker] was a very jovial person – he used to play the mouth organ and the clappers and he'd play an accordion. He used to black his face up and we used to have quite a bit of a sing-song. Perhaps a few of the kiddies or the neighbours in. He could entertain.'

A Salford railway goods checker had perfected much the same routine: black face, and, in this case, an imported fiddler: 'And so heavy, the dancing would go on, that the furniture, we had to hold the drawers, for the vases dropping off. The floor was creaking and cracking. They'd say, "Oh we'll send the floor if we do much dancing".'
A Halifax labourer, remembered as 'always jolly', enjoyed pushing his children centre stage: 'If he came home [from the pub] and we weren't in bed – if he bring somebody with him – he used to say, "Come on, recite. Say that recitation." And we used to do and he'd give us a penny.'[8]

In that instance the authoritarian lurks beneath the *bon vivant*. The recollection evokes, as well, the fact that many good-natured fathers found it easier to enjoy themselves away from the congestion of two or three rooms. A tiny house might more readily accommodate a week-end song and dance, in which all the family stayed up to participate, than a week night's conversation between a man and his workmate, constantly interrupted by children's squabbles or by a wife's admonitions to speak softly for the sake of a sleeping baby. Opportunities for a quiet read at home, should the husband crave one, were no better than the chance for conversation. A sober-minded crane operator, at work all day in a blast furnace, lamented his lack of a place to call his own at home: 'If he wants to read or study he is constantly being interrupted by his wife doing her household duties or by children running in and out, and he often gives up his book in despair and goes out to his club . . .'[9]

Families recognized Sunday as dedicated to the rest and enjoyment of husband and father. Most middle-class observers, writing of the manner in which Sundays were designed to gratify the working man, remarked upon their ritual and their dullness. 'Up at twelve,' Booth wrote, 'to be ready for the "pubs", which open at one; dinner any time between two and four, then sleep, then off with wife and children to hear the band on the common.'[10] 'Gazing from windows of the Blocks into the tenement facing my own,' Reginald Bray reported in *Studies of Boy Life*,

I have often watched the preparation of the sacred meal. I have seen the girls seated at the window shelling peas or peeling potatoes; they are wearing their oldest week-day clothes, and their hair is tortured into stiff wisps of paper and unsightly rags. I have caught glimpses of the mother's face in the bright firelight as she bends over the oven. As the hours pass I have observed the father lay aside his pipe and draw on a coat of black, while the boys appear in the glory of Sunday suits. Then, too, the tresses of the girls are loosed, ringing their heads with a halo of rippling locks, and the shabby frock gives place to flimsy muslin or gaily coloured prints. Finally, in the dim shadows of the room I have visions of many people drawing chairs around a table. And I have never watched this scene without feeling conscious that I am the witness of some solemn and mystic ceremony, a kind of sacrificial feast celebrated at the shrine of family life, and laid on the altar of the home.[11]

George Gissing saw the rituals of countless Sundays as little more than deadly, mindless routine:

Then began the unutterable dreariness of a Sunday afternoon ... The greater part of the male population of Lambeth slumbered after the baked joint and the flagon of ale. Yet here and there a man in his shirt-sleeves leaned forth despondently from a window or sat in view within, dozing over the Sunday paper.[12]

Two points deserve to be made. First, the manner in which the ritual focused upon the man of the house. Bray's description is of a ceremony designed not just to celebrate family life, but also to honour its head. While the wife and children prepare the 'feast', the husband smokes his pipe. In turn the celebrants don their ceremonial clothes. The food is spread upon the table and, we can be sure, the honoured man is first served. Sunday dinner is a tribute to what he has achieved for them in the week past. The second point regards the matter of dullness. Monotony for the middle-class writer or social worker might be luxury for the hard-working labourer. To sit still in an armchair smoking a pipe, to lean on a window sill studying those who passed beneath, to fall asleep by the fire as the newspaper slipped into one's lap – these 'monotonous' moments were a delight to men who spent five and a half days a week in a noisy factory, who were on the go from five in the morning until six at night. They savoured the 'dullness' of not having to do anything, anticipated and then treasured the times they could absolutely call their own.[13]

Nor was Sunday afternoon always devoted to this sort of static relaxation. Parks and playgrounds drew increasing numbers, though habit and location determined the extent to which these facilities were patronized by workers and their families. A social worker, complaining of a Sunday 'vacancy of mind' in Leeds, a vacancy 'which wanders up and down and *does nothing*', did note that the 600-acre Roundhay Park was at least three miles from the slums.[14] Victoria Park, on the other hand, in the heart of East London, was a haven to which the poor turned in the knowledge that they could enjoy its pleasures among their own kind: 'No West End face is to be seen there, no well-dressed man or woman; only workers bent on enjoying their one day of relaxation, on making the most of the few hours they can call their own during the week.'[15]

An East London district like Poplar, enjoying some sense of itself as a community, could succeed in the organization of 'Pleasant Sunday Afternoons', occasions devoted to the dissemination of mild politico-religiosity, and quite popular. Will Crooks described the gatherings as 'not religious in the orthodox sense', but as incorporating talks on social questions, Biblical subjects or educational matters, preceded by some sort of musical entertainment.[16] 'Services' of this sort were as close as the majority of the non-religious working men of England were willing to come to orthodox worship.[17] Those with more eclectic tastes could almost always find entertainment to suit them on Sunday afternoons in a large city. Arthur Morrison contrasted the monotony of bleak, Sunday-blighted dwelling houses with the vitality of noisy speakers' platforms:

> At the dock gates it was mostly labour and anarchy, but at the other places there was a fine variety; you could always be sure of a few minutes of teetotalism, evangelism, atheism, republicanism, salvationism, socialism, anti-vaccinationism, and social purity, with now and again some Mormonism or another curious exotic. Most of the speakers denounced something, and if the denunciations of one speaker were not sufficiently picturesque and lively, you passed on to the next. Indeed you might always judge afar off where the best denouncing was going on, by the size of the crowds, at least until the hat went round.[18]

Smaller towns could offer the worker fewer diversions of this sort. Instead they gave him the chance to walk out into the countryside, an experience almost lyrically recalled by a Halstead ironmoulder's son:

> On a Sunday evening we'd walk sometimes, the family would go for a walk to Greenstead Green, to a village about three miles off, walk through the meadow, and the children would sit on the green while the parents went into the public house. We'd have, say, a bottle of ginger beer and a packet of crisps and that was really a great treat. And I can remember vividly walking down the lane. I've taken my wife down these lanes, and snapping these what we called 'shirt

buttons', these little flowers. You know, they have these seeds, you know, just snapping these little 'shirt buttons', but we were perfectly happy on those things, yes.[19]

Men who spent time with their families on Sunday more often than not enjoyed what few weekday leisure hours they could afford in the company of other men, workmates or neighbourhood acquaintances. Habits varied in accordance with predilections and circumstance. A teetotaller would remain at home, where a beer drinker would walk to his pub for a pint or two. A man recently arrived in a neighbourhood would be shy at first about stopping in at a pub where he was not known, and would consequently stay put in his own kitchen. Whatever his fancy, if he had little money, he had little chance of indulging it. Though the rhythm of all but the bleakest lives allotted some time for pleasure, and though the Edwardian working man found himself encouraged by propagandists such as Robert Blatchford to satisfy his natural craving for enjoyment, he might discover to his sorrow that to desert thrift for pleasure, even to the extent of a glass or two of beer, was to put his entire family in jeopardy. Wages of twenty-five shillings a week, budgeted down to the last halfpenny, might not allow for even that meagre extravagance.

Workingmen's clubs afforded him a chance to enjoy his few leisure hours in a pleasant and generally seemly fashion. The product of a movement founded in 1862 by a former Unitarian minister, the Rev. Henry Solly, the clubs initially boasted a patronage list of dukes, bishops, and other establishment worthies, and the professed goal of rescuing working men from radicalism and the pub. By 1900, however, the clubs had grown from a 'movement' (philanthropy *for* the working classes which was accepted *by* the working classes')[20] into a collection of meeting places run by workers to suit their particular needs. The process resulted in an ultimately successful effort to eliminate the patronage of well-intentioned middle-class reformers. It produced, as well, a change in the sort of programmes the clubs promoted, a reflection of a similar change in the goals their members espoused. The struggle between those anxious to preserve the clubs for serious political debate, often of a radical nature, and those ready to encourage evenings of song and entertainment had, by the turn of the century, been won by the latter group. Many old-timers blamed the victory on youth. One report in the *Club and Institute Journal* for 1892 complained that the young had let older founding members do all the hard work before joining, and that 'these fellows' had then worked quickly to alter the tone of the club: 'They elected most of their friends upon the committee, and our notions of making the club a well-behaved, respectable and educational centre soon got knocked to the winds.'[21]

A 1904 survey found that the large majority of the 992 clubs affiliated to the Club and Institute Union were social in nature. Two hundred or so still called themselves 'political'; the rest either dedicated themselves to relaxation and sociability pure and simple, or combined those purposes with such endeavours as the organization of a brass band, a bowling team, or a local Friendly Society.[22] Many of the clubhouses, located for the most part in former dwellings or small warehouses, contained libraries, as well as bars, billiard rooms, and entertainment halls. One such, described in 1895 by T. S. Peppin, contained 800 volumes, behind glass, 'the cases carefully locked, being opened only when books are borrowed or replaced'. Activity centred about the hall, where hired entertainers performed standard music hall turns, and about the bar, furnished not only with the normal fixtures and appurtenances, but with tables and chairs for cards and bagatelle.[23] Some clubs sponsored occasional lectures and instructional classes, often on politics or other topics of the day; sometimes, as in an instance Peppin reports, on a more general topic, in this case the very popular one of 'British Seamen'. Few clubs operated by working men themselves essayed the sort of heavy educational diet provided by organizations such as the Workers' Educational Association, or by those various local settlement houses whose management lay in the hands of middle-class philanthropists. Nor, had they wished to, could the clubs' directors have assembled the talent that the Manchester Every Street Settlement provided its members in the early 1900s: P. J. Hartog on chemistry; J. J. Mallon and L. T. Hobhouse on politics; J. H. Clapham on economics; G. M. Trevelyan on history.[24]

But they did not wish to. As B. T. Hall, the secretary of the Union, admitted in 1904, the purpose of the clubs was, in the eyes of their members, to provide a place for 'talking, drinking, smoking and association'.[25] In most cases, socializing was conducted in a decorous enough manner. Hall congratulated the club movement for its civilizing influence:

> He who heretofore held that a man 'that is a man' must 'speak his mind' to, 'pick a bone' with, or be 'thumbs up' with some other person at short intervals, becomes, under club influence a gentle man, holding the uplifted hand to be the rankest of sins, condemning the angry altercation as sheer noisy vulgarity disturbing the peace of mind of the disputants and the reposeful leisure of all others. This

is no fancy picture. This is the evolution which is daily progressing in every workmen's club.[26]

Even in clubs catering to those accustomed to 'ruder speech and coarser habit', rules and regulations tutored them to behave themselves. Hall naturally painted a picture of club life which he hoped would serve the Union well among its middle-class sympathizers. Yet there appears to be little question that the institution was a thoroughly respectable one. Rowntree printed the balance sheet of a York Workingmen's Club for 1899. Its budget amounted to £2,744, and reflected an enterprise conducted by responsible stewards and committeemen. Rowntree, as a temperance reformer, deplored the amount expended on drink, an average of £5 8s 10d per member per year, but acknowledged that although many members appeared to be heavy drinkers, little drunkenness and disorder occurred on the premises.[27]

For this reason, the clubs' proponents claimed that membership sustained rather than undermined the working man's family life. Overcrowded housing and a natural desire to associate with his mates, Peppin argued, were bound to drive a man occasionally from home of an evening. Far better that he be where his wife knew she could reach him, where she knew she would be respectfully treated should she come in search of him, and where she knew that she too was welcome on entertainment nights and occasional outings.[28] Whether a wife viewed the club as friend or rival depended on a good deal more than Peppin allows for: her weekly budget, her husband's proclivity for drink, and her own expectations as to the role he should play at home. There can be little doubt that a working man of moderation, who spent his leisure hours in a well-managed and generally reputable club, was contributing not only to his personal enjoyment but to his neighbourhood image as a respectable and responsible member of the community.

Those without a club never lacked for a pub. Statistical evidence abounded to prove the ease with which English working men could buy themselves a drink. There was one licensed premise for every 193 men, women, and children in East London, one for every 215 in Birmingham, one for every 176 in Sheffield, one for every 195 in Bristol. After deducting children and an estimated number of teetotalers, Joseph Rowntree concluded that the average yearly *per capita* consumption of beer in 1899 was 57 gallons per man and woman – more than a pint a day – and, of spirits, 1·93 gallons.[29] Manchester, in 1902, contained 486 public houses and 2,394 beer and wine houses. The figures, which did not include clubs, matched those of the other cities: one pub per 189 inhabitants.[30] Robert Roberts calculates that there were fifteen pubs in his Salford 'village', though but one establishment licensed to sell more than beer.[31] Roberts's account substantiates the statistician Leone Levi's calculation that at least two-thirds of the nation's yearly drink bill of 162 million pounds was rung up by the working class.[32] Opinions varied as to whether or not working-class drunkenness had declined since the mid-nineteenth century. Booth argued that, if measured by consumption, it had; Rowntree that, if measured by arrests, it had not.[33]

No one argued the fact that working men drank a great deal – a great deal too much to suit most reform-minded observers. Beer, the average working man's beverage, cost 2d a pint. A man, therefore, able to withhold 4 shillings a week from the money he entrusted to his wife, might buy himself as many as 24 pints of beer from Friday to Friday. Booth declared it was not uncommon for labourers to spend one-fourth of their earnings on drink, and still generally appear quite temperate. A witness stated that a steady artisan might drink as much as two quart pots of beer a day. Roberts reports his father's normal ration, 'to maintain his strength', was double that amount. More common than occasional bingeing was this 'habitual soaking', so characterized by C. F. G. Masterman, and classed by him as one of the nation's primary social problems.[34]

Working men drank in Edwardian England for much the same reasons that men have always drunk: to socialize and to escape. Men who enjoy each other's company but are forbidden it at home by the size of their families and their houses will naturally congregate at a public house. Seebohm Rowntree's unsurprising conclusion, that York pubs were a centre for neighbourhood socializing,[35] reinforces the testimony of the bachelor house-painter Philpot, a character in Tressell's *Ragged Trousered Philanthropists*: 'It ain't the fact that I likes the beer, you know, it's the company. When you ain't got no 'ome, in a manner of speaking, like me, the pub's the only place where you can get a little enjoyment.'[36] 'But you ain't very welcome there,' Philpot adds lamely, 'unless you spends your money.' Socializing meant treating, an important and expensive adjunct of pub ritual.

Philpot had no home. But his mates, who did, found the pub as necessary to their lives as he declared it to be to his. For them, as for Philpot, it brought not just sociability; it promised a way out of the life they were leading. It wasn't just the drink; it was, as Roberts suggests, the drink and the atmosphere in which it was drunk:

After the squalor from which so many men came there dwelt within a tavern all one could crave for – warmth, bright lights, music, song, comradeship, the smiling condescension of a landlady, large and bosomy, forever sexually unattainable, true, but one could dream, and her husband (the favoured called him by his first name) . . . But above all, men went for the ale that brought a slow, fuddled joy. Beer was, indeed, the shortest way out of the city. Then, driven at nearly midnight into the street, their temple shuttered and barred, the company lingered on, maudlin, in little groups, loath to face a grim reality again.[37]

To some workmen, drink came to mean more than a social life or an escape. Occupation had a good deal to do with the making of an alcoholic. Painters, boilermakers, and printers were often cited as particularly susceptible. A South Shields boilermaker's daughter, whose father worked at night and claimed the heat made him drink, recollects his addiction:

> Me mother used to often tell me, go and see if your father's all right. And I used to go way down to the Low Street . . . in South Shields and I knew all his haunts, all the pubs, and sure enough I'd find him in one of the pubs. And he'd sit there all day and never come home.[38]

If it was heat that drove the boilermakers to drink, it was sheer physical exhaustion in the case of the chainmakers whom Robert Blatchford despaired of in *Dismal England*:

> Once a week [an old foreman tells Blatchford] a lot of 'em goes off on the beer; a spree they calls it. But the truth is the poor devils is exhausted. Many of the smiths get ruptured through twisting and swinging the heavy links cross-hip. Strikers is used-up old men at forty. It's no use talking about the drink. *They must have it.* Oft enough they cannot touch a bite of breakfast 'til they has a pint. The work tells on 'em so severe of a morning.[39]

The prevalence of drink, if not of drunkenness, evoked a temperance movement which, like worries over money, helped to induce guilt in the minds of pleasure seekers, even when it failed to stop them from seeking pleasure. Especially in the traditionally Nonconformist north, teetotalism was a social force which a drinking man would, at some time in his life, almost certainly have to face down. The three generations which grew up between 1860 and 1914 all felt the pressures of temperance propaganda. 'To this day,' Stella Davies recalled in *North Country Bred*, 'I cannot go into a licensed premises without feeling that I ought not to be there.'[40] Brian Harrison, in his excellent study of drink and the Victorians, argues that by denying working men their pubs, the movement effectively denied them both a social and a political meeting place. Yet Ben Turner's *About Myself* contains descriptions of temperance cafés which suggest that, again in the north at any rate, they too might afford men a congenial place to congregate outside the home. Describing the cafés of Leeds, Bradford, and Huddersfield, he observed that they were often patronized by older radicals. 'Mayors and prospective mayors', he declared, 'were regular habitués.'

> At Huddersfield, Thornton's was a regular debating place, and when I used to go there, one could learn about politics, science, religion and social topics, including town affairs. The same at Laylock's at Bradford. Liberals, Labour men, Radicals, Agnostics, Church and Chapel men and noted teetotalers made this a most famous debating house.[41]

Those who craved more stimulation than conversation alone provided, and sought it in the pub, found themselves forced to confront propagandists determined to break them of their habit. The Manchester Temperance Society sent open lorries through working-class neighbourhoods on Sunday, one displaying a tableau of 'the home that doesn't drink'; the other of the home that did. 'The one that took drink was in rags and them that didn't take it was dressed in their best. The publicans didn't like it, you know, but we used to enjoy it,'[42] recalled one witness, who also reported that both her mother and father drank, the latter quite heavily. The temperance movement undoubtedly kept many men from drink. It kept others from enjoying their beer without at least a twinge or two of conscience.

Drink played a major role in the celebration of the few special occasions to which workmen could look forward throughout the year. Tressell's description of the painters' annual 'beano' in *The Ragged Trousered Philanthropists* heightens with a macabre brilliance but does not basically exaggerate the anticipation and excitement attendant upon such affairs. Important not only for the few hours of enjoyment they afforded participants, their significance can be measured in the manner that, taken together, they marked out yet another sustaining rhythm in the life of a working man. 'The period between Christmas and Easter', Alfred Williams wrote of the railway factory,

> is one of hope and rising spirits, of eager looking forward to brighter days, the long evening and the pleasant weekend ... From Easter till Trip and August Bank Holiday – notwithstanding the terrible trials of the summer weather in the case of those who work at the furnaces – the feeling is one of comparative ease and satisfaction. A

series of little holidays is included in this period. The men are encouraged to bear with the heat and fatigue through the knowledge that it will not be for long, a holiday in sight goes far towards mitigating the hard punishment of work in the shed ... From August till Christmas the feeling is one almost of despair. Five whole months have to be borne without a break in the monotony of the labour. The time before the next holiday seems almost infinite; a tremendous amount of work must be done in the interval. Accordingly, the men settle down with grim faces and fixed determinations. The pleasures of the year are thrust behind and forgotten; day by day the battle must be fought and the ground gained inch-by-inch.[43]

Men doggedly pursued whatever day-to-day diversions were available to them. Besides pubs and clubs, they were not many. In northern towns, choirs and brass bands might attract those with the time and talent to contribute. 'I could name nearly half a dozen choirs; male choirs and mixed choirs,' a Darlington furnaceman's daughter recalled.[44] For the rest: pigeon raising, bowling, gardening, cycling – though this last was a sport more favoured by the bachelor than by the married man. Alfred Williams reported his railway factory hands infected by football mania, a pastime that 'has come to be almost a disease of late years'. The young played it; their elders watched it and bet on it. Betting, in the opinion of some social reformers, was as much the curse of the working classes as drink. Booth deplored the habit while acknowledging that little or nothing could be done about it. Police, he reported, took little notice of bookies operating beneath their noses. Following the running of an important horse race, working-class streets came alive with the appearance of newsboys hawking results: 'Off rush the little boys shouting at the tops of their voices, doors and factory gates open, men and boys tumble out in their eagerness to read the latest "speshul" and mark the winner.'[45]

A lucky win might enable the workman to indulge with his wife in an evening at the local music hall. 'A night out for a shilling' meant two seats at the hall, 6d; a pint of beer, 3d; 4 ounces of sweets, 1d; and either two tram fares or a packet of cigarettes, 2d.[46] Performances, usually twice a night, lasted two hours or so, and, depending on the talent, were wretched or sublime or something in between. Roberts disparages the culture of the music halls, describing the bulk of the songs sung as 'airs painfully banal and lyrics of an inanity that even the sub-literate rejected.'[47] Yet the best songs and the best singers – 'My Old Man', 'The Houses in Between', 'The Old Kent Road'; Dan Leno, Bessie Belwood, Marie Lloyd – could carry even the weariest labourer out of himself for a moment or two. They transported him only far enough that he might laugh or cry at the everyday foolishnesses and disappointments of his own life. The songs were down-to-earth; the singers as often as not exchanged badinage with the audience as with each other. Harry Gosling recalled Bessie Belwood begging off her encores with, 'It's all very fine, but I've got to get home and bathe the kids.' Audience identified with actors as people: 'Ow my, 'ere's Johnny Armstrong [the actor in the part of villain],' a voice from the circle calls, 'Down't 'e look naughty?'[48] Pleasure lies in the immediate and identifiable. There is little or no romance in it all, no longing for transportation out of the here-and-now – confirmation, perhaps, of an impression that, once married, the working man had little inclination for extra-marital flings.[49] His world confined him by routine assumptions and habits of mind, much as it did his wife. He found his pleasures within that world's boundaries, wishing for more, but only more of the same.

Conditions under which men worked in Edwardian England were as varied as we have seen they were for women. Many thousands of men in the Sheffield and Birmingham metal trades continued to work in shops where they might enjoy a close association not only with their mates but also with their foreman or employer. A weaver at a small Bolton shed claimed to have experienced no sense of change at all as he passed from home to shop each day: 'We used to say it were going from home to home ... Because the bosses talked to you and all that, you know ... They were all right bosses. 'Course they were village people, you know what I mean. You knew them more or less.'[50] C. V. Butler, in her 1912 study of social conditions in Oxford, remarked that one of the advantages in working in a town of that size was that 'the workman gets into close contact with the master, or, at least, with his foreman, all parties often know about each other privately, and there is every reason for them to get on well together'.[51]

So it was, apparently, for the Bolton weaver; so it may have been for some in Oxford. Anyone familiar with the picture of savage enmity between master, foreman and labourers painted by Tressell in *The Ragged Trousered Philanthropists*, however, will know that Butler's assertion needs a correction. Often a small enterprise meant only a tiny margin of profit for the master, and hence a greater degree of insecurity among those few he employed. Booth discovered that wage-earners in the London furniture trade were extremely wary of those employers who depended for money to pay the wages of their men on sales made during the preceding week. But, as he discovered, 'This is what so many do.'[52] A small operation, a building firm such as Tressell describes, for example, held out the promise to foremen of promotion into the ranks of management, if they would but prove their mettle. Bob Crass, Tressell's foreman, proves his by harassing the men beneath him unmercifully, much as Hunter, his general manager, badgers Crass. And at the novel's end, Crass, sporting Hunter's top hat and walking in Hunter's place, assumes the position he has craved as he marches in Hunter's funeral. Firms of this sort could breed jealousies and ambitions that made them far from pleasant places to work. Far better, in those cases, the large impersonal factories – an iron works, a railway factory – or at any rate a job in which lines between 'them' and 'us' were clearly marked out, and a man, if he never saw his master, might at least trust his mate.

Wherever he worked, he ran the risk of accidental injury or death. In 1912, the Board of Trade reported a total of 3,995 industrial fatalities, exclusive of seamen.[53] The figures fail to include the men who died of industrially caused disease: anthrax among textile workers; lead poisoning among pottery workers; silicosis among cutlery workers. Nor do they take account of the thousands of industrial accidents that resulted in injuries which kept men either temporarily or permanently from their employment and therefore from their wages. In a speech to Parliament in 1911, upon the publication of the annual report of the Chief Inspector of Factories and Workshops, Arthur Henderson called attention to the unnecessary risks workmen were continually forced to run in the course of their normal labour. Objecting to the inspector's matter-of-fact tone in noting that 'the number of accidents due to molten metal was again very large', Henderson declared that he had himself many times carried molten metal in ladles across areas 'so dark and dirty . . . and so often blocked with boxes and plates which have been used in connection with castings, that they are almost impassable.' He complained that the visits of factory inspectors were much like those of angels – 'occurrences which happen very seldom'. And he declared that until the government acted more forcefully than it had, little if any change for the better was likely to occur.[54]

Factory inspectors, in turn, answered that the men themselves were often at fault for taking unnecessary risks. An inspector for the Midland division in 1910 had claimed that many foundry accidents were the result of the workers' unwillingness to wear proper boots: 'There is a general consensus of opinion that if foundry workmen could be induced to wear boots of a suitable type or place strips of leather over the lace holes, or "spats", the number of accidents from molten metal would be greatly reduced.'[55] The inspector fails to include in his report how much a pair of suitable boots would be likely to cost the workman.

Whatever was ultimately responsible for industrial disease and accidents, the weight of their toll fell upon the shoulders of those who suffered them. Even after the passage, in 1906, of a workman's compensation Bill with teeth, workers were obliged to carry the burden of claiming and collecting. As L. G. Chiozza Money, one of the drafters of the Bill, himself acknowledged after its passage, it would prove little more than cold comfort to the working class: 'The law we made in 1906 is necessarily complicated, and I, who helped to make the law, always take care to look it up before I dare define liability under it. How, then, is an injured agricultural labourer, or the widow of a deceased builder's labourer, to be expected to know where he or she stands?' And even supposing the worker's mastery of such knowledge, he was too often prevented from claiming his just deserts by unsympathetic or uncomprehending medical and legal experts. Chiozza Money cites the case of a 'fine' moulder he calls Burrage, who initially won compensation of half pay for seven months as the result of losing an eye. Reviewing his case, a judge, acting counter to the testimony of Burrage's doctor, reduced payments to only 4s a week and declared him fit to return to work. 'He ignored the fact', Chiozza Money remarks,

> ... that an iron founder must carry molten metal and that his employer had very wisely not allowed him to do so on his resumption – a clear recognition of a clear case of incapacity. He ignored the fact that Burrage was a 'fine' moulder, to whom good sight and binocular vision to enable proper judgment of depth and distance is a prime necessity. He appeared to think that a man of fifty-two years of age, with only one eye, assisted by spectacles, could earn full or almost full wages in competition with young men of normal vision.[56]

The harvest of accident and disease was frequently either permanent unemployment or reduction from the ranks of the skilled to the unskilled. Rosalind Nash wrote of the depressingly widespread state of industrial disability in the potteries at the turn of the century:

> Case after case might be quoted of workers whose lives have been ruined, not only by such calamities as blindness or insanity [as a result of lead poisoning] but by repeated illnesses [particularly by the respiratory disease of phthisis] which cut off earnings, involve families in debt and misery, send children and married women into the factory, and so force mothers to leave their babies untended as to die of improper feeding.[57]

Though industrial disease was particularly prevalent in the potteries, it remained a problem everywhere. In York: 'Now, not only are his hands so disabled that he can never work rapidly again, but often enough, as his wife says, he looks like death.' In Birmingham: 'He has lost all his lower teeth through lead-poisoning in the factory where he used to make medals, etc.; he suffers from colic and is turned 60; it is fourteen years since he had any regular work; he is now fit for nothing but carrying sandwich-boards and doing odd jobs.'[58]

Those fortunate enough to work in trades where disease was less common were confronted by the fact that, with but few exceptions, the work they would perform five and a half days a week for most of their lives was arduous, monotonous, and debilitating. Hours varied greatly from trade to trade, a few, by 1900, working eight-hour shifts, the vast majority still geared to at least a 54-hour week. With short breaks for meals, with the press of overtime, common when times were 'good', with journeys to and from the factory, a man might be away from home for as long as twelve or thirteen hours a day. The smaller the enterprise for which he worked, the greater the chance that he might find himself prevailed upon to disrupt his own schedule to suit that of his employer. A woman whose father was a crane-slinger in a London timber yard, while acknowledging the benefits his overtime pay packet bestowed on the household, made clear at what sacrifice he obtained it. On Fridays he worked from 6.30 in the morning until 8.00 at night, came home for a quick supper, then returned to the yard to work from 9.00 p.m. until Saturday noon. 'He'd get home at 8.00 to have his supper or tea, then my mother would rush round and get a meal ready and pack it up, and he'd take it back with him and be back just after nine.'[59]

For ten hours or so a day, men lived in surroundings which, whether spacious or confined, were often dirty and uncomfortable. Tom Bell, the engineer, wrote of the foundry in which he worked that it was 'vile, filthy and unsanitary':

> The approach to the foundry resembled that of a rag and bone shop, or marine store. The entrance was usually strewn with all kinds of scrap iron and rubbish. The inside was in keeping with the outside. Smoke would make the eyes water. The nose and throat would clog with dust. Drinking water came from the same tap as was used by the hosepipe to water the sand. An iron tumbler or tin can served as drinking vessel until it was filthy or broken, before being replaced by a new one.[60]

Even Lady Bell, apologist though she was for conditions in the Middlesbrough foundries, could find nothing good to say about the red ironstone dust, the white furnace dust, the black chimney dust, and the brown stove dust that together covered everything and everyone:

> One of the most repellent phenomena at the ironworks to the on-looker is the process of expelling the dust from the stoves, for which purpose the valves of the stove are closed, the stove is filled with air at high pressure, and then one of the valves is opened and the air is forcibly expelled. A great cloud of red dust rushes out with a roar, covering everything and everybody who stands within reach, with so intolerable a noise and effluvium that it makes itself felt even amidst the incessant reverberation, the constant smells, dust, deposits that surround the stoves and the furnaces.[61]

'To the onlooker' – Lady Bell presumes that because the worker is accustomed to the dust, he no longer finds it repellent.

The atmosphere in textile factories, far more benign than in an iron foundry, was still oppressive and monotonous. Temperatures demanded that spinners exchange their outdoor clothes for thin shirts and drawers. They worked bare-footed to avoid slipping on oil-soaked wooden floors. Spinners began work at six, took half an hour for breakfast, then worked through the morning until half-past twelve. Their task, with two assistants, was to mind spindles, piecing the thread should it break, 'in a hot room, amid machinery roaring so loudly that one can only converse with those close at hand, and only then at the top of one's voice, amid whizzing wheels, and bands, and swift-straps, which would snatch off a limb for a second's carelessness'.[62] For ten hours, excepting his breaks for meals, he was on his feet watch-ing and tending his machines.

Hope of steady wages and lack of any real alternative kept a man at his unpleasant job. Often rushed, often bored, often both at once, he might withdraw defensively into a kind of physical and mental torpor. One spinner-turned-journalist wrote that the surroundings in which he had worked ultimately laid him low: 'I was called at 5.00 o'clock each morning, with the most disgusting feelings in my head and stomach – nearly always inclined to vomit, my body being in a feverish condition ... It seldom takes a mill hand long to lose nearly all his elasticity and energy of body and mind – especially the latter, and, as a whole, they are a most uninteresting class of people.'[63]

Repeated rhythms become monotony; they can, at the same time, afford a man some measure of psychological comfort. Routine, so often a support to working-class men and women, came to their aid on the job as it did elsewhere. Williams traced the pattern of life inside his railway factory not only in terms of the seasons of the year, but of the days of the week and the hours of every day, a comfortingly familiar pattern of psychological crescendos and diminuendos. Monday, 'an extremely dull day'; Tuesday, 'the strong day'; Wednesday, 'very similar to Tuesday, though the men are not quite so fresh and vigorous'; Thursday, 'the humdrum day'. 'By Friday morning, the barometer will have risen considerably. Notwithstanding the tiredness of the individual, he is nerved to fresh efforts and induced to make a final spurt towards the end of the weekly race.' Saturday, 'the day of final victory'. The daily barometer charted a steadier rise, from early morning sullenness, through mid-day normality, to the 'good fellowship' that followed tea-time.[64]

Determined as were Williams and others who described factory life to expose its harshness, they did not deny those moments of good fellowship or try to insist upon the shop floor as a living hell. As monotonous as much work was, it did not necessarily turn workers into industrial zombies. Accidents and disease, though in the opinion of most far too prevalent, were not the central fact of their reports any more than they lay at the centre of the consciousness of those who risked them. Yet constant unpleasantness and hardships were undeniable, and these observers wrote to ensure that they would not be denied.

One emerges from the mass of evidence with two perceptions: the first, of the bone-weariness with which most workers must have returned home night after night. A second perception is of the readiness on the part of management – as their own perhaps unconscious insistence on depersonalization was leading employers to call themselves – to think of workers as a different breed, less sensitive to dirt and unpleasantness than others. Working men expected to work long and hard, and at often difficult, dirty and unpleasant tasks. They did not believe that they should be asked to sacrifice their humanity in the process. Many of the deficiencies noted by inspectors and others could easily have been remedied, had management attempted, from time to time, to look at the factory through the workers' eyes. A report from the North East Division in 1911 noted that 'the majority of foundries are darker and dirtier than they would be were the walls limewashed yearly'. Of those visited, 74 were washed yearly, 33 every other year, 57 at periods ranging from three to ten years, and 49 had never been washed at all.[65] Williams complained of water closets designed to serve five hundred or so men:

> The convenience consists of a long double row of seats, situate back to back, partly divided by brick walls, the whole constructed above

a large pit that contains a foot of water which is changed once or twice a day. The seats themselves are merely an iron rail built upon brickwork, and there is no protection. Several times, I have known men to overbalance and fall into the pit. Everything is bold, daring, and unnatural. On entering, the naked persons of the men sitting may plainly be seen, and the stench is overpowering. The whole concern is gross and objectionable, filthy, disgusting, and degrading. No one that is chaste and modest could bear to expose himself, sitting there with no more decency than obtains among herds of cattle shut up in the winter pen.[66]

Williams does not attempt to discover why the factory's managers had done nothing to clean up this mess. If asked, they might have replied, as others did, that workers, because they were neither chaste nor modest, did not object to the present arrangement.[67] Williams reports that some did object, and refused to use the facilities at all, thereby inflicting upon themselves the unnecessary discomfort of chronic stomach disorder. What is important is not so much the answer as the fact that the managers never apparently asked the question of themselves. Concerned with workers only as so many 'units of production', they had yet to learn what present-day personnel managers know, that it is wiser not to treat them as such.[68] Those members of the middle class who saw beyond the economic calculus nevertheless often assumed that a worker was somehow a member of a race apart, with feelings foreign to the ken of a conscientious yet alien sympathizer. Many an observer, Lady Bell remarked, seeing an iron foundry for the first time, might shudder 'at what seems to him the lot of the worker among such grim surroundings as these. But there is many a man employed in the works to whom these surroundings are even congenial, to whom the world coloured in black and flame-colour is a world he knows and understands, and that he misses when he is away from it.'[69] 'Them' and 'us': the factory could impart that perception, the central ganglion of a worker's consciousness, with a certainty that shaped his life and his family's as well.

The distance separating 'us' from 'them' widened during the years before the First World War as the result of technological innovation and changing methods of production in factory after factory. The demands of a maturing capitalist system, which required an increasing turnover of new products, and the determination on the part of management to manufacture those products by means of further specialization and standardization, meant that working men found themselves forced, often in very short time and without understanding why, to relearn a skill. Having done so, they might also discover that the task they had now to perform was being taught to a great many who had never before possessed any skill whatsoever, and that management's technological advance had been at the expense of their position within the hierarchy of labour.

Engineers, to take but one example, were confronted by what their historian has termed 'a revolution in tools', particularly in the years between 1900 and 1914. Capstan and turret lathes, milling machines, vertical borers, radial drills and carborundum grinders were among the tools introduced to insure greater precision and efficiency and to increase production: 'The micrometer left the manager's drawer to become, as an advertiser claimed in the *A.S.E. Journal* of 1905, "an essential possession of every engineer". Verniers, protractors, and squares appeared alongside the trusted calipers and rule in the engineer's tool chest. Slowly but surely decimals began to oust fractions from the drawings.'[70] In industries demanding far less skill, workmen either had to learn a new job, or how to perform their old one in a new way. Bigger steamships, if they were to pay, had to be turned around at the docks faster than their smaller predecessors. Dockers accommodated to the fact or looked elsewhere for jobs. Ferro-concrete forced changes in the building trades. Linotype machines threatened compositors; pottery 'jiggers' displaced hollow-ware pressers. Mass production substituted cooperative for individual effort, as in Williams's proto-typical railway factory. Cheaper goods brought the compulsion for constantly changing fashions, a compulsion that could be satisfied only if workers adjusted to speed-up and pattern change. A Birmingham member of the Glass Makers' Society lamented in the 1890s:

> At one time you would have found a hundred tons of stock in manufactories where you will not find one today. Fashions change quickly, and articles which have gone out of fashion can be sold only at a great loss. This does not apply to our trade only; I have seen electroplated articles which have gone out of fashion sold for a tenth of cost price.[71]

Management was determined to keep the inventory low and to keep it changing, depending upon the worker to master whatever new tech-niques and skills that dual goal demanded. Capitalist competition was reshaping men's work patterns, bringing stress, anger, and confusion in the wake of that redefinition.

Though English workers had not experienced technological change so intensely, and in so many areas at the same time, since the early years of the industrial revolution, they were familiar enough with the process to have built up a defensive mythology opposing what they mistrusted and feared. An article on 'the old wool combers' in an issue of the 1892 *Trade Unionist* told a tale that workers in the 1890s insisted was of direct relevance to them:

> From that time [1825] the history of the wool combers was that of a deadly struggle between man and machinery ever growing more severe. The hopeless fight was marked by strikes from time to time, each strike being the signal for the fresh introduction of machinery, and all the time the busy brains of Lister and Co. were at work perfecting the 'devils' which were to take the men's places ... Their capital was their specialized skill, and it was destroyed by the machine.[72]

Historical polemic fused with personal recollections of a more recent past to fire the indignation of working men. Those in the boot and shoe industry might recall the extent to which their 'technological' revolution of the 1850s and 1860s had created as many new jobs for hand workers as for machinists. Yet in the ensuing years, machinery had forced the pace of hand work until clickers and cutters, the aristocrats of the trade, saw their places filled with barely trained boys and youths.[73]

Few workers wished to scrap machinery and return to some sort of pre-industrial world of handlooms and spinning wheels. That fantasy was the almost exclusive property of the middle class. The more thoughtful among the workers recognized that the handloom weavers were, in a sense, not the victims of industrial revolution but of industrial decay. They were prepared to tolerate the introduction of new machinery and new technology, but only if they were afforded the chance to determine the conditions under which they were introduced, and the opportunity to ensure that the machines did not, in the process of increasing the profit margin for 'them', make machinery of 'us' in the bargain.

Without that chance, workers were made to risk the alienation that Engels had described when he wrote of Manchester in the 1840s, and that psychologists continue to define and describe. Alienation, in this sense, results from an inability to exercise at least some control over the processes of one's job – when to pick up a tool and put it down. It communicates to the worker a sense of disconnectedness from himself as a human being: 'Reacting to the rhythms of technology, rather than acting in some independent or autonomous manner, he approaches most completely the condition of *Thingness*, the essence of alienation.'[74] One man's sudden awakening to the fact of his own 'thingness' made a lasting impression on his mate, Tom Bell. Day after day he filed points on sewing needles at the Singer Company's Clydebank works:

> Every morning there were millions of these needles on the table. As fast as he reduced the mountain of needles, a fresh load was dumped. Day in, day out, it never grew less. One morning he came in and found the table empty. He couldn't understand it. He began telling everyone excitedly that there were no needles on the table. It suddenly flashed on him how absurdly stupid it was to be spending his life like this. Without taking his jacket off, he turned on his heel and went out, to go for a ramble over the hills to Balloch.[75]

Some never woke up to their own condition. Alfred Williams provided his readers with what may have been part truth and part parable, but was even so a vivid picture of the way new technology and speed-up could eat into a man. Pinnell, a stamping shed worker, found himself the victim of his reputation as a hard worker when American machinery was introduced there. He was to demonstrate just what the machines could do; the work they were able to wring from him was to determine the standard expected of his co-workers:

> Everything was designed for the man to start as early as possible, to keep on mechanically to and from the furnace and hammer with not the slightest pause, except for meals, and to run till the very last moment. His prices were fixed accordingly. Every operation was correctly timed. The manager and overseer stood together, watches in hand. It was so and so a minute; that would amount to so much an hour, and so much total for the day.

Wages were calculated on the basis of Pinnell's work during the morning hours, when he was fresher, and when he could be expected to accomplish more. Piece rates were 'weighed, chiselled, and pared with great exactness, even to the splitting of a farthing'. In the end, 'broken' to the new conditions, Pinnell could do nothing but bury himself in his work, 'a very part of the machinery he operates'. Nothing could keep him from the shop floor:

> Ill or well he was sure to be at his post. Sometimes, when his wife exhorted him to stay at home and recuperate and locked the doors against him, in the early morning he escaped to work through the window. There was no detaining him at all; he felt bound to come to the shed and endure the daily punishment.[76]

Clearly Williams is writing more than description. The language is that of a cautionary tale: Pinnell – who may or may not have been a real person – the 'much be-fooled' victim of a 'cruel and callous system'. No matter if the details are 'accurate'; they bespeak a state of mind that was real enough. Whether or not conditions had grown that much more oppressive with the introduction of new technology, the workers believed that they had. They did not so much resent harder work as they did the pace and rhythms to which it was now bound. In former days, Williams declared, workmen were not 'watched and timed at every little operation'. Nor were they confronted with the constant need to relearn: 'As the job had been done one day so it would be the next.' Not any more; experience no longer seemed to count for anything. An old and experienced hand lost his self-respect when he began to see himself as he believed his managers saw him: unwanted, both because his wage was too high, and because, in a period of rapid industrial change, he had learned too much and could not forget it fast enough. 'He is not pliable.'[77]

Tensions such as those Williams described were widespread. Piece rates replaced hourly wages in those industries where management calculated that the change would result either in a reduced payroll or increased production, or both.[78] Men in textile factories joined women in complaining of the 'driving system'. Though instinct taught them to work with their mates, they now found themselves compelled to work against them. The competition took its toll; Allen Clarke predicted that the 'driving' system would soon make work unbearable even to the strongest, quickest worker.[79] Foundry men bridled at the same treatment, striking at a Bradford works for two years to re-establish their breakfast break, and arguing, as other unions argued, that speed-up, whatever it might mean in terms of mounting production figures, meant a mounting accident toll as well.[80] The confusions and distress evoked the concern of investigators, of the unions, and, above all, of the workers themselves. Deploring the decline of the small family employer, a Salford iron founder in 1908 wrote to his union's monthly *Report*, as uncertain as he was angry:

These firms have vanished, and been replaced by the strictly business hustler on their side, and the animated dividend producer on ours . . . [Our] working conditions can be summed up as follows: The speeding up of both human and inanimate machinery intensifies all along the line. Men complain of a multitude of petty tyrannies and humiliations in the course of workshop life. The pace grows hotter, and the working period of a man's life grows shorter. Work is harder to keep and harder to perform with every day's development. Improvement in tools are increasing man's productive capacity, almost indefinitely, making the unemployed problem more difficult of solution every day.[81]

The author of the letter wants to know what is to become of him. His certainty is limited to the 'producers' on his side and the 'hustlers' opposed to him. Yet to make their new technology pay, managers constantly attempted to persuade workers that there were no longer two sides, that higher production and greater efficiency would reap rewards for both capital and labour together. The working man refused to believe that particular gospel. If he worked for one of those firms whose production schedule demanded the preaching of co-operation, the chances were good that his experience would instill in him what a recent analyst calls 'factory class consciousness', which, far from promoting a belief in common goals, would convince him, instead, of the importance of opposition to any such notion.[82] After 1880, world economic forces compelled manufacturers, if they were to remain competitive, to press ahead with rationalization and speed-up to an increasing degree. Those very processes, because they encouraged managers to think of workers as 'objects', almost guaranteed that workers, in their turn, would resent that objectification and stiffen their resolve to oppose it.

As Arthur Kornhauser has pointed out, even in those cases where employers are able to persuade workers to increase production for 'the benefit of all', there remains the thorny question of how to divide the higher earnings in a manner that 'all' believe to be fair: 'The percentage of return to the owners and workers is more flexible the greater the margin of profit, and hence subject to more argument and more struggle. Some of the most militant and aggressive unions are found in companies and industries where the margin of profit is high.'[83] Finally, thoughtful workers would find it difficult to trust employers' pleas for united effort while the employers themselves were in the process of organizing a federation whose specific purpose was to counter union demands. If the struggle between capital and labour was about to take on a national rather than a local character, the president of the Trades Union Congress declared in 1897, then labour would have to respond to that challenge with stronger federations of its own: 'As capital has started the ball in this direction they must be prepared to play the game, and they cannot complain if labour should at any time enter the field and challenge them with their own weapons.'[84] One of management's most common devices to encourage co-operation took the form of the 'premium bonus' introduced in Glasgow in 1898. Time study experts, along with plant foremen, determined a time 'standard' to which all workers would be expected to conform. Those who exceeded the standard would receive half the profits from their extra endeavour, the other half accruing to the company. Labour was all but unanimous in its opposition to this scheme. Many argued that it resulted in nothing more than further speed-up. The Sheet Metal Workers, in their annual report of 1912, complained that 'standards' had become so unrealistic that in some cases workers found themselves having to spend twice the time at their job as the technical experts allowed.[85] The Ironfounders, following an inquiry in 1910, declared their reasons for opposition to the bonus:

1 That it destroys the principle of collective bargaining;
2 That it is destructive to trades unionism and encourages disorganization;
3 That it is one of the causes of unemployment;
4 That it leads to scamping work;
5 That it prevents the proper training of apprentices;
6 That it promotes selfishness in the workshop; and
7 That it promotes workshop favouritism.[86]

A further and understandably basic objection had been voiced the previous year by a deputation from the United Pattern Makers to the Admiralty. By restricting the 'bonus' to only half the excess profit workers earned, management was depriving them of the full value of their labour: 'The value of the men's labour is appraised by the employer at a certain figure, and then a reduction of that is made, which goes to the employer.'[87]

If technological change resulted in furthering factory class consciousness and increasing class division, it at the same time contributed to a restructuring of the working class itself. The tendency inherent in persistent mechanization to chip away at distinctions between the skilled and the unskilled deserves further comment at this point. Nothing more clearly evokes the dislocations working men were suffering than an advertisement in an 1890 brochure, circulated by the Marsden Process Marker Company of Wigan, calling manufacturers' attention to a newly patented process for cutting cloth, 'designed to ensure that all garments are planned out of the least possible quantity of cloth and scientifically marked in within the space of two to five minutes ... a mechanism by which the less skilled marker can cut garments as perfectly and economically as the designer himself.'[88] Once introduced into the manufacturing process, sophisticated machines of this sort made it much simpler for a heretofore unskilled worker to pick up a trade, while driving the skilled artisan back into an ever-increasing pool with him, as fellow member of a semi-skilled limbo.

J. W. F. Rowe, in his careful survey of changes in the engineering trade, has shown the need for a certain degree of qualification when addressing this problem. Moulders and pattern makers continued skilled craftsmen, despite the introduction of new methods of production. Fitters and turners, on the other hand, found themselves reduced in status as they were forced to adjust to less technically demanding routines. Generally, Rowe concludes, there occurred a 'tremendous increase in the proportion of semi-skilled men',[89] not only in engineering, but in other industries as well. His conclusions, drawn in 1928, reflect contemporary impressions. Arnold Freeman, writing in 1914, declared that many of the operations performed in Birmingham factories and workshops could, by that date, be mastered in a few days; 'Others require not more than a few months. Such employments as require years of laborious training are few, and are diminishing in number.'[90]

As the author of a book on boy labour, Freeman was particularly struck by this phenomenon, since in many instances it was boys, hired at low wages, who were learning the new 'skills' and thereby replacing their higher paid seniors. Boys would be put to work on machines and paid at a lower rate than men at the same job. At the first opportunity, the men would be dismissed or, at the least, forced to accede to a reduction in their own pay.[91]

Perhaps the building trades suffered as much if not more than any others in terms of this rapid reordering of workers' skills. Two members wrote to the *Transport Worker* in 1911 to urge all workers to unite in opposing a system that had already resulted in the deterioration of their own position:

> The ever-increasing use of so-called labour-saving machinery is more and more casualizing the trade. Today we are confronted with the problem of the semi-skilled or so-called unskilled labourer, displacing artisans who have had to serve an average apprenticeship of five years to become proficient. Buildings are everywhere being designed to this end. The introduction of ferro-concrete, stereotyped ornamentation, etc., must needs awaken the sectional unions to the fact that as building is rapidly being revolutionized so must the unions change their methods, and quickly.[92]

Skilled workers recognized that technology might reduce them not just to the level of the semi-skilled but to the ranks of the unemployed. After 1900, unemployment among skilled workers was not significantly lower than among unskilled, a reversal of general trends in the second half of the nineteenth century.[93] Ramsay MacDonald, addressing a conference on the abolition of unemployment in 1910, described what had occurred during the preceding twenty years in Leicester. Machines 'of the most delicate construction and the most complicated movement', had replaced men. Workers found themselves out of a job, not because trade was bad, but for the stark, simple reason that machinery had made human labour more productive, 'and under the present system of industry a large percentage of human labour that used to be necessary had therefore come to be necessary no longer.'[94]

Technology, if it did not make men more skilled, forced them to become more specialized, to learn the ways of one machine at the expense of a more general knowledge of their trade. Employers boasted to investigators that innovation was eliminating the totally unskilled. More and more men were learning to play at least a small part in the increasingly technical process of manufacture. But the fact that they knew no more than that one small part meant that if their particular speciality was not in demand, their only recourse was a job as a common labourer. The new demands made upon fitters and turners, while reducing them to the ranks of semi-skilled operatives, transformed them into specialists as well. They ceased to be the 'all-round' workmen they had been, J. W. F. Rowe found, as engineering firms began to adapt to one or two particular lines, and sub-division of labour grew with the introduction of mass production. What was true of engineering was true of other industries as well. 'Specialists', a builder informed N. B. Dearle,

> . . . are largely taking the place of the ordinary artisan and navvy. His foreman told me that things were getting very specialized now, the idea of 'one man one job' being carried to an extreme, and each having his own particular sphere. This is largely the result of the new processes and materials replacing the old familiar methods . . . The concrete labourers, for instance, form a type of their own, being little recruited if at all from the ranks of the artisans they have displaced or of ordinary labourers.[95]

Technological change brought confusion and resentment. Most workers accepted its coming as inevitable, perceiving, however, that they would be pressed to increase their productivity, without enjoying any compensation in the form of an appreciable increase in their standard of living. Never fully reconciled to that fact, they turned to trade unions for help in ameliorating the consequences of its galling paradox. In theory, unions taught individual workers 'to feel' – as one idealistic engineer declared in 1896 – 'that they are not single units, each fighting for his own hand, but that, within certain limits, each is responsible to his fellow workers'. Standing in 'strong and united opposition to all forms of industrial opposition' they bred 'the spirit of firm independence' grounded in mutual reliance upon each other's sympathy and interest.[96] That was, at any rate, the ideal: 'One for all and all for one', the motto which appeared on the banners of union after union. And that ideal was particularly appealing to men who had experienced the threats and pressures of technological innovation. To credit the growth of trade unions in the years before the First World War to the fear which those threats and pressures engendered would be to ignore other equally important explanations of the phenomenon: a sharp increase in living costs, for example, a long stretch of full employment after 1911, and the institution of national insurance payments through union bureaucracies.[97] Yet unions did represent one defence against inroads by the unskilled and semi-skilled. Labour aristocrats had, from the 1850s, relied on their unions to preserve for themselves the benefits a maturing capitalism was affording them. Profiting from their skill and from their employers' willingness to reward that skill for the sake of industrial peace and increased production, those unionists had seen no reason to ally themselves with the vast unorganized majority of the British labour force. Now, the threat of new machinery and consequent dilution of skills compelled them to rethink their situation and their strategies.

In some unions, changing circumstance merely reinforced traditional aloofness. The general secretary of the Iron Founders' Society sounded a warning in 1889 that labour aristocrats were to repeat often in the years to follow. In answer to his own rhetorical question, 'Should we let in the unskilled?', he said:

> Such a course would be most unwise because the invention of new machinery and the supply of unskilled labour are practically unlimited ... Employers could practically flood our society with relays of this class of members which would soon end in exhaustion of funds.[98]

Craft unions, recognizing the futility of fighting against machines, tried to ensure that their introduction would not immediately result in a flood of semi-skilled rivals and consequent wage reductions. In January, 1897, the Engineers won a temporary victory when, after a nine months' strike at Hull, the Amalgamated Society, in the words of its *Journal*, 'forced recognition of the principle that machines which supersede hand-skilled labour should be manipulated by skilled and

143

full-paid men.'[99] In both Leicester and Northampton, socialist members of the Boot and Shoe Operatives led the fight against the introduction of machines. In Leicester, they organized a campaign, as well, to restrict their output once the machines were introduced, in an attempt to convince management that the new equipment was more trouble than it was worth.[100]

Not all unions stood as adamantly against change; some perceived that the longer they continued to shut out semi-skilled workers the greater the opportunity and the determination of many of the latter to join the 'new' unions which, since the late 1880s, had been campaigning for their membership. The semi-skilled not unnaturally resented aristocratic exclusiveness, a fact that was not lost on the more perceptive members of the trade union leadership. Charles Hobson, secretary of the Metal Trades Federation, warned in his union's journal that unwillingness to extend membership would only serve to damage the movement as a whole.[101] Of fourteen existing local societies among forgers of tools and cutlery, six were unions of hand forgers who refused to admit machine forgers, although they manufactured precisely the same product. The result was 'the greatest antipathy between the two sections of workmen, although they may work for the same firm'. By 1904, the leaders of the ASE, recognizing the futility of further opposition, proposed the opening of a 'machinist section' within the union to accommodate the semi-skilled workers in their trade. Rank and file opposition compelled them to abandon the plan, as it did five years after a scheme was eventually adopted in 1912. The Pattern-makers, on the other hand, faced with a sizeable increase in unskilled and unapprenticed membership after passage of the National Insurance Act, reacted with less hostility than the Engineers and with a sense that the pressures they were experiencing would be worth enduring in the light of the increased strength they seemed to guarantee:

> Although considerable risk is taken by some of the more highly-skilled trades in admitting to membership youths whose future competence and industry are largely matters of conjecture, still there cannot be the least doubt but that [the] advantages far outweigh the risks, and that the general tendency to throw open the trade union to a youth as soon as he has commenced to learn his trade in earnest is based on sound commonsense.[102]

Some of that was surely brave whistling in the dark. The Pattern-makers could hope that advantages would outweigh risks, but they could not know. As with all unions, uncertainty argued caution while circumstance dictated change. Nor were their problems limited to the

1  The landscape of the working class. Preston, Lancashire. 'Neither good
enough to promote happiness nor bad enough to produce hopelessness.'
(W. G. Hoskins, *The Making of the English Landscape*, 1955.)

2 Cannon Street, Leeds. The clothes line and the chairs in the street suggest the residents here shared in each other's lives to an unusually high degree.

3 The forbidding emptiness of respectability. A working-class street in the railway town of Wolverhampton.

4 Nos 66–71 Rea Street, Birmingham. Bow windows and carved lintels are evidence of the surrender of a once better neighbourhood to urban decay.

5 Columbia Square, London. Model housing for the working class, built in 1859–62 by Angela Burdett-Coutts, the Victorian philanthropist.

6 Katharine Buildings, London. 'The prevailing ideas were that ... the fittings should be of the simplest in view of the destructive habits of the tenants, the buildings airy and wholesome, and the rents low.' (J. Parsons, *Housing by Voluntary Enterprise*, 1903.)

7 Saltney Street, Liverpool. Water from a communal pump; garbage in communal bins: the trials of working-class housekeeping.

8   East End, London, 1912. The compulsion to keep yourself to yourself confronted with the well-nigh impossible task, in this case, of doing so.

9   Matriarchy. Circus Street, Liverpool, c. 1895.

10   Moss Street, Bankside, London, 1896. Houses on Moss Street are coloured black and dark blue on Charles Booth's survey map. Black: 'Lowest class. Vicious; semi-criminal.' Blue: 'Very poor, casual. Chronic want.'

11　Whitechapel Street, London, 1911. The ladders are possible evidence of an all-too-rare improving landlord.

12   Necessity and invention: lamp-post into maypole. London, 1892.

13 Policeman's funeral. Lambeth, London. An occasion which must have varied the rhythm of neighbourhood life. Note the lowering model tenement in the background.

14 'Woman of the time', Manchester.

15 Crisp Street, Poplar, London, 1904. 'Row after row of coster barrows weighed down with tempting or deceitful offerings; line upon line of shoddy shops where reeking masses of meat and vegetables and over-ripe fruit poison the air.' (Winifred Blatchford, *The Woman Worker*, 1909.)

16  A phalanx of working-class respectability. Monday Afternoon Mothers' Meeting, Heyrod Street, Manchester.

17  Afternoon Assembly. The antiseptic authority of the Board School.

18 Working men outside a Manchester pub. 'The shortest way out of Manchester.'

19 An East London fair, 1912.
'... shows, shies, swings, merry-go-rounds, fried fish stalls ... You may be drunk and disorderly without being locked up – for the station won't hold everybody – and when all else has failed, you may set fire to the turf.' (Arthur Morrison, *Tales of Mean Streets*, London, 1894.)

20 Yarmouth Sands. 'You Can Do a Lot of Things at the Seaside That You Can't Do in Town.' (Music Hall refrain.)

21 Labour Party propaganda. Class consciousness and the law.

**SPECIMEN.**

**WHIPS FOR LABOUR'S BACK.**

This block can be supplied for 5s. Candidates and Secretaries will find a pictorial handbill of the greatest use for announcing meetings, distributing in workshops and on the streets, with the Candidate's name, &c.

22 Ben Tillett addresses workers during the 1912 Transport Strike. 'Capitalism is capitalism as a tiger is a tiger; and both are savage and pitiless towards the weak.' (Ben Tillett, 1912.)

matter of dilution. Often just as thorny were questions of demarcation, again the result of technological innovations which were shifting boundaries that had for years separated one craft from another. Raymond Postgate, in his *Builders' History*, took the plumbers as an instance in point, 'unable to grapple with the difficulties involved in the new processes', and convinced that 'their only remedy was to claim that whatever had before been done by plumbers should still be done by them, though iron or china had taken the place of lead.'[103] Problems were particularly acute in the shipbuilding industry, where increased specialization required minute redefinitions of the tasks each union might perform. Excerpts from a demarcation judgment involving the Boilermakers and the Shipwrights in 1899 suggest the tensions that could build between one union and another:

4   Portable Rifle Racks. The Shipwrights mark off position, make moulds, and mark off material when made, and when these come on wood, finish the fastening. When they come on iron, the Shipwrights mark off holes for hole-borer: if tapped, the Caulkers follow up and finish the work: if plain holes, the fixing is done by Riveters or Caulkers as the case may be . . .

23   Fire Bucket Hangers. These depend very much on the position in which they are stowed. As a rule they are stowed by both Carpenter and Joiner, if on wood. If fixed on iron, Shipwrights mark off position and holes for hole-borer; then if tapped, the Caulkers follow up and do the tapping and finish the job. If, however, the holes are plain, the Shipwrights or Riveters, as the case may be, finish the job . . .

28   Levelling Beams. If in ordinary work the Shipwrights sheer the deck lines and put the ribbands on deck to carry up the weight of the beam, then the Caulkers help or cut the holes on beam knees to raise or lower the beam as required. If on an upper deck, the Caulker will cut off frame tops by or to the sheer line. If it be a double bottomed ship, the beams are usually made fair, and any discrepancies made up by angle corner pieces on tank margin plate. These pieces are fitted by Ironworkers.[104]

Many trade union leaders, and some members of the rank and file, noted the wasted time and effort of endless demarcation disputes, and urged amalgamation. Leaders of the Boilermakers and Iron and Steel Ship Builders, in their 1907 report, argued that to continue as disunited as they were at present meant that all the unions in the shipbuilding industry would run the risk of losing ground to their well-organized opponents in employers' federations: 'We then have on one side a

well-organized body of employers governing and controlling each of
the two parts of the shipbuilding and engineering industry, both closely
interwoven with each other; and on the other side a loosely federated
body of trade unions, some well organized, others just the reverse.'[105]
And all of them were too often disputing with each other rather than
uniting against the impositions of management. When unions did
attempt amalgamation, they as often as not foundered on points such
as those raised in a letter from a rank-and-file iron founder to his union's
monthly report for June, 1908, opposing a merger with the plate
moulders. The latter, the writer noted, at present worked at lower
rates in almost all the factories employing iron founders. If the plate
moulders are now to receive the higher rates, the lower paid founders
will justifiably ask for an increase as well. If the moulders are to continue to work at their present rate, what will prevent employers from
lowering founders' rates to the same level? 'Thus at one blow we ourselves reduce wages to the plate moulders' level, and maybe throw
moulders on the funds ...' Furthermore, amalgamation will not in
itself resolve the question of demarcation: 'We know how employers
keep attempting to let plate moulders do odd jobs, loose patterns.
What position should we be in if they were our members?'[106]

Members were even more chary of any scheme that hinted at industrial unionism, the grouping together into one union of all those
workers engaged in a single industry. The 'all-grades' movement, that
less radical means to something like the same end which we have seen
ASE rank-and-filers opposing, met with the opposition of other skilled
workers as well. Ben Turner recalled the difficulties he had in persuading textile workers 'to take in the guinea a week man and the 12s
woman as well as the £2 a week man and the 25s a week mender ...
The spinner felt himself a different class from the piecener, a cut above
the weaver, and a long way above the willeyer and fettler who did the
hard preparatory work in the mill.'[107] Harry Gosling of the Thames
Watermen and Lightermen credited the success of his 1911 strike to
his ability 'to drop the individual unions, and speak of the whole of
the trades as a federation'. In his memoirs he declared that consolidation
was, in the minds of most men, a matter of convenience and not affection, and that even as he wrote, in 1927, sentiment remained what it
had been two decades earlier.[108] Federation, a joining together for
particular purposes while preserving to each union its separate existence, funds, and bureaucracy, represented the limits of most members'
readiness to experiment with grand reorganization. Even among unskilled 'new' unionists, unwillingness to risk the destruction of their
painstakingly constructed and still fragile organizations soon came to

outweigh whatever hopes they may have harboured for victories gained through militant and united class actions.

Debates over consolidation represented one of many areas in which rank and file union sentiment might stand at odds with official aspirations or intentions. Success was breeding union bureaucrats, bound in the organizational paraphernalia of their new offices – leaflets, rule books, balance sheets – and, in the minds of members, too often ready to bargain as if their constituency was a clientele instead of a collection of fellow workers. As an example of this new breed, 'a prototype of the twentieth century trade union leader', Alan Fox cites Ted Poulton, general secretary of the Boot and Shoe Operatives after 1907. Poulton worked eight years at the bench before assuming the position of branch secretary in 1890. The same year he founded a trade union club in Northampton and served as its first secretary. Two years later, as president of the local trades council, he helped organize the Midland Federation of Trades Councils. Soon his name appeared on various municipal boards and councils: School Board, 1895; Town Council, 1898; Northampton Technical Instruction Committee; Northampton General Hospital. In 1906, he was elected the city's first working man mayor. Poulton believed in the virtues of union centralization, maintaining that negotiators should be allowed to bargain unhampered by restraints imposed upon their actions from below. He argued as a confirmed and convinced bureaucrat: 'The whole trend of events . . . was in favour, so long as men efficiently performed their duties and honestly carried out the rules of their Union, of giving them these powers, because they were put into position as being considered the most capable of conducting the business.'[109]

The power should be theirs because the power was theirs: so the argument appeared to rank-and-filers who consistently opposed Poulton's attempts at consolidation. They, along with workers like them in other unions, suspected those who had moved beyond the branch level of the qualities of habit and mind which bureaucracy sanctioned and encouraged. A negotiator taught himself to see problems 'in the round', to understand the two sides to every issue. As the Webbs described it in their *History of Trade Unionism*, a further unconscious bias began to work within him: 'Whilst the points at issue no longer affect his own earnings or conditions of employment, any disputes between his members and their employers increase his work and add to his worry. The former vivid sense of the privations and subjection of the artisan's life gradually fades from his mind; and he begins more and more to regard all complaints as perverse and unreasonable.'[110] The result was the sort of weary exasperation expressed by the Boilermakers' Executive in 1907 after the union's membership had rejected a plea for financial reorganization: 'To deal in a pettifogging manner by cutting off here and there a few pounds from official salaries, as suggested by some branches, is to miss the real object of the meeting together of the Committee and as well as being both mean and contemptible is also a mockery and a sham.'[111]

Battles between leadership and rank and file were not consistently drawn in terms of reactionary head versus radical tail. 'Advanced' proposals for consolidation and amalgamation, the projects of a union bureaucracy, were often voted down by a more conservative membership. In the minds of rank-and-file union members, participation as often meant a sharing in the benefits of certain tangible results as it did involvement in the process of democratic decision-making. Relatively few joined the radical authors of *The Miners' Next Step* in thinking through the meaning of democratic leadership, or in declaring with them that unity and loyalty derived from 'an interest and a policy which is understood and worked for by all'.[112] Lack of time and inclination left most union members unprepared to pursue the implications of a declaration such as that. They were ready to entrust leadership to others, but only so long as those others remembered where they came from and who they spoke for. Once officials talked as if they alone 'knew best', they spoke with the accents of an authority the working class had taught itself to mistrust and disbelieve.

'Union' implied a horizontality – a cause in common with one's mates. Working men welcomed that relationship with a warmth that they would never feel for their vertical connections to a distant hierarchy. Organizers understood that sentiment, and wherever possible capitalized upon it as they worked to increase membership. Persuading often ignorant or apathetic men to join a union was hard work. The unskilled had difficulty believing in benefits that appeared problematical; the skilled wondered if unions existed for any purpose other than levelling wages down to a standard rate.[113] Ben Tillett expressed the exasperation of many organizers when, in his account of the 1911 transport workers' strike, he despaired of the 'dull indifference' or 'dull wondering interest' that he and others continued to encounter 'in spite of ardent service year in and out for the past fifteen or eighteen years'.[114] Against such a background, loyalty and solidarity were more readily understood when preached with direct reference to bonds that were local, familiar, and concrete.

Evidence of the strength of those bonds appears in the April, 1908, *Iron Founders' Monthly Report*. There, the executive committee chronicles its ultimately successful battle to force Manchester Branch No. 1

to transfer those of its members working at a shop in Reddish to the union's Stockport branch. The committee argued its ruling on the ground that the shop was closer to Stockport than to Manchester. The Manchester branch fought the decision in the belief that to send its members to Stockport would result, not simply in the loss of their dues, but in their banishment from a branch where they were well known and where they believed they belonged. The year-long correspondence, printed in full in the *Report*, illustrates the acrimonious divisions that could arise between leadership and rank and file. The letters evoke, as well, bureaucracy's unwillingness to sympathize with local sensitivities and its annoyance with the seemingly petty grievances which were, except rarely, the substance of union life at the branch level:

> You could not [the Executive Committee wrote] have chosen a worse time to ask for the case to be submitted to the vote of the society, as you must know that we are very busy with the annual report, and scarcely know which way to turn, and this is no ordinary case of appeal, as owing to the length of time the case has been pending the voluminous correspondence will require a great deal of time to seek out and arrange for the printers, much more time than we have at our disposal at present, and certainly if you are determined to persist with your appeal it will have to wait until we have time to deal with it.[115]

Strikes probably imposed the most severe strains experienced between union members and their officials. The leadership was generally prepared to undertake strike action if it considered the dispute a serious one; if it could be convinced that a negotiation in good faith had at least been attempted; and, most importantly, if it believed it had a good chance of winning. Officials often found themselves driven by local discontent to lend support to strikes which failed to meet those generally cautious criteria. The Patternmakers, in 1913, deplored the willingness of their Southampton members to press ahead with a strike which, in the opinion of the leadership, was a lost cause from the start. 'It takes more courage at times to remain at work than to come out on strike, and many of the Southampton workmen have had abundant cause to regret their lack of courage on this occasion,' the Executive reported angrily.[116] A group of labour worthies, including Will Crooks, Arthur Henderson and George Barnes, attempted to legislate against precipitate action at the annual meeting of the Trades Union Congress in 1911 by proposing a mandatory thirty-day notice of all intended strike action. The move, rejected by the membership, reflected the attitude of trade union bureaucrats, who expressed the hope that the procedures of conciliation and arbitration might eliminate the need for strikes. As a device for the intelligent solution of industrial disputes, strikes were, the *Metal-Worker* reported in 1909, 'becoming more disastrous every year ... Now we have arbitration courts which bid fair to be impartial, we should, as far as possible, make them serve our purpose and obtain through them our due, and their use of our funds for constructive purposes.'[117] Arbitration would succeed only if rank and file could be convinced their leaders had won them a fair settlement.

To suggest, in the matter of strikes, a clear division of opinion between conservative officialdom and adventuresome rank and file would considerably oversimplify and distort an extremely complex pattern of behaviour and beliefs. Ben Tillett was not alone among union leaders in deploring the apathy of the mass membership. In the course of any strike the attitudes of those most directly involved – the strikers – can shift quite suddenly and dramatically as the very nature of the strike itself undergoes change. The authors of a recent study compare a strike to a row between husband and wife: 'A row over something that would ordinarily seem ridiculous; but as it progresses more fundamental issues are raised which put in question the very idea of marriage. Likewise a strike, whether the participants are always aware of it or not, puts in question the whole basis of employment.' And in addition, the authors might have added, the whole question of trade union structure.[118] Strikers might down tools with reluctance in support of members in another shop or in another town; once in the fray, consciousness of a more vague and general grievance against their own employers might turn them into diehard advocates of an all-or-nothing settlement.[119] Initial enthusiasm, on the other hand, could well wane when workers began to experience the privations a strike imposed upon themselves and their families. In those instances, moral pressure might hold them to their course, still loyal to the cause but no longer committed to the action.

Strikes worked real hardships. Wives pawned whatever they could spare, while husbands waited in line for meagre strike benefits. A man whose father struck with the General and Municipal Workers in 1912 recalled the bleak state of affairs at home:

> I know the day my mother was taken ill she never had ... a crust of bread in the house. And we were waiting to see if there was any strike tickets [redeemable union vouchers]. And on the Sunday morning the secretary of the branch of the union came down and

knocked and gave father some. And I went down on the Sunday morning and got a piece of meat and some bread and stuff.[120]

Neighbourhoods as well as families experienced the tensions. Blacklegs found that the price they paid for employment was ostracism or worse: 'One man had such a hell of a time that his wife made him move out of the East End [during a strike against a furniture factory there]. When he moved his furniture, the wardrobe was so big it had to be lowered through the window and as it came down to the ground, the strikers seized it and smashed it up.'[121] Once the strike was over, and even assuming it successful, the member for a time faced the unpleasant necessity of increased assessments to rebuild his union's strike fund. Despite these often prolonged and unpleasant consequences, working men were increasingly prepared to engage in strike action after 1900. Their willingness was a testament to their growing determination to make union membership count for something important.[122]

Unions, however powerful, could not guarantee their members' jobs. Unemployment remained the working man's most constant worry.[123] Its causes varied from place to place and man to man. Economic slumps, taken for granted by most as an unavoidable evil, were the most general. Depressions brought both dismissals and short time in their train. Skilled workers suffered, once technological change introduced semi-skills and encouraged employers to save money by hiring and firing accordingly. Unskilled workers in many trades suffered the effects of seasonal demand and, more severely, of casualization. Bicycling was a seasonal sport, and the employment patterns of bicycle manufacturers reflected the fact. Paul de Rousiers reported that a Coventry company which employed as many as 700 in the summertime expected to dismiss 'the large part' over the winter. 'Just now', a company representative informed him, 'we are changing our models, and as soon as the new ones have been introduced we shall work at high pressure to profit by the movement's popularity, and then we shall wait till next summer.' De Rousiers inquired what became of the men in the interval. 'If they belong to a union, like the black-smiths, they apply for out-of-work relief, and others shift for them-selves.'[124]

Seasonal work imposed a greater burden the further down it struck on the scale from skilled to unskilled. As Gareth Stedman Jones has remarked, the unemployed piano maker could turn to cabinet making, and the marginal cabinet maker to street selling, firewood chopping and the docks. But an unemployed docker had very few options, and was that much closer to his 'last resort, charity and the poor law'.[125] Those who had no skill stood the least chance of escaping from the pools of casual labour that mired large portions of the working class in every major city. Londoners suffered more than others, but the problem was general. William Beveridge, in his 1909 study of unemployment, explained its universality and its apparent inevitability in terms of trade cycles, and of capitalism's need for an expendable reserve army of labour ready to answer an employer's call in boom times while conditioned to accept its dismissal in periods of depression.[126]

Age, as well as degree of skill, determined a man's chances of continued employment. Here, as in so many instances, technology extracted its toll. The older a man, the more difficult for him was the task of relearning a skill or adapting to a new machine. Once or twice, a working man might undertake retraining successfully. But like wire, Booth wrote, 'He does not gain in suppleness from much bending.' When he can no longer bend at all, 'his special acquired value is gone, and if he is old he may even be found to have no industrial value at all.'[127] And at that point, Alfred Williams observed, he is without ceremony 'removed from the manufacturing cycle and presented with a broom, shovel and wheelbarrow'.[128]

Perhaps the most dispiriting experience a man underwent was the search for work. Hampered by lack of an intelligence system to alert him to the existence of a distant job and, often, by the lack of a way to get to it, supposing its existence known to him, he found himself retracing his steps over and over as he canvassed the familiar territory for jobs that did not exist: 'There is a state of things where the search is without system or method, and, a few of the nearest and most available sources being exhausted, the workman finds himself utterly at a loss.'[129] As often as possible a man would make use of connections: friends or relatives at work in other factories, or his union, if he belonged to one. However he went about it, looking for work was almost always discouraging and often humiliating. Seebohm Rowntree described a 31-year-old unemployed railwayman, who had held nothing but odd jobs for four years:

> Conscious of a patched coat that cannot possibly hold together much longer, and of unspeakable shoes, he keeps well in the background. He has walked eight-and-twenty miles today in search of work, with only a crust of bread for breakfast and more bread for supper on his return; he says the walk 'nearly did for him'. His feet, hidden, or half-hidden, by the apologies for shoes, are blistered and swollen, his attitude and the very set of his shoulders, are those of a man who is giving up all hope.[130]

Extended periods of unemployment debilitated a man, leaving him less confident, and conscious of his failure to sustain the role within his family that custom had assigned him. The Victorian middle class had done its best to teach his father that the fact of his unemployment was no one's fault so much as it was his own. Not until the 1920s and 1930s, when millions were out of work at the same time, did working men and women come to a full realization that they need not burden themselves with individual guilt for a problem that was community-wide.[131] If a normally industrious early twentieth-century working man found it hard to shoulder all the blame for his unemployment, his perceptions were seldom clear enough to lead him to understand that the burden rested with the unregulated system under which he found himself forced to work. His tendency was to curse his luck, and to keep looking until he convinced himself that his luck had run out. That process might take as long as several months, by which time most men would have found themselves at least some sort of casual employment. If not, the physical and emotional pressures were almost certain to take their toll.

Figures from a study by Seebohm Rowntree show that 28 per cent of a group of unemployed workers in York had lost their jobs for reasons of 'physical or moral unfitness'. But, of the same group, 51 per cent of the men were judged by interviewers to have reached the same stage since they had been without work. 'It is obvious,' Rowntree wrote, 'even if we underestimate rather than exaggerate the value of the figures, that strong adverse influences have been at work, and almost all the men in this class are undergoing a more or less rapid process of deterioration.'[132]

Deterioration did not begin and end with the worker. His family naturally suffered along with him. Workers were without recourse in times of acute distress. Some unions had established out-of-work funds to tide members over brief periods of unemployment. The National Insurance Scheme of 1911 provided unemployment benefits in certain industries.[133] The multitude of charitable institutions which had proliferated throughout the nineteenth century continued to afford relief in amounts great and small, and in accordance with a wide range of stoutly defended eleemosynary principles. And in the end, there was that humiliating but certain alternative to starvation, the Poor Law.

Every step in the process of applying for relief carried with it some embarrassment to the applicant: the appearance before the Guardians to plead one's case; the visit by an overseer charged with determining the extent of one's 'deservedness'; the weekly journey to receive one's dole. Each experience demanded the willingness of recipients to demean themselves in their own eyes, and in those of their neighbours and of authority. A desire to remain independent of 'them', the certainty of being patronized and the fear of being tyrannized – these attitudes and concerns explain the reluctance of the unemployed to entrust their well-being to the Board. The wife of a hospitalized plumber, whose family was the subject of Collet and Robertson's investigation of family budgets, recalled that it took almost two weeks for the Board to grant her and her children support, during which time they were 'almost starving'. Their stipend of 2s 6d per week was stopped as soon as the husband returned home, and before he was able to work again: 'The misfortune of the time, the tardiness of the relief, and the surliness of the overseer, are looked back upon with some bitterness of recollection by the man, who is devoted to his wife and children.'[134] A London laundress, mother of seven and married to an invalid, requested assistance of the Canning Town Board. An inspector arrived to discover fish and meat in the house and children's clothes on the line. His recommendation that the family receive no aid was eventually overruled by the Board. 'Well, you know what they give her? Two loaves. Two loaves of bread for a week and a ticket for . . . a bit of meat and stuff. And he said, "Don't eat cakes with the . . . ticket," he said.' Another laundress with seven children, wife of a paralyzed Stoke-on-Trent miner, received a four-pound loaf and a shilling a week. Because the bread was a particular shade of brown, the woman carried it back to her house in a bag, so that neighbours would not know of her plight.[135]

The ultimate degradation was commitment to the workhouse. Men and women wore a peculiar uniform which identified their pauper state to all who saw them when they walked abroad. Few workhouses could have been held liable for disregarding the famous charge of the reformers of 1834; conditions within their walls remained, in almost all cases, 'less eligible' than those a working man might hope to encounter outside. In return for 'task work', inmates were fed and housed in a degree of comfort or discomfort commensurate with standards established by the Board. 'If you were on relief,' a Lancashire foundry worker recalled,

> the parish official, a big overfed swine, would walk in while you were having breakfast. Anything on the table that hadn't been allocated and you'd be in trouble. You weren't paid money on relief but given vouchers for certain foodstuffs. And you had to take what you were given. And if you refused to go to do the task work, no relief.[136]

In some establishments attempts were made to segregate the steady and respectable from the drunk and disreputable. In others – Rowntree cites York as one – all inmates lived together. One Londoner interviewed by Thompson and Vigne had attended a special Poor Law school during periods when his father was out of work and on relief. Students boarded there, separated from their parents, and scrubbed floors for their tuition. When reminiscing with George Haw, Will Crooks, who with George Lansbury was responsible for the humanitarian reforms instituted in Poplar at the turn of the century, recalled his own school days in a poorhouse, and his father's unsuccessful attempt to smuggle a suet pudding in to him.[137]

Such is the stuff that myths are made of, and there is little doubt that, though much of a working man's fear of relief and the workhouse stemmed from unpleasant firsthand experience, much was the result of stories told and retold. Robert Blatchford, an able mythmaker, concluded a generally favourable report on a workhouse school at Swinton with what can only be called a 'vignette', probably true but clearly designed to enforce the stereotype firmly lodged in many working-class minds. As he was about to leave, Blatchford reported, several children came up to him to touch him.

> 'That', said Mr Birkky [the Master], 'is a peculiarity of all workhouse children. They will touch you. They will handle and kiss any glittering thing you have about you. It is because you are from the outside world.'[138]

Fear of unemployment was, more than any other, the sensation that most directly linked the working man's two worlds together for him in his mind. At work, he contended with economic and industrial forces he seldom fully comprehended, but which he recognized might suddenly threaten his livelihood. At home, his understanding heightened by habits and affection, he confronted the human circumstances which gave that threat its meaning. As he lived out his life, his consciousness, a collection of individual enthusiasms and concerns, reflected as well the common apprehensions that his place in a changing and confusing social order imposed upon him.

# 6 Children

SOCIAL INVESTIGATORS entering working-class neighbourhoods for the first time wrote that they saw children wherever they looked.[1] The lower a family's income, the more children it tended to produce. And the working class was generally continuing to produce large families at a time when the middle class was limiting theirs.[2]

Statistics on family size included only living children. Had they incorporated figures on deceased infants, they would have provided further evidence of working-class fecundity. Far more working-class children died within their first year than did the children of the middle class. Infant mortality rates were highest in the most densely populated and poorest wards in any given city, and in those manufacturing towns which contained the greatest proportion of working-class families. Figures from a Parliamentary Report of 1913 show that while the infant mortality rate was 77 per 1,000 births in the upper and middle classes, it was 133 per 1,000 in the wage earning class, and 152 per 1,000 among the families of unskilled labourers. Sixteen of the twenty-five towns showing the highest rate were clustered in a belt across industrial Lancashire and Yorkshire.[3] Individual surveys confirmed the more general findings: the 1908 rate for Birmingham as a whole was 145 deaths per 1,000; that of the working-class wards of St George's and St Stephen's was 213 and 232 per 1,000 respectively. The population density per acre in those same wards – 162·1 and 137·7 – compared with an average of 44·2 for the city. The 42 families Pember Reeves investigated had produced a total of 201 children, but 18 were born dead or died within hours of birth, and 39 others – over one-fifth of those remaining – died before the age of 16 or 17. Pember Reeves saw a direct correlation between income, living conditions and infant mortality. The death rate among those who paid less than 6 shillings a week rent was 38 per cent; among those who paid 6 shillings, 36 per cent; among those who paid over 6s 6d, 24 per cent.[4]

Children who survived their infant and childhood years grew up less healthy than children of the middle class. A. L. Bowley and A. R. Burnett-Hurst, in their study of working-class households in Nottingham, Warrington, Stanley, and Reading, discovered that 27 per cent of the 3,287 children in their statistical sample lived in families whose income prevented them from leading a healthy existence.[5] The poorer the family, the greater the chance that its children might suffer from chronic bronchitis, pneumonia, or pleurisy, the commonest and most debilitating of childhood diseases. The greater, as well, the likelihood that they would not grow up as tall or as robust as children from the families of better paid working men. Rowntree found that the average height of thirteen-year-old boys from the poorest class of workers' families in York was 3½ inches less than that of boys from the highest class, and that they weighed 11 pounds less.[6] A mother of ten children reported in her letter, published in *Maternity*, that her children were all nearly two years old before they ran: 'My eldest girl was three years before she ran; I never thought she could live, but, thank God, she has lived, and is nearly twenty-two.'[7] Perhaps it was because she was the eldest that she was so slow to develop. Pember Reeves discovered that the eldest child tended to suffer since, at the time it might have been expected to venture outdoors on its own, the mother would find herself confined with the birth of another, and her toddler thenceforth lived in the kitchen, 'dragging at its mother's skirts, much on its legs, but never in the open air'.[8]

Inspections across the country by medical officers and by private charitable agencies confirmed the toll that poverty took upon the health of children. In Birmingham a spot check in October, 1911, revealed that 88,000 children were in need of immediate dental care, that 14,000 suffered from eye defects, 11,500 from ear and throat defects, and 1,400 from ringworm. A doctor studied the health of 200 Westminster children over a six-month period and found 59 per cent of the five-year olds with decayed teeth, 41 per cent with tonsilitis, 23 per cent adenoidal and 18 per cent in need of eye-glasses. Of the one-year-olds he examined, he could declare 79 per cent 'normal'; but of the five-year-olds, only 6 per cent, thereby confirming the generally accepted argument that the older a working-class child, the less healthy.[9] A survey of infant schools in Oxford in 1910 discovered 61·5 per cent of the boys and 62·5 per cent of the girls in sound nutritional shape, 54·5 per cent and 61·5 per cent, respectively, in satisfactory physical condition. In each group almost one-third of the boys and girls were placed in what the inspectors termed an 'intermediate' category, that is, 'unsatisfactory but easily capable of being made satisfactory'. If the family's income was only marginal, the chances were good that by the time those very young children reached adolescence, they would be listed among the unsatisfactory,[10] a part of that class which produced the high number of service rejects so alarming to those concerned for the state of the country's efficiency.[11]

Social critics despaired. If the poor could do little to improve their children's diet, they might at least see to it that they changed their clothes often enough to prevent the presence of body lice and other vermin. The first time children in Bradford schools were subjected to physical examination, doctors learned to their horror that over 100 had not had their clothes off for from six to eight months.[12] Alexander Paterson deplored the practice, common among the very poor, of wrapping children up in unnecessary clothing even in summer: 'The prevalence of vermin . . . is largely due to the wearing of two unwashed shirts and a perpetual jersey underneath other clothes.'[13] This apparent perversity was no mystery to men and women who had themselves grown up in the midst of poverty. The labour leader Tom Maguire accounted for it in a letter written on a cold January day in 1895, a few months before his death: 'The poor do not like cold, because they *feel* it; the sick are the same . . . Coldness is death. I have never been able to get over the misfortune of being born in December.'[14] Among the very poor, common sense taught that the comfort of enough warm clothes – and the physical security derived from their presence on one's back – was well worth the risk of vermin, a risk the children of the slums would run in any case, too many clothes or too few.

Not all working-class children were sewn into their clothes, only the most underprivileged. The evidence of Thompson and Vigne is of once-a-week baths, of washdays and fresh linen. But if working-class children as a whole did not suffer to the extent of the worst off, they suffered enough to distinguish themselves in reports and charts from their healthier and better nourished middle-class counterparts.

Working-class parents brought up their children according to a set of psychological presuppositions that imparted a particular pattern to the relationship between generations. Parents were forced to acknowledge to themselves that however much their own age and experience might enable them to dominate their offspring when very young, financial reality declared their eventual reliance on the earnings of their sons and daughters, both in the short run, when the elder children went to work as adolescents to help support the younger, and in the more distant future when, prematurely aged or infirm, the older generation might find itself almost completely dependent for its livelihood upon its progeny. Working-class children received their share of parental love and parental discipline, but within the seldom articulated, generally unconscious framework of this generational economic calculus.[15]

That calculus may have encouraged contemporary observers to believe that working-class parents were unprepared to deal with their children in a self-conscious way *as* children. 'The difference between a child and an adult', Alexander Paterson observed, 'is everywhere regarded as one of degree rather than of kind.' The Frenchman Paul de Rousiers concurred: 'Children are treated as men. Their little ambitions are not laughed at, nor is their spring of action broken by the words "You are only children". On the contrary, they are always treated as grown-up persons.'[16] De Rousiers exaggerated to make his point; certainly in matters sexual, working-class parents believed that children were best off knowing and hearing less. And it may well be that the assumption of a child's incipient adulthood was more pronounced the further down the economic scale a family lodged.

Though parents may have thought of their children subconsciously as adults in miniature, most did not live together with them on those terms; nor does it seem likely that the children expected or desired such a relationship. Roberts speaks of a 'gulf that stood between parents and children'[17] which appears to qualify Paterson and de Rousiers. The Thompson and Vigne interviews sustain this impression of distance:

> Mother usually got into our minds by questions. If she wanted to know what we were thinking we'd get questions. I can't think that we were encouraged to converse. We were taught to listen rather than talk. We would never volunteer to join in a conversation.

> There was a certain reserve between parents and children that was well kept and it was almost like respect, you know, you'd show them.[18]

Children of working-class parents, Elizabeth Bott has argued in her recent study, lead lives that are segregated by generation. The division increases as the children reach adolescence, and is far more pronounced among boys than girls: 'From the age of three onwards . . . boys spend a great deal of time with groups of boys in the local neighbourhood, and these relationships may continue over a considerable number of years, even into adulthood.'[19] Against this thesis of accepted and institutionalized segregation one must balance the undoubted fact that, within a few years of adolescence, mothers and daughters, far from encouraging distance between each other, wherever possible practised the close sort of communion that so characterized the quintessential working-class family network. Nor can one conclude that generational separation, if it did exist as a particular working-class phenomenon, did so at the expense of familial affection. Reginald Bray, in his 1904 account of the working-class boy and his family, argued that until a boy reached the age of about ten, his mother not only felt but expressed what often amounted to a 'ferocious affection' for him. In the case of the poorer mother, Bray suggested that the attachment in all probability 'had its origin in the sentiment of property or owner-ship. The boy is her own, to be dealt with as she pleases' – and to be dealt with in that particular way since she herself recognized that in a few years it was he who would call the tune of their relationship. Among mothers of a higher stratum, affection originated, Bray wrote, 'not so much in the pride of possession as in that feeling which gathers round any object for which one has laboured long and suffered much'. As her child grew, she resented his increasing independence and feared his unwillingness to conform to the respectable mould into which she had tried so hard to shape him.[20]

When Thompson and Vigne asked about the extent and the manner of parental affection, they received as broad a range of answers as one might expect. Some recalled specific evidence: 'When you come in from school she had her arms ready for you and she used to say, "Well, what have you done at school?".' Others found the question more difficult because their impressions remained far less certain: 'She ... didn't like ... what you'd call affection – we never used to kiss much, you see, anything like that – only when we'd say goodbye or anything, or going away – wasn't very affectionate that way.' Still others pointed out that it takes time to demonstrate affection, if not to feel it. Most working-class parents had as little time to enjoy that pleasant luxury as they had money to indulge themselves in others equally desirable:

I think that our parents always had too much to do to play games. That was the difficulty. I found that with my mother that she didn't give me the time that I should have liked. [The speaker was one of six children.] She fed us, she clothed us, but I think they were so busy with that side of life – she saw that we had good reading matter and were encouraged to sew and knit.

I don't mean that we didn't get love. But there wasn't time for, you know, we were never fussed because nobody had the opportunity or the time.[21]

Generational segregation is probably best explained by that last, simple declaration.

Segregation was implied in the strict disciplinary standards imposed upon working-class children in all but the most disreputable house-holds. Among the poorest families, parents veered irrationally between over-indulgence and thoughtless mistreatment of their children.[22] Elsewhere, boys and girls were expected to adapt and conform to the respectable standards their parents preached and, in the main, practised. No one could hope that fame or fortune would make the man. If anything succeeded in doing so, it would be manners. Punishment could be severe and was generally corporal:

> [Mother had] a little stick . . . what they called cat-o-nine-tails on the table, and if we was all sitting down to our meal and we mustn't speak, you had to get on with your meals – and no putting off your plate on the other one's plate what you didn't like . . . you had to eat it.

A Durham railway guard kept a strap which he took to his son only once, upon the occasion of his lingering in the street with pals after the call to Sunday dinner: 'I just got one round the back of me neck. And that was enough. That – that did me. In – in the face of me pals and I didn't like it. And it never occurred again.' As punishment for the theft of three pieces of chalk a girl suffered a subtler and apparently equally effective form of degradation. The three purloined chalks were placed on the mantelpiece 'until they were nearly black. And me Dad said, if you touch those chalks – he says, you'll know about it. I daren't have touched those chalks for all the tea in China.'[23]

Though discipline was designed to teach children right from wrong, or to implant the seeds of respectability, it served the more immediately practical end of maintaining some sort of order in households that, without it, would have been chaos. ('We daren't say anything wrong to them . . . They were strict in that way, brought us up – properly, but . . . when you're living in one room . . .'[24]) One almost universally observed rule was an early bedtime for children: 'At home and in bed – generally 8 o'clock. But – never outside the house – never out-of-doors after half past eight or nine. If we were out after nine o'clock, my goodness we got into trouble.'[25] Only after the children were in bed could husband and wife hope to enjoy an adult solitude. Rules that kept them respectable in their neighbours' sight helped them maintain an emotional equilibrium as they faced themselves and each other.

Household discipline demanded that the children should perform a prescribed set of daily and weekly chores: cleaning the stains off cutlery, scraping the mud from boots, carrying water or coals, running to the neighbourhood shop for provisions. The tasks were a part of a boy's or girl's regular life until the time he or she left school. Then, semi-independent and able to strike their own bargain with their parents, they passed the jobs to younger brothers and sisters, their contribution to the family's well-being now appearing in the tangible and necessary form of shillings. Some chores were the task of all the children in turn; floor scrubbing, for example: 'It was a flagged floor and we used to have to scrub it in our turns. And there were a great big stone sink, and we had to wash up in there and then scrub the sink all down.'[26] An eldest daughter would often have the additional assignment of acting as nursemaid to her youngest brother or sister, or of undertaking a week's shopping if her mother were ill or confined with the birth of yet another child.

Life was by no means all discipline and drudgery. Children depended on themselves and each other for amusement; parents were not expected to join them in games and did so only rarely. Given the general state of overcrowding, children were shooed outside to play all but quiet games such as Ludo or Snakes and Ladders: 'We didn't look upon the home as a place to play in at all except when father could spare a few minutes to play a game of draughts or teach us something like that.'[27] Boys spent hours refining their collections of cigarette cards: 'God, we had thousands and thousands of them . . . We had sets, as we called them . . . We used to go on all over swapping . . . And I had train cards, birds, cricketers, football.'[28] If their fathers raised rabbits or pigeons, they might well lend a hand with the care and feeding. And those who had the money to spend indulged themselves in *Magnet*, *Gem* and similar comics, often forbidden in more straitlaced homes, despite the undoubted propriety of the famous Greyfriars Series.[29] Piano lessons, that talisman of the respectable, imposed upon children whose parents could manage to afford both the instruction and the instrument, were seldom considered anything but a chore by the boys and girls forced to endure them.

In all but the ultra-respectable working-class neighbourhoods, recreation took place in the streets or vacant lots, and required no more equipment than children could devise for themselves – often no more than an ear for rhymes and rhythms inherited from immediately preceding generations of boys and girls. 'Cherry Holes' was a card cut with holes, and cherry pips to toss through them. In 'Dead Man, Arise' some children buried themselves beneath piles of old clothes while others hid elsewhere. 'It' called out, 'Dead man, arise!', followed by a player's name. If under the clothes, he was forced to come forth and become the next 'It'. 'Tippy Cat', a form of street cricket, was played between two sharpened stakes driven into the ground.[30]

Most games reflected their local urban origin. Barrel organs and one-man bands, common enough in working-class neighbourhoods, led children to improvise their own street dances.

We'd do the cake walk . . . cocking your legs and swinging your legs and doing this business you know and all. It was good and we used to get crowds around us watching us, but of course it wasn't for long – about a quarter of an hour, 'cos he used to get a collection and then go off to somewhere else.[31]

In rougher areas, children played at 'being drunk'. 'A life school exists in every street,' Walter Besant reported disapprovingly of East London, 'and the fidelity with which every stage of drunkenness is represented by these young actors would be remarkable even on the boards of Drury Lane.'[32] Two folklorists who studied children's street games in and around North Shields discovered the rhyme 'One o'clock' was based on the local custom of firing a cannon at that hour daily as a signal for men to return to work. The verse said something of the way in which standards of respectable conduct were ingrained into a little girl's subconscious:

> One o'clock – the gun's gone off,
> I dare not stay no longer;
> For if I do,
> Mama will say
> I've been playing with the boys out yonder.[33]

Another rhyme from the same collection reflects the extent to which working-class children shared their parent's mistrust of police authority:

> O lady, O lady, keep off the tram lines,
> Or the Bobby will come and take you away;
> He'll give you a payment or a week and a day,
> O lady, O lady, keep off the tram lines.[34]

Street games often brought a run-in with the local policeman – a cuffing at the least or, if the children were older and more abusive, a court summons and a fine for 'obstruction':

> If we'd been playing football or something like that in the street and there used to be a policeman, we used to call him Flash Harry . . . And he used to throw that cape as you ran away and he'd fetch you down with it – he'd turn it right between your legs . . . He never – just used to cuff you round the ears.[35]

Mothers concerned for their families' respectability cited such encounters as justification for keeping their children indoors and off the streets. A boy bent upon mischief, however, would have a go at it despite restrictions. Walter Greenwood, in his autobiography, recalls the delightfully malicious game of 'arson':

> Occasionally unsuspecting visitors to the privy could be surprised by boys and youths in search of revenge. Waiting at the known habitual time that the victim was in the habit of answering Nature's

daily call the revengeful stood at the flap-door in the back entry listening in silence. They were armed with a slat from an orange box at whose end stood a candle stump fixed in its own grease. They waited until the victim made himself or herself comfortable and was lost in the study of the evening newspaper, then, quietly, raised the flap-door, took a sighting, applied the burning candle to the naked target, and on the ensuing howl of agony, disappeared.[36]

Mothers anxious for the reform of their unruly children might enlist them in a Sunday School or the often affiliated, teetotal-propagandizing Band of Hope. Just as often, parents used the institution simply as a device to get the children out of the house on the weekends. Certainly in a great many households where the adults never attended church, the children were in the habit of going to Sunday School, sometimes in both morning and afternoon. The children of a Nottingham stall-keeper kept the following Sunday observances:

Sunday School, 9–10 a.m.
Church, 10.30 a.m.
Dinner, 12.30 a.m.
Sunday School, 2–3 p.m.
Tea
Church (children's service) 6 p.m.
Church, yet again, 6.30 p.m.

'Father wasn't at all a religious man, but my word he brought you up to it.'[37] In some families, particularly in the Nonconformist north, Sunday was kept as the Sabbath: no game playing, a cold tea. 'Sunday was Sunday,' a Keighley Baptist recalled.[38] Yet most children did not feel themselves unduly repressed, and enjoyed Sunday Schools, at least for a time, as a pleasant break in the week's routine. Church or chapel meant not just services but magic lantern shows, concerts, rabbit pie, and cheese and onion suppers – all entertainment out of the ordinary. 'We went', recalled a man raised in one of the roughest of London's working-class neighbourhoods, 'to see the magic lantern . . . used to get a bit of fun out of it. 'Course there's always a clique of us, about half a dozen of us; we was more of a nuisance than anything else.'[39]

Band of Hope meetings offered, in addition to the standard fare, lectures on the evils of drink: 'Oh, we had demonstrations with alcohol, to show how it burnt! Oh yes, scientific demonstrations to show how dangerous alcohol was.' Roberts recalls the desperate attempts of tee-total young men to prove that one could enjoy oneself and still remain sober, 'capering on the stage in song and uproarious sketch . . . soon under the influence our own pleasure frothed over and ran reckless among the benches . . . Chaos crept near. But a stern call to the closing hymn, in which each and all remembered pledges made, returned the meeting to its high purpose.'[40] Both Sunday School and Band of Hope afforded loyal members the chance of at least one yearly outing, a chance that city-bred children anticipated with pleasure and enjoyed thoroughly. 'Whit Walks', for example, in Nottinghamshire, led children from chapel to chapel, the Church of England refusing to participate on the grounds that it was denied its rightful place at the head of the procession. The children returned home from high tea on market carts cleaned especially for the occasion.[41]

Whether institutionally sponsored or undertaken as a private pastime, walks were a favourite recreation of working-class children, as they were of their parents: 'We prided ourselves on the distance we could walk . . . and then there was the walk home, and if we'd twopence in our pockets – we might have had a penny or twopence which we'd saved up for the occasion . . . and the last penny would be spent on a ha'penny worth of chips and a bottle of pop on the way home.'[42] Walks provided parents and children with one of their few chances to enjoy life together. Bray recorded one boy's account of an outing with his father and brothers and sisters:

At half-past six [on Sunday morning] we had finished our breakfast and equipped ourselves . . . I carried the provisions in a bag. And we started for Chislehurst at seven o'clock. We reached the Tiger's Head tavern, where my father bought some gingerbeer for us and had a glass of ale for himself. The time was about ten o'clock when we arrived at Chislehurst when we sat down under the shade of an oak tree, from which, after much climbing, I secured an oak-apple. For the next hour we wandered about picking blackberries which grew plentifully on the bushes. At the end of that time we sat down to some dinner, which consisted of a drop of herb-ale and bread and butter with a few blackberries. When we had finished eating, we went towards Sevenoaks, where we obtained some large cones and a few ferns. At about six we started home with about seven pounds of blackberries in our possession. It was about nine o'clock when we reached home, where we had supper and retired to bed.[43]

Walks were a means used by boys to cement relationships with their peers, to establish themselves as part of a group outside home and school. They afforded pre-adolescents the opportunity to taste the independence of the adulthood that would soon be theirs. Even if the journey took its travellers no further than a range of slag heaps, as a

Newcastle man recalled, it carried them to a kind of freedom their confined life made them appreciate all the more sharply: 'One fellow supplied from home purloined potatoes, another the salt, another butter or dripping, and the result was excellent, though we did not bother to wash the tubers, or consider the morality of the meal . . .'[44]

Middle-class social reformers, who spent much of their time considering the moral state of working-class boys, believed them much better off away from their own urban bonfires, enjoying themselves instead in clubs designed to provide them with more worthwhile recreational opportunities. The club movement for boys and girls paralleled in many respects the club movement for working men. Middle-class patronage, together with a programme of worthy and uplifting instruction and recreation, was expected to improve the children's lot as it was their fathers'. The fathers, who managed eventually to secure the management of their own clubs for themselves, and to reshape them to their own tastes, never ventured to intrude on middle-class attempts to mould their offspring's character. Mothers and fathers appear to have taken a less than pronounced attitude to their children's joining or not joining, recognizing that whatever else membership might entail, it would not alter their children's character or outlook to any marked degree.

The clubs were of various sorts, some little more than junior branches of larger and more general philanthropic enterprises: Ragged Schools, for example. Others, such as the one organized by a Miss Vernon in Ancoats Hall, Manchester, catered for both boys and girls, and centred their activities around programmes of music, magic lantern shows, and theatricals.[45] By far the most effective and pervasive organizations, however, were the Lads' Clubs, established in various cities at the end of the nineteenth century, boasting large memberships, substantial budgets, and elaborate, varied activities. C. E. B. Russell and Lilian Rigby, in their 1908 survey of club activity, report active enrollments of over 2,000 in the Salford club during the years 1903 to 1908, and the participation of nearly 200 annually at Hull.[46]

The directors responsible for maintaining those figures at their respectable levels struggled constantly to design regulations and programmes of a sort that would serve both an educational and moral purpose, while continuing to attract high-spirited and often untamed boys to their doors. They aimed particularly to capture the interest of youths at the time they were leaving school and beginning work, experiencing their first heady dose of adult freedom. They might stock their libraries with *Tom Brown*, Mark Twain, Henty, and Manville Fenn, but they recognized that most boys, if they came, would come to play games, and, in most cases, to play football. Russell regretted the clubs' lack of success at teaching cricket: 'Few boys have ever been *taught* cricket, and few even watch the arts of the game as played by an expert, whereas most lads are keenly observant of the tricks employed by a first-class football player.' 'Outdoor games', Russell observed, to most Manchester boys 'have only one meaning, and that is football, as played under the Associaion Code.' Nor were many working-class boys willing initiates into the mysteries of middle-class sportsmanship and team spirit. Again, the distressed Russell: 'Where leagues are formed for youths of a particular age it is a common practice for those of a higher age to lie and cheat in order to join, and so endeavour to make certain of winning whatever trophies may be offered. The play is frequently unfair, and too often foul and violent tactics take the place of strenuous play.'[47]

One is reminded of similar findings reported in Brian Jackson and Dennis Marsden's recent study, *Education and the Working Class*. Huddersfield working-class boys attending grammar school pressed for the organization of teams in their sport, rugby *league* football. The school countered with reasons why rugby *union* teams might be difficult to field – the expense of equipment, for example. 'The whole point', Jackson and Marsden comment, 'of the rugby playing was lost in this, for the school failed to see that whereas rugby league was very close at heart to northern working-class life, and whereas soccer could occupy a kind of neutral and classless position, rugby union was almost as remote as lacrosse, and not what was wanted at all.' Much the same sort of misconceptions arose over the matter of sportsmanship and team spirit, though in this latter-day instance, the compulsion to win was the school's, while the working-class boys – recognizing the chance to act as subtle saboteurs – played with a casualness 'that was not quite the same thing as "sportsmanship". It carried with it a freshness, almost an ironical touch, a readiness to take rests, to applaud the opposing team, to enjoy the game but to be not much troubled whether the school had won or lost.'[48]

Despite the tentativeness of an enterprise contending with the subtleties of class consciousness, the clubs did succeed in providing thousands of youngsters with a chance to read, to play games and, in summer, to spend time outside the city, chances they would otherwise never have enjoyed. The Ancoats Lads' Club owned a cottage for weekend excursions, used by 900 boys in the summer of 1907. In Whitsun Week, 1908, eleven Manchester Clubs sent 2,500 boys to camps in Wales.[49] Reginald Bray criticized such activities, and clubs in general, as destructive of a boy's home life. And Booth warned that in their effort to maintain a 'high character', clubs too often found themselves catering to a clientele 'somewhat above the class for which they were originally intended', a fate, he adds, very common to all attempts at social improvement.[50] Against such caveats, one can place the testimony of an Oldham boy whose week away from home was clearly a treat and an adventure, and recognize the way in which a club could often satisfy working-class children on their own terms:

> ... Tuesday myself and a friend resolved to spend in Llandudno, so we started about 9.30, crossed the river Conway by the ferry, and walked through some splendid country to our destination. Here we spent the morning, donkey riding, bike riding, and sauntering about the Pier and Parade. After dinner we had a walk up Orme's Head, passing through the Happy Valley on the way. Finding a nice piece of turf, we had a lie down and a look round ...
>
> On Saturday I had a climb up Penmaen Mountain, and saw a very pathetic scene – a sheep lying on the ground dead, and a lamb just by bleating sorrowfully – the sheep had not been dead long for it was quite warm.
>
> We went for a row in the afternoon, and a fellow-shipmate was quite sick when we landed. Sunday morning was spent in packing up and thinking about work, and where all the money had gone to.
>
> This is my first experience of Camp, and I hope it is not my last. We had the luck to have a fine week, and a fine set of officers, to whom every praise is due.[51]

Whitsun Week was but one of the holidays that marked off a child's year. Like his parents, he enjoyed the security that routine and ritual provided, the succession of recurring special occasions that imparted to his life both excitement and steadiness. Hoggart evokes them as he describes the rhythm of neighbourhood life: 'Pancake Tuesday, Voting Day, which is always a holiday, Hotcross Buns on Good Friday, the Autumn "Feast", Mischief Night, and all the week of cadging and collecting for Bonfire Night.'[52] May Day found streets decorated with a pole – a broom handle decked with streamers of coloured paper or ribbon. 'A ring of girls,' Walter Greenwood recalled, 'each holding a ribbon, in attendance on a diminutive May Queen veiled with a piece of old lace curtain and carrying a basket of posies and a collecting tin for the hoped-for halfpenny contributions.'[53] Christmas was the occasion of the year, far more elaborately celebrated than birthdays, which came at irregular times during the week and were therefore more difficult to fit into the household's normal routine. No matter how poor the family, parents made an effort to procure toys for their children and to deck the house out to mark the holiday:

> Father used to do himself well that time; he'd spend money on us, then, to get a present each, and other things . . . all the children have the goodies, he used to buy that . . . He did us very well for Christmas, although, as I say, things were very poor some years. But other years they'd be better, and then we got more.[54]

The other grand occasion, for those fortunate enough to afford it, was the annual week's summer holiday. Rowntree found that among York families with an income of over 30 shillings a week, a holiday of a few days – to Scarborough, as a rule – was the growing practice.[55] Southport and Blackpool, Colin and Rose Bell point out, 'were the new towns of the industrial revolution just as much as the great manufacturing cities or the mill villages'.[56] In its issue for 2 June 1911, the *Cotton Factory Times* carried advertisements for 113 Blackpool boarding houses, and for others at Morecambe, Southport and elsewhere: 'Mrs Peel, "Brooklyn", 100 High Street. Two minutes from Talbot Road Station, Sea, New Parade. Terms 1s each person. Board from 4s 6d. Piano.'[57] Those unable to afford boarding-house rates might get out of the city for a visit with relatives in the country. A Bradford girl recalled sojourns with her aunt in Ripon: 'We went nutting and blackberrying, which girls didn't usually do. We paddled in the river, and went with fishing nets, you know, catching minnows in the river near. Oh we loved Ripon. We still do.'[58] The recollection reminds us that city-bound though the working class was by 1900, some could still reach back into the countryside to sustain themselves in a network older than the one they had woven inside the industrial towns. Few could boast, with a Darlington woman, that 'we had relations all over England' ready to take them in.[59] But those children with even one rural aunt or grandmother close enough for visiting led a richer life and had a fuller sense of what family could mean through her existence.

The rhythm of children's daily life was measured against the routine of school. Boys and girls in all but the very poorest and most ill-regulated families went to school regularly for a period of seven to nine years. A sizeable minority of their parents remained functional illiterates: Pember Reeves found eight of the 42 women in her survey could neither read nor write. Lady Bell discovered an illiteracy rate of 12 per cent among the Middlesbrough working class; Roberts's mother estimated that, among women in her neighbourhood, as many as one in six were deficient.[60] Yet their children were growing up in the period which was to see England change from a predominately illiterate to a predominately literate nation.[61]

Not only were more children being educated than ever before, they were being educated in a more humane fashion. A school might amount to very little and still represent a marked improvement over the 'permanent mass meetings' – Harry Gosling's description – that constituted the majority of schools for the working class in the years immediately following the passage of the Education Act of 1870.[62] By 1900, standards set by school boards were improving the conditions even in Voluntary (that is, privately supported) elementary schools such as the one which Gosling recalled. In almost all areas, however, Voluntary schools were inferior in apparatus, teaching and curriculum to the rate-supported Board schools.[63] Reginald Bray, writing in C. F. G. Masterman's *The Heart of the Empire* in 1902, deplored the number of Voluntary schools in which 'the classroom system is still practically non-existent, one or two apartments have to do duty for all the pupils, and three or four teachers may be seen wrestling with their children in the same hall. An air of gloom and rusty antiquity seems to pervade the whole place.'[64]

Though Board schools generally maintained a standard well above that of the Voluntaries, conditions in those built or converted for the use of working-class children were nothing like ideal. Classes in elementary schools often numbered as many as sixty children; learning frequently took place in unpleasant physical surroundings. A 1905 survey sponsored by the Brassworkers' Union contrasted schools for working-class children in supposedly up-to-date Birmingham with those in Berlin, and discovered no grounds for complacency. Classrooms in Berlin were washed down daily; in Birmingham, only seven times a year. Toilets in Berlin schools could be flushed after each use; in Birmingham they were flushed but once a day and 'smelled offensively; a pool of strong-smelling urine lay in the entrance to the urinal, made by the lads who preferred not to go further inside ... In comparison with the Berlin school, everything was very dirty and untidy.'[65] A Manchester health officer blamed crowded, unhealthy and unventilated school rooms for the fact that children grew less while in school than while at home on holiday.[66]

When Boards built new schools, they frequently made an effort to provide the best within their means.[67] School boards were attempting, as well, to vary and broaden the curriculum in elementary schools. In line with the country's general policy of education by class, they were reluctant to encourage students to learn more than what was assumed proper to their station in life. Working-class children moving beyond the three R's found themselves venturing in the direction of courses in handicrafts, cooking, laundering, and housewifery.[68] But Board schools did offer, as well, elementary courses in geography, science, and history. And in the better schools, imaginative instruction had begun to replace the cramming and rote-learning that were standard before the revised educational code of 1890 in great part abolished the system of payment by result. Still, the truly gifted teachers continued to lament that the code could not be stretched, that the child was to be fitted to the code, and not the code to the child.[69]

Teachers demanded of working-class children the same standard of deportment that most of their parents insisted upon at home. Booth remarks upon the perfect discipline of the classroom: 'From end to end, through the whole school, in every department it is the same. The turbulence of the streets is subdued into industrious calm.'[70] The Thompson and Vigne interviews confirm the impression. An East Ender recalled shying inkwells at the teacher; most talked of the order in classrooms ruled by teachers as anxious as parents to instil habits of respectability into their charges. In a Bolton classroom of 100 boys and girls 'you could hear a pin drop'. Some teachers rewarded exemplary behaviour with membership in 'Guilds of Courtesy'. All of them punished a lapse from the expected standard with the cane. Canings – usually on the hand – were part of the educational routine: 'They used to take us down into . . . the lavatory, where the wash basins and that was, and we used to get the cane then.' In this case, the headmistress, and not the teachers, administered the punishment.[71]

Regular attendance at school depended, more than anything else, upon the parents' determination to see their children educated. Attendance figures had risen dramatically since the 1870s when, in London, no more than 75 to 80 per cent of the enrolled students came to class on any one day. By 1904, London's record had improved to 87·2 per cent, well above the national average (excluding London) of 83 per cent.[72] One explanation for London's success was its devoted army of school board visitors, used both to enroll pupils initially and to pursue persistent truancy cases. Averages masked the fact that attendance remained far lower in schools patronized by the working class. Booth divided London's Board schools into three categories – lower, middle, and upper – and discovered that in six of the lower group, the schools attended by the very poorest, only 52·5 per cent of the children came regularly to class.[73] One ingenious London truant was in the habit of pressing a button to the skin of his throat as he entered the classroom, and then showing the mark to his teacher who would send him straight home, diagnosed as a case of ringworm: 'I was away from school three or four months at a time.'[74] A Salford Board school headmaster's records suggest the extent to which non-attendance was not confined to London working-class districts alone:

> 19 February, 1894. All teachers present and admitted three boys, but attendance is very poor. Many boys are said to be selling cards at the race course.

> 11 June, 1894. Only 251 present this morning. [The total enrolment is not given, but the headmaster notes that an attendance of 300 would please him.] The excuses are various, e.g., minding the baby, going on errands, and visiting the pawn shops appear to be responsible for many absences.

> 14 October, 1895. 70 absent with apparently no other reason than the indifference of their parents.[75]

Parental indifference was assumed to increase along with a family's poverty. Mothers of large families might send their younger children off to get them out of the way, and keep an older child at home to run errands or mind the baby, as the Salford headmaster observed. But more than mere convenience was involved. Although working-class parents no longer had elementary school fees to pay, as many did during the years immediately following passage of the 1870 Act, education represented one further burden on an already overburdened family exchequer. School children, if they were not to disgrace the family, needed decent-looking clothing and boots, as well as the frequent penny or two for notebooks, pens, or other student equipment required by the teachers.

In addition, children old enough to work, yet still at school, represented a financial sacrifice many parents told themselves they could not afford. Surveys provided convincing evidence of the extent to which families depended on children to supplement weekly income. 'The importance attaching to the earnings of the children in the families of the poor', Rowntree reported, 'reminds us how great must be the temptation to take children away from school at the earliest possible moment, in order that they may begin to earn.'[76] A child of twelve who had passed the Education Code's Fifth Standard, or had attended school for at least 300 sessions over the past five years, was eligible to begin work as a half-timer, working alternate days or half days at mill and school.

The number of half-timers had by the turn of the century begun to decline significantly – 84,298 in 1908 as compared with 175,437 in 1890;[77] almost all worked in the textile mills of Lancashire and Yorkshire. Trade union leaders joined social workers in urging the abolition of the practice. Yet, as J. W. Ogden of the Weavers' Union remarked, following a TUC vote in favour of such a motion in 1911, rank-and-file workers in the textile industries remained unwilling to support the reform. Ogden complained that he was forced to vote, as his union's representative, against a change which he himself favoured: 'But the last ballot of our members on the question went very strongly against us.' Ogden described the campaign his union had waged, and pledged to continue the effort.[78] He was contending, however, against notions such as those expressed two years previously in a letter to the *Woman Worker* from a thirty-six-year veteran of Yorkshire mill work, asserting that the movement to abolish half time was nothing more than an attempt on the part of do-gooders to spoil the children of the working class with too much education: 'They are pampered and catered for in all sorts of ways until they get the idea into their heads that they are superior to a bit of fair, honest work. Their time is spent in games, and in little tinkering experiments in chemistry.' Teachers, the writer continued, when they questioned children about their absences, too often tried to persuade them that it was 'the smell of the mill' that had made them sick. 'Is not this calculated to rear a generation of those of whom we have too large a stock already – idlers?'[79]

Parents without prejudices as extreme as these, and who accepted readily enough the arguments on behalf of a sound elementary education for their children, found it difficult to sympathize with the campaign being waged to extend the school-leaving age and to open up the experience of secondary education to children of the working class. The years before the First World War witnessed a struggle – generally futile – on the part of some trade union and Labour Party leaders to achieve something like a democratic educational system for England. The much vaunted 'scholarship ladder', enshrined in the Education Act of 1902, was to become instead a 'broad highway', carrying working-class children by means of maintenance scholarships as far as their abilities would allow them to travel.[80] A variety of related factors did the reformers in: principally, the middle-class assumptions of conservatives like Robert Morant and of socialists like the Webbs, whose concern was not democracy but state efficiency.[81] The movement could claim little rank-and-file support, however, among members of the working class. Economic necessity had bred a tradition decreeing that a child was 'educated' by the time he was twelve or thirteen. Further years in school wasted the youngster's time while depriving his family of much needed income.

Habit and assumption reflected themselves in statistics. Board of Education figures for the year 1906–7 showed 99 per cent of the children in England and Wales in school at the age of 11; 98 per cent at the age of 12; 77 per cent at 13; 35 per cent at 14; 23 per cent at 15; and 18 per cent at 16.[82] In working-class districts children bunched in the lower standards. An inspector for London schools in 1904 reported that 74 per cent, 72 per cent, and 69 per cent of the pupils at the Notting Hill, Lambeth, and Finsbury schools attended the lower three standards. These figures compared with 45 and 51 per cent in two schools in Wandsworth Common.[83] To cite figures such as these is not to say that, from the turn of the century on, the number of working-class children who remained in school beyond the age of 13 did not increase. But those who did stay on were a tiny minority and came either from families of the 'aristocracy' or from those in which other, older children were already at work; where comfortable economic circumstances could afford the luxury of a continuing education for the youngest.

For many parents a concern to ease budgetary strains was coupled with a view that further education might make life, in psychological terms, harder rather than easier both for themselves and for their children. A generation of parents, many of them only one remove from illiteracy, would never have an easy time coming to terms with the phenomenon of mass education. Working men and women were accustomed to hear that an education could mean advancement. A Bradford woolsorter recalled a stock phrase of his youth: 'Any child who gets something under his cap has no need to take his coat off.' The saying was to his father's generation as much a threat as a promise. When a day-school teacher suggested that the lad be encouraged to continue in school, his father retorted, 'I took my coat off at thirteen and he will do the same.' 'So I knew where I stood,' his son adds. 'First the mill, then woolsorting if I could get it.'[84] A bright child might be a source of pride to the ambitious parent. But to most his incipient erudition would appear, as Reginald Bray remarked, 'mysterious and a trifle uncanny. [Parents] feel their own inferiority and prefer to turn to subjects where their own preeminence is unquestioned.'[85]

Parents, when they considered their children's education, were contending with an institution designed for them by the middle class, and, to that extent, with something alien. Working-class fathers and mothers were not particularly welcome at school: 'There was no such thing as what they call now an open day ... when parents can go to the school and the teacher would tell them how they were getting on ... but there was nothing of that kind.'[86] When a mother went to see the teacher about her child it was usually because he was reported to be in trouble, or had been dealt with by the teacher in a way that his mother considered unwarranted or demeaning. A young girl was called to account for a dirty wrist which was disfigured by a birthmark. The child came home, boiled water, and scrubbed at the offending spot in hope of giving satisfaction. Her mother worked herself into an understandably righteous fury: 'I'll pull her blooming hair off.' And her daughter was certain she would at least have hit the teacher had not she herself intervened to prevent the confrontation.[87]

Children were no more anxious than their parents to subject themselves to predictable and apparently unnecessary stress. Family and friends expected them to work as soon as the law allowed, and they themselves looked forward eagerly to doing so: 'Work was a wonderful thing. It was a wonderful thing to be a workman and earning a wage, and that's all you thought of. It was as if your brain was closed in. So I was right glad when I left school. I thought that was the finish of that, and I was right glad to get a job. Like I said your mind gets closed in, but you're satisfied and you're happy.'[88]

Work began for many children before they left school. A 1908 investigation found that approximately 9 per cent of all school children, or about 200,000, worked outside school hours.[89] The figure did not include half-timers; nor did it take into account the many children of the very poorest who, as the Thompson and Vigne interviews inform us, scouted up broken flower boxes to sell as scrap for 2d a bag, who fetched bread and tea for men in the lock-up, who jumped aboard cabs at railway stations to earn 3d unloading baggage, or who used their wits in any number of ways to earn themselves or their families a few pennies extra a day.[90] Nor, we can be certain, did the figure include the boys whose inventiveness sparked money-making schemes such as the one Walter Greenwood describes, in which an enterprising lad hawked annual reports of the local Cooperative Society as the 'Record and Balance Sheet' inside pubs on a Saturday night for a penny apiece, and managed to make himself 1s 3d before the evening was over.[91]

The work of most school children paid far less than that, and called for the employment of far less imagination. Milk rounds, paper rounds, window washing, errand running – these were the common lot of employed schoolboys. Girls most often earned money as baby minders or, if their mothers were engaged in home-work of some sort, in the completion of the monotonous tasks such labour normally entailed. Clementina Black's inquiry into sweated industry reported, among others, the cases of Jane B., aged 13, her brother, aged 9; and of Alice J., aged 11:

Jane B. Standard 6. Age 13. Father a potman at 25s a week. Mother machines uppers of boots; common goods, 10d a dozen; better, 1s

3d a dozen. Jane sews on buttons, cuts apart work, inks round button holes. A little brother, aged nine, does buttons (i.e., I suppose, sews them on).

Mother, who does sometimes three dozen in a day, sometimes only three pairs, begins work at 7 a.m. Jane begins at 7.45. She goes to the shop for work in the morning, and carries it in – a heavy load of three dozen pairs sometimes – when she comes home from school. She gets late for school, and is only in time in the afternoons.

At the same school, a girl of eleven, Alice J., pastes in the soles of babies' shoes and sews together the pairs . . . These are white buck shoes, and are paid at the rate of 1s 1d to 1s 3d a dozen. Two dozen can be done in a day. The father is a cabinet maker in regular work; the mother a cleaner (apparently at an office or warehouse). The sister, of 18 or 19, makes 10s a week. The little Alice works from 12 to 1, and again from 5.30 to 6.30, doing in that time a dozen or fifteen pairs; she reckons that it takes her five minutes to finish a pair, or perhaps twenty minutes for six pairs.[92]

Jane, Alice, and the rest, when they began to work full time, in all likelihood continued at their same trades, entering into the 'adulthood' of their ten- or twelve-hour day with none of the enthusiasm one senses in the remarks which hymned work as a 'wonderful thing'. Yet most children, and especially most boys, anticipated the day they would begin work as a day of emancipation – from school, from home – and took to their employment with real zest. The noise of hammering in the workshop, a journeyman cooper recalls, 'falling as it did on the ears of a young boy starting his first job, was an exciting sound, for it meant the end of childhood and the beginning of manhood, the first wage packet to be taken home heralding the new independence from parents, the chance to smoke openly and (I thought) the chance to swear like a man.' (The fastidious coopers refused to grant him the latter privilege.)[93] The hero of Walter Greenwood's *Love on the Dole*, who worked while still a schoolboy as a pawnbroker's assistant, pined for a job on the shop floor, far more respectable in his eyes than the clerk-like duties he was required to perform for his present ill-tempered master. His friends 'talked, intimately and in terms of magic; entrancing names such as "machine shop", "foundry", "riveting shop" slipped from their tongues with spellbinding ease. They were men already; their speech and swagger made him an outcast, filled him with gnawing envy.'[94] The bright, 'go-ahead' lad was not the one who stayed on in school, who pushed a menial pen. He was the lad who took as little time as he possibly could to leave childhood and became a man with a full-time job.

Just what that job would be depended, in large part, on two factors: a father's willingness and ability to interest himself directly in his son's career, and simple chance. In some families tradition demanded that a son follow in the calling of his father, his brothers, or his grandfather. A Croydon shoemaker, in a letter to Alan Fox, historian of the Boot and Shoe Operatives, illustrated the way in which his career was determined for him:

> My grandfather had something to do with selling the early sewing-machine and was – according to the standard of those days – a successful and prosperous man. His brother was an out worker ... his wife and daughter were closers; all the work was done in the kitchen, and the meals were cooked during working time. Many other members of the family were in the industry either as managers, pattern cutters ... clickers, skivers, and closers. Nearly all families were more or less connected by marriage.[95]

A network of that sort presumably left a boy little choice. The trade was in his blood, its particular skills and the lexicon of terms to describe them a part of daily life since early childhood. Harry Gosling, great-grandson of a Thames waterman, recalled imbibing the lore that pre-ordained his own life's work: 'The River Thames runs through all my boyish recollection and through the stories of my early life that have been told to me by my father and others.'[96]

Kinship played an important role in recruiting new workers into unskilled trades. In this case, casualization, not tradition, encouraged a father to speak up to the foreman on his son's behalf. Without such an introduction, the recruit was almost certainly doomed to the recurring fate of 'last hired, first fired'.[97] Employers' practice in favouring the sons or other relatives of present employees varied widely. Some made a conscious effort to fill vacancies from the families of their own men, others informed employees of vacancies in the course of advertising a job more widely. Some made no special efforts of any kind. N. B. Dearle, surveying the subject of industrial training in 1914, suggested that the custom of passing a trade from father to son was diminishing. Men increasingly aware of the disadvantages attached to their own trade might work actively to discourage their sons from following them in it. A father whose own job was threatened by mechanization, and whose son had the chance to work at something else, was not likely to impose the less promising choice upon him.[98]

Despite a pattern of inherited callings which can be traced in certain trades, evidence suggests nothing like a universal custom of advice and consultation between father and son on the eve of the latter's emergence into the world of full-time employment. Arnold Freeman, in his 1914 study of Birmingham, *Boy Life and Labour*, discovered that in only six out of 71 cases in which sons had begun careers in skilled trades had fathers talked at any length with the boys or attempted 'to open the boy's eyes to the path he was taking'.[99] Often when son followed father into a trade it was not in pursuit of familial pride of calling, but rather the line of least resistance. Freeman, deploring the number of talented boys who remained content to follow in their unskilled fathers' footsteps, remarked that

> there is almost a caste-system in the various grades of labour; and the fact that the father is unskilled seems to act like a bias carrying the son also towards unskilled labour. Heredity, the father's narrower circle of ideas and his lack of influence in the industrial world seem to predetermine the career of his children.[100]

Choosing a job afforded a boy and his father perhaps the best chance they would enjoy to come to know each other. Pride and affection encouraged some to make the most of the opportunity. Incipient jealousy – the threat any newly independent son implies to his father's authority – this plus the general indifference engendered by the 'caste system' Freeman describes, continued to breed that reserve which appeared to govern the relationship between most working-class fathers and sons, and which they accepted as normal.

When neither family tradition nor a father's concern steered a boy in the direction of a particular job, chance and local circumstance frequently decided the nature of his employment for him. If born and raised in a mill town, he would, in all likelihood, join his fellow townsmen at the mill. Freeman discovered that the majority of boys he interviewed had little notion as to what they wished to work at. 'They plunged headlong into industrial life', often taking the first job that came their way, refusing to spend more than two or three days looking for work after leaving school. Only an exceptional few had later found it possible to break a pattern of aimless shifting from one job to another, and to make a conscious decision about the direction their life should take. Even when a boy took himself in hand, his efforts to better his lot were easily thwarted by circumstances beyond his control. Freeman cited the case of an exceptional boy anxious to find work that would allow him to master some particular skill. His father had been unable to afford the cost of apprenticing him to a trade, so his Odyssey from job to job had been a discouraging and unproductive one: errand boy for a ring manufacturer at 5 shillings a week; errand boy to a firm of platers at 6 shillings; then to a manufacturer of letter presses, where he was laid off for lack of orders: 'He is a boy who has moved judiciously from one job to another, trying to better himself in all respects. He writes a clean, neat, sensible letter, is a most taking fellow, and, in physique, a young giant.' Freeman concluded that in this case natural ability might eventually win out over initial bad luck: 'With such gifts, perhaps he will force his way into skilled work.'

Other case studies in Freeman's survey argued against such optimism. A lad with a widowed mother to look after, determined to learn a skilled trade, went first to a silversmith's, where in eighteen months he was taught nothing more than simple soldering; to a cabinet maker's, where he lost his job due to slackness; to a brass foundry; to an electrician's shop; back to a brass foundry where he was at present working on an emery wheel, where he expected to remain, and where he was convinced he would fall victim to grinder's rot. 'What is certainly true', Freeman observed, 'is that there is no prospect here for him of a wage much above £1. He realizes it plainly, but says he must keep on for the present, because his wages [17s] are very high for a boy and his mother badly needs him.'[101]

Unskilled labour often brought a relatively high wage to young recruits, thereby tempting them away from an apprenticeship, with its long period of indenture at wages of almost nothing at all. Apprenticeship in the formal sense had degenerated by 1900, for reasons having more to do with the broader patterns of technological change than with the particular matter of a long, low-paying indenture. Industrial innovation, as we have seen, made the protracted teaching of a particular skill a waste of time. Once mastered, it stood a good chance of being almost immediately superseded. Nor could workers see much point any longer in attempting to use apprenticeship as a means of limiting entry into their trade, when employers could with such apparent ease call upon the growing army of the semi-skilled to pick up in no time at all whatever simple techniques a new method of production might require. The result, as the Webbs reported in 1897, was that apprenticeship regulations were enforced in unions with a combined membership of only 90,000, that regulations were on the books but virtually unenforced in unions with a further membership of 500,000, but that unions with a membership of 900,000 had no apprenticeship regulations whatsoever.[102] Dearle found that, in London, apprenticeship in the traditional sense existed only in the printing trades and among the Thames watermen.[103]

Though formal apprenticeship was by 1900 becoming an industrial anomaly, employers had by no means abandoned the system whereby they could obtain young, unskilled labourers at very low wages. What had been indenture now became 'improving', or 'following up'. Lads would contract – not with a union but with a firm – to work at a particular task for a period of from five to seven years, and for a wage that would increase annually as their training progressed. Too often, that 'training' consisted of nothing more than assisting a more highly paid worker to accomplish a task to which very little real skill attached. C. E. B. Russell described the system in Manchester engineering firms:

> Once admitted, [the boy] finds that he is set to some work which only calls for intelligence of the meanest kind, or at least for so little that all that is needed for its proper discharge is very quickly learnt. At this work he remains week after week, year after year, his mind dormant, his hands moving with the precision and dullness of an engine.

His years of 'apprenticeship' over, the worker, now a young man, discovered to his alarm that he really knew little more about his trade than he did the day he had entered the factory years before. 'He is, in fact,' Russell declared, 'in a worse position ... for his mind is heavier and he moves less readily.'[104] The team comparing the life of Birmingham and Berlin brassworkers complained of the very same system. Boys were employed, not to learn a trade, but to master a process – that is, to work continuously at one operation, edging or filing, for example. They never proceeded beyond 'boy's work', never learned a 'man's occupation', and the result was precisely that which Russell deplored in Manchester. The young semi-skilled trainees, in supply which generally exceeded demand, threatened both each other's livelihood and that of the older men with whom they had worked for the past five or six years.[105] Unmarried in most cases, and willing therefore to continue work for less than their elders, the members of this new generation of adult labourers found themselves looking back apprehensively over their own shoulders to see yet another phalanx of adolescents, cheaper still than they were and quite prepared to take their place. 'So long as boys are cheap,' Freeman wrote, 'work will be done by them rather than by machines or men.'[106]

Others joined Freeman in lamenting this system which, though economical from the point of view of the capitalist manufacturer, appeared to squander potential natural ability to an alarming degree. Reginald Bray, surveying boy labour and apprenticeship in London, found that over two-thirds of the graduates of elementary schools there moved immediately into deadening 'blind alley' jobs that doomed them almost certainly to adult life as an unskilled labourer.[107] How to make better use of that wasted talent was a question constantly debated and never satisfactorily resolved. What was needed, William Beveridge argued, was a revival, not of apprenticeship, 'but of the principle underlying apprenticeship – that no youthful worker should be regarded merely as cheap labour, that every youthful worker while being employed should also be undergoing preparation for a future career.'[108]

Too much conspired to prevent the achievement of that well-meant goal. Capitalist economics and its insistence upon simplification and standardization encouraged a sketchily trained, under-motivated work force. A national educational system designed to afford the vast majority of its beneficiaries nothing more than a rudimentary education, turned thousands of adolescents loose upon the labour market each year at a time in their lives when serious future planning was as unnatural to them as it is to all but the exceptional thirteen-year-old. Simple 'boyishness' was the problem in too many cases, Freeman concluded. Knowing he could find another job without much trouble, the young factory worker succumbed to his natural resentment of authority. Training at a skill meant learning, a task the boy assumed he had left behind him at school. Rather than apply himself, he often bridled when instruction was afforded him and moved off to an easier and better paying job. 'Even where there is method in his madness,' Freeman wrote, 'and he moves definitely in response to the money-stimulus, he is neglecting his future welfare because of his adolescent ignorance.'[109] Still a child in an adult world, he passed from job to job, every step in his almost unconscious progress further condemning him to a life's work that would bring him as little personal satisfaction as it would financial reward.

Reformers worried less about the recruitment and training of girls than of boys, assuming that the great majority of girls would cease to work after eight years or so in order to marry and raise a family. 'Apprenticeship' for them was in most cases as nominal as it was for boys, and for the same reasons: the nature of their employment, which required far less skill than it had formerly, and their own desire to make as much money as they could, and as soon as possible. 'The important point', MacDonald observed in his book on women in the printing trades, 'is not so much the nominal length of apprenticeship, but the fact that the work which an "apprentice" now does is less educative than it was, and that wage-earning considerations now enter at an earlier stage into the apprentice's thoughts'.[110] Edward Cadbury's study, *Women's Work and Wages*, produced evidence that in some trades – French polishing, for example, which demanded a thorough knowledge of graining – something like a genuine apprenticeship system still existed. Even in that case, the understanding between master and trainee was characterized as informal, and the period of apprenticeship usually lasted no longer than two years.[111]

In many instances 'apprenticing' was a euphemism for sweating. One so-called apprentice to a Bradford dressmaker earned only a shilling a week. 'I suppose it was the accepted thing at the time you know, but – it was certainly not much, it was just a matter of pocket money ... no more than that.'[112] Because so many of the girls lived at home or shared the not very heavy expenses of a furnished room or two with a co-worker, they remained willing, even at the end of an apprenticeship or training period, to accept low wages as a tolerable enough fact of their lives. Cadbury remarked on the generally 'un-complaining nature' of factory girls. Those who worked in the metal trades 'accept [their work] as a kind of fate, never think of trying to understand their legal safeguards, and when an accident happens, rarely of their own initiative claim compensation. They are afraid of any new teaching or suggestion that could by any possibility offend the master.' The docility was a further reflection of the childishness Freeman had found among adolescent boy workers. So delighted were the girls to be earning money of their own, to be out and about in the world of adults, that they had little time to worry over the complicated, long-range problems which agitated those anxious about their exploita-tion in the mass. Cadbury went on to describe their 'enviable freedom from worry or anxiety'. Other than their concern about lay-offs and short-time, he discovered them 'careless and happy as soon as released from work'.[113] MacDonald reported a similar mood among the girls in the printing trades, who admitted even to the enjoyment of their life inside the workshop, 'frankly confessing that factory life especially was a joke, particularly when they had overtime', and who 'above all enjoy the larger life that they meet in a factory just as girls in another social scale enjoy public school or college life'.[114]

Only occasionally did this general, high-spirited bonhomie translate itself into an *esprit de corps* both tight enough and militant enough to produce concerted campaigns for improved wages and working conditions. The London match girls provide the most notable case in point. Booth found that they not only worked together, but lived together or near each other in Bow, Mile End, Stepney, Limehouse and Poplar. They clubbed together to buy their clothes and their feather hats. They enjoyed each other's company and the company of almost no one else, especially those 'whom they consider too aristocratic to associate with on equal terms'. Their proximity to each other, the shared experiences of their work and of their pleasures, bound them together in a way that gave them a sense of common cause.[115] In this they were almost alone. The great majority of young factory girls, if they did not look upon work as a lark, viewed it as a daily penance to be accepted as natural, and endured uncomplainingly as payment for the pleasures it provided. To hand over even as little as a shilling or two as her own contribution to the family's weekly earnings, and to spend all that remained on whatever struck her fancy: the gratifying self-importance implicit in both those delightfully adult-seeming actions left the factory girl without much need for further ambitions or goals.

Factory labour induced in a girl sensations of responsibility and freedom. Hence its increasing appeal to a class of employees whose only realistic alternative was work as a domestic servant. Figures showed that, proportionate to the population as a whole, the number of indoor domestic servants was declining. The census of 1911 reported a total of 1,359,359, however, an increase of 1·3 per cent from 1901.[116] More girls were entering service at a later age than had formerly been the case, one observer suggesting that they did so only after they had tried and failed to hold a factory job.[117] Wages began at somewhere between 2s 6d and 3s a week, plus room and board, and rose to something like 8s after several years in service. C. V. Butler, who surveyed the pre-war domestic service industry in 1916, had argued in her study of social conditions in Oxford four years previously that, for many a young woman, such an apparently rock-bottom scale might actually provide as much or more money, and certainly greater security, than she could count on as a factory hand. Butler estimated that the domestic's savings on food, lodgings, and washing – 10 or 12 shillings a week – when added to her wage, brought her weekly compensation to about a pound, at least two or three shillings more than she would have been able to earn in the factory.[118]

Perhaps the adolescent working-class girl reasoned in like manner; perhaps her parents did for her. More probably, she went into service, if she did, because other young girls on her street – her older sisters included – had done so before her. Such a tradition was far stronger in rural villages than in urban working-class neighbourhoods; recruits came with far greater frequency from the country than from the city. Butler observed that the city child was accustomed to far too many distractions to settle comfortably into a routine which was at best both tedious and demanding. 'The country girl', she suspected, 'feels the change much less in this way, but even she must be removed from the human interests of home.'[119] Butler maintained that the livelier girls shunned domestic service for factory work, and that it was generally the 'quiet, rather dull members of very poor families' or the 'steady-going daughters' from 'really good' working-class homes who went off as servants.[120] Letters from workers solicited as part of the Cadbury study tend to confirm Butler's observations. Those who preferred domestic service did so because it afforded them a security and respectability which factory work could not guarantee:

> ... Service in a good home is better than factory in some things, they have less temptations for if their Mistress is good they have good food and money for clothes ... I think they keep themselves cleaner and nicer because the home they are in makes a difference ...

> ... To be a servant is much healthier and comfortable. Girls who are in service are generally much more quieter and more ladylike than those which work in a factory ...

> ... Being in domestic service you avoid a great many evils to which you are subject to in a factory. Of course, in a factory there are so many people of all kinds. Some will want you to go with them to places where you would rather not be seen ...

Many girls found loss of freedom too high a price to pay for the advantages that appealed to the quiet and steady-going. Nor did a preference for factory work necessarily imply a willingness to tolerate a more rough and tumble working life. One of Cadbury's most genteel respondents composed an essay for him entitled 'Why I Prefer to Work in a Factory':

> ... You have only got one to serve and you can go to as many classes as you like in a week, you have got Saturday and Sunday to yourself and you can see a bit of life and we are not shut up all day ... We have only got one amount of work to do in a day and we can help other girls to go the right way ... There are one or two things that can be approved of [improved]. The Master ought to have a Lavatory so that you can come out respectable when you were done. There hadn't ought to be any bad words to be put out, most factories there is ...[121]

A respectable yet freedom-loving girl could rise above foul toilets and coarse language, but not the housemaid's cap, that stigma that so many young female servants considered the trademark of their servitude. Maids who answered Butler's questionnaires remarked that 'owing to their hated headdress, they cannot put their head out of doors without being called "skivvy" by passing workmen or errand boys'.[122] The cap betokened a loss of control over one's own life, and a tacit admission that one no longer existed as a person. Employers discussed private affairs while servants waited upon them because they assumed that servants had ears only for a command or for the bell: 'It was expected always that ... you weren't human – you were expected to be on the run. ... If she rang the bell wherever she was in the house you were expected almost to be there – before the bell stopped ringing ... you weren't supposed to be out of breath either.'[123] Nor were you expected to require, let alone request, the assistance one thoughtful human being might ordinarily accord another. Upon the occasion of a tennis tea: 'I had to carry a great heavy tray ever so far down the garden. There used to be half a dozen young fellows lounging around and never, never helped you with a tray or said can I take it.'[124] The industrialist enjoyed complimenting his wife on her ability to run the household like a well-oiled machine. His domestic servants were the anonymous cogs in that machinery as surely as their fathers and brothers served in the same alienating, anonymous capacity in his factory. On those rare occasions when servants were not summoned for orders, they were nevertheless called upon to acknowledge their inferiority to those they worked for. 'I was allowed to go and look at her,' one woman recalled, of the time when a daughter of the house was presented at court. 'And she was in her court dress with her ostrich feathers and her dress. I thought of course that it was heaven ... It was a ceremonial thing. You see, the servants were allowed to go and see this grand thing happening.'[125]

A maidservant's life was seldom punctuated with events that exciting. Her routine was as monotonous as it was strenuous. Mrs Beeton, in the 1912 edition of her celebrated treatise on household management, laid down standards that all respectable middle and upper-class households attempted to achieve or at least to approach. Here is her description of the duties incumbent upon a housemaid, between the time she herself arose in the morning and the time she set the table for her employers' breakfast:

On coming downstairs [the housemaid] should go to ... the sitting-rooms, to open all the shutters, and, if the weather be fine, the windows of the various apartments.

She then arranges the breakfast-room, and gets it ready for the the family; for this she brings upstairs a carpet-broom, dustpan and some damp tea-leaves.

She should first remove the fender and fire-irons, and roll up and remove the rug; take off the table-cloth, shake and fold it; also shake and fold any antimacassars that may be in the room, and place altogether on the table, which she should cover with a dusting sheet. She should also cover the sofa, if there be one in the room, and the easy chair, and place the other chairs one seat upon the other, and get all the furniture as much together and in the middle of the room as possible. She should then, having sprinkled the carpet all over with the tea-leaves – sweep the room, beginning at the door going into all the corners; when it is swept all round, moving the furniture and sweeping where that stood, and bringing all the dust to the hearth-stone, where she should collect it in the dustpan and remove it.

She should then shut the door, and while the dust is settling sweep out the hall and down the doorsteps, using for this not the carpet-broom, but the common house-sweeping brush. She should also take out the hall mats and shake them.

She should then return to the breakfast room, bringing with her the housemaid's box, well supplied with brushes, blacklead, emery paper and leathers. The cinder-pail, a small pail of hot water, a house-flannel, a piece of hearthstone, a large coarse cloth, and paper, firewood, coals and matches to light the fire. She should then, first laying down the cloth before the fireplace to save the carpet; clean the grate, fender and fire-irons.

She should first clear out of the grate all the remains of the fire of the day before, placing the cinders and ashes in the cinder-box.

Then blacklead the grate, laying on the blacklead with a soft brush, rubbing it off vigorously with a harder one and finishing it off with a polishing brush. Then rub with a leather all the polished steel portion of the grate, which should not be touched at all with the blacklead or brushes; where any spots appear, rubbing first with the emery paper, and afterwards with the leather. The fender the same way; any portion that is of polished steel being cleaned with emery paper and leather. The fire-irons always with emery paper and leather only.

She will then light the fire, proceeding in exactly the same manner as the cook does with the kitchen fire. Then wash the hearthstone, washing it very thoroughly, rinsing it quite free from all dirt and black; then, while wet she should rub it well over with the hearth-stone, but in doing this she must be very careful to let none of the water or stone touch the grate, fender, or fire-irons.

She should then remove to the scullery all the tools and utensils she used for the grate and fire, and bringing up a clean duster, she should thoroughly dust the breakfast-parlour. In doing this, she should go over every article carefully, not flapping the duster about, but wiping the dust off with it. She should go over the backs and legs of the various pieces of furniture, and should lift every small article from chimneypiece and sideboard and dust under them. She should also dust round the cornice of the room, dust the door and the window-panes, sills and ledges.

She should then re-arrange the furniture all in its proper place, and everything being in order, she should leave the room, shutting the door after her.

Before returning to the breakfast room to set the table, the housemaid was instructed to clean the ladies' boots and shoes; then, having washed her face and hands, and put on a clean cap and apron, to carry hot water to the bedrooms.[126]

The Thompson and Vigne interviews demonstrate the extent to which actual emulated ideal. The between-maid who had been allowed to admire the household debutante recalled the following daily routine: clean and light the kitchen range; prepare the servants' breakfast; clean the steps and brasses; clear the breakfast and wash up; assist the house-maid until 11; prepare the sevants' mid-morning snack; clean vegetables for the cook; lay the servants' noon meal; wash up after the meal; clean the copper cooking utensils, 'which had to be kept very clean and bright and which had to be cleaned with vinegar and silver sand and something which was awfully bad on my hands'; rest; prepare the servants' tea; clear it away; prepare the vegetables for the evening meal 'and do all the little ugly jobs the cook didn't want to do'.[127] In the end the girl went on a hunger strike in desperation and was sent home sick.

Mrs Beeton writes of a thorough daily dusting. Another former maid recalled what such work entailed: 'The sideboard was one whole mass of silver. Little tiny silver pepper pots and things like that. It had all got to be cleaned once a week.'[128] Mrs Beeton takes stairs for granted in a way that servants, particularly those called upon to wash them down, never could:

> I had the back stairs to do up to my bedroom. . . . It was like cottages made into a big house. And then when you were downstairs you had so many steps to go into the front. And then there was the back stairs to the cook's room. There was my stairs through the pantry. . . . All steps, you know. It was a real hard house. But it was a good house.[129]

What often made a hard house a good house was the presence of con-genial fellow servants. Their absence could mean terrible loneliness. Perhaps the most poignant testimony among the Thompson and

Vigne interviews is that recalling an incident in the life of the young girl whom hard work and lack of companionship finally drove to the hunger strike. In her teens, while engaged as a between-maid in a London household, she was by more than ten years the youngest servant in the house: the cook-housekeeper was 35, the lady's maid 50, the parlour maid in her 30s, the housemaid 28. She spent her half-days off with the housemaid, but found herself desperate for companionship. One morning while polishing the front brasses, a gentleman from the neighbourhood, whom she had observed passing the house on other occasions, stopped and addressed her, asking if she would like to spend an evening out with him. 'I would give you a good time,' she recalled him telling her. 'And I was flattered beyond words.' Before she could respond, the cook emerged from the basement, and the gentleman moved off. 'And I was all sort of blushing and thrilled. You see how easy.'[130] The ease recalls the observation of the author of *My Secret Life*: 'As to servants and women of the humbler class . . . they all took cock on the quiet and were proud of having a gentleman to cover them. Such was the opinion of men in my class of life and of my age.'[131] Further evidence, as well, of the 'thingness' of domestic servants in the eyes of their employers, and of the nature of the risk run by a respectable working-class girl employed in a 'proper' upper-middle-class household, far greater than what she might expect in factory or workshop.

Apologists for the institution of domestic service ignored the evidence of such risks, arguing instead that employment in a well-regulated, middle-class menage offered working-class girls excellent training for their role as future housewives, and that the chance of exposure to 'better' life made them more genteel and, by implication, more deferential.[132] Though undoubtedly individual instances here and there could be found to support the contention, it was difficult to sustain as a generality. A girl entering service at fifteen and leaving for marriage five or six years later would have had little chance to rise very far from her menial position as kitchen or between-maid. Her 'apprenticeship', like that of her sisters in the factory or mill, consisted of little more than conditioning to hard and monotonous work. She was hired not as a learner but as a labourer. Nor did her duties impart to her a knowledge of working-class household management: budgeting for five or six on a weekly income of 25 shillings. As for fastidiousness and deferential behaviour, they depended on a girl's particular character and on the length of her time in service. If she remained unmarried and rose within the domestic ranks to a position of some importance, the habits and assumptions of her 'family' might in time come to reflect preferences and prejudices which she would consider her own. If her term of service was shorter she might return to marriage and the world of the working class to find herself in a kind of limbo, rejecting the values of employers who had used her in a manner she could not approve of, while discontented and distressed by a pattern of life which she now found herself compelled to consider hard and crude.[133]

The same dilemma faced those working-class girls who chose to work as shop assistants. In many cases the compensations of their position were even fewer than those of the housemaid. Subject to a severe system of fines and expected to work as many as 15 hours a day, the girls often found themselves required as well to live in bleak dormitories, sharing windowless cubicles with other girls they did not know.[134] Employers, who preferred the 'living-in' system as a means of ensuring maximum performance from their assistants, argued for it on the grounds of the girls' youth, and their need for supervision and protection.[135] The younger the girls, however, the less likely they were to tolerate the confinement of the dormitories, preferring, if necessary, simply to wander about the town, a greater prey to moral temptation than if they had lived in rooms by themselves.

In one important respect, the job of assistant was even less attractive than that of domestic servant. Whereas a girl who remained in service to a household over a period of years had a good chance to better her position, either there or elsewhere, a shop assistant too often found herself redundant after the age of 25 or 30, easily replaced by a younger woman, and forced to take on even less appealing jobs in order to earn enough money to eat. The predicament was particularly acute among teashop waitresses. 'For the girl who belongs to the great majority which is average and commonplace,' wrote the social investigator Barbara Drake in 1913,

> and who misses her vocation to marry, the outlook is a poor one. With no taste and less skill for further work, with little hope of another berth, she is discharged for a trumpery fault; or she is shelved at a lower wage as a counter-hand; or she is driven from the beloved haunts of the City or the Strand, to the limbo of the waitress, the teashop of the suburbs.

Drake suggests that the woman would consider herself fortunate if able to obtain work at that time in her life as a household domestic.[136] Neither alternative appealed to an increasingly large number of working-class girls who, like their brothers, welcomed release from school into the freedom of a life which for a few years they could enjoy as their very own.

'The apathetic content of the old and dying is thus balanced by abounding vitality and eagerness for pleasure in the young.'[137] Though Booth evoked that spirit more persuasively than most social investigators, he was reporting nothing more than what they all discovered and felt the need to describe. Some expressed a further need to disparage a frivolity considered heedless, and a cheek they mistrusted as disrespectful. 'Girls for whom underclothing hardly exists', sniffed Helen Bosanquet, 'somehow manage to deck themselves with some external finery, to dress their hair in the East-End version of the latest fashion, and even to break out into marvellous but inexpensive jewelry ... It is a pathetic little outburst of vanity in most of them. ... after marriage they relapse into the hopeless slatternliness of their childhood ...'[138] S. F. Jackson, in an essay in J. J. Findlay's survey, *The Young Wage Earner*, deplored the yearning of working-class youths for an escape from learning to freedom where, contrary to the best interests of society, 'they mate earlier' than their middle-class counterparts, 'and without the apprehensive circumspection that others take.'[139] Circumspection has never been one of youth's virtues, and it may be that working-class adolescents possessed even less than their share of it. The confined nature of a working-class childhood – cramped quarters, routine schoolwork – propelled boys and girls into their teens with an extraordinarily intense desire to put all that behind them, eager to live as uncabined a life as possible, and ready to flash out in hostility when anyone challenged their right to do as they pleased.

Booth, although admitting along with his reforming confrères that 'something should be done' to curb that feckless indifference to the long run which they all deplored, appeared more willing than most to take working-class youth on its own terms. His description of the London factory girl is the best of many:

> She can be recognized on ordinary days by the freedom of her walk, the numbers of her friends, and the shrillness of her laugh. On Saturday evenings and Sunday afternoons she will be found promenading up and down Bow Road, arm in arm with two or three other girls, sometimes with a young man, but not nearly so frequently as might be imagined. On those occasions she is adorned and decked out, not so much for conquest as for her own personal delight and pleasure, and for the admiration of her fellow women. She wears a gorgeous plush hat with as many large ostrich feathers to match as her funds will run to – bright ruby or scarlet preferred. Like all the working women in the East End she wears good tidy boots on all occasions, perhaps with high heels, but generally suitable for walk-

ing although a little higher always than those adopted by the Rational Dress Society.[140]

The type was not confined to London. Tom Maguire celebrated her northern counterpart in his ballad 'The Duchess of Number Three':

> ... I will do as I like as long as I dare,
> What's fair to me is my own affair,
> And I'll please myself anyhow – so there!
> Says the Duchess of Number Three.[141]

If the Duchess's less exuberant co-workers forebore from singing out their independence as she did, they joined her in flaunting it on their backs, their heads, and their feet. Clothes expressed the young workers' freedom to spend their own money as they saw fit. When the factory girl had less than enough to buy what she wanted, she resorted to clothing clubs, contributing 6d a week for fifteen weeks with fifteen other girls, and thus assuring herself a new pair of shoes.[142] Again the middle class disapproved, declaring that mill girls were fools to follow fashion and wear corsets, concerned lest working boys permanently damage their health, by stinting themselves on food in order to dress in a fashion unbecoming to their station.[143]

As children turned into young men and women, they grew less willing to continue faithful attendants at the clubs and missions provided for their entertainment and further education. Flora Freeman, a social worker in Poplar, described her initially futile efforts to begin a dancing class, and her ultimate success in taming her charges:

At the last about ten of them [mostly laundry girls] began to come regularly. Their only idea of amusement was to rush about the room, shrieking and knocking each other over. Rolling on the floor was a favourite pastime; also climbing on to each other's backs, and galloping wildly around the room ... We sternly quelled those original games, and taught them instead, 'Sir Roger de Coverley', and 'The Swedish Dance', and in time they became comparatively orderly.[144]

Not all working girls cavorted with the abandon of Miss Freeman's charges, or with the saucy indifference of Booth's East Enders. These descriptions must be read against what has already been said about parental discipline and working-class respectability. Yet even the most respectably raised boy or girl might be expected at the age of fourteen or fifteen to bridle at past do's and dont's, or at present attempts to teach them the manners of their 'betters'. All codes but their own struck them as alien. When life for the first time was so obviously for the living, 'respectability' was neither psychologically appealing nor socially necessary. 'We *are* sorry for you,' a girl announced to her club leader. 'Why, if we wants to talk to a chap, we just knocks off 'is cap. You 'as to wait till you're hintroduced!'[145]

Boys and girls had began to walk out together by the time they reached the age of sixteen. Before that, boys spent their spare time in company with each other, going once or twice a week to picture palaces or to a football match. Freeman asked several of his Birmingham informants to keep weekly diaries. Here are excerpts from three accounts of Saturday afternoons and evenings:

> Had dinner at 12.30. Went to a football match with our shop and Cape Hill Mission. I ran the line for them and shouted them up a bit. I came home and had tea at 6. Then went to the pictures. I enjoyed myself nicely thank you and went to bed.

> Read the *Birmingham Weekly Post* till 2.30. Then rote to London for a list of Banjo Music, went out to buy a cap and tie, came home and got ready for the night. After tea I change myself and went a walk around town until 8.30 and then went to the Empire. The top of the bill was George Mozart in his thumbnail sketches, I think he was very good, as I take great interest in acting.

> At about 1.30 went with some friends and played football for about two hours and then went to the match Birmingham *v.* Preston North End ... In the evening I got ready and then we walked all about the town through the market hall and then we came down Jamaica Row, the Rag Market in which we walked about watching things being sold at about half past nine we came home.[146]

Other boys spent their free time less circumspectly. Roberts writes of Ancoats street gangs battling each other to establish sway over 'territory' they assumed to be theirs, or avenging wrongs perpetrated by the member of a rival group on one of their own.[147] 'Forgiveness', Russell discovered, 'is most rare among working-class boys; they will carry the remembrance of little wrongs with them for years, looking for an opportunity of "getting their own back", of being even with the boy they imagine has injured them.'[148] The gangs educated their membership in more than the techniques of sporadic warfare. They were themselves 'clubs', spontaneous and self-generating, in which boys taught each other what, by common agreement, they most needed to know: the techniques of finding and holding a job, the form and fortunes of local football clubs, the mysteries of the opposite sex.

A good deal of the mystery would probably remain even after boys began to seek the company of girls. In most cities there existed, by common agreement, one or more thoroughfares to which working-class youths flocked on Saturday and Sunday nights to meet casually for an hour or so of walking, joking and general flirtation. To some, the custom was known as 'stagging', a term well known to pigeon fanciers, used to describe the despatch of a tame pigeon to other cotes to bring back other pigeons.[149] Though noisy and crowded, the congregation was a generally good-natured one, boys and girls often travelling together in bunches of four or five until inspired to pair off for the rest of the evening. Russell, describing Sunday night in Manchester's Oldham Street, concluded that a kind of rowdy innocence prevailed, and found little but the occasionally off-colour remark to condemn:

> From Hulme, from Ardwick, and from Ancoats they come, in the main well dressed, and frequently sporting a flower in the button-holes of their jacket. But the motive is not so much that of meeting their friends, as of forming an acquaintanceship with some young girl. Girls resort to Oldham Street on a Sunday night in nearly as large numbers as the boys . . . [The boys] exchange rough salutations with the girls, who seem in no way less vigorous than the boys themselves, and whose chief desire, one would think, was to pluck from the lads' button-holes, the flowers which many of them wear.[150]

From this ritual of introduction, young working-class men and women moved through a pattern of further encounters, at club-sponsored dances, perhaps, or if they were earning good money and could afford the purchase of a bicycle, on weekend jaunts as members of a cycling club. Not until they had all but decided to marry would the man come to call at the girl's house. Once given tea by her parents, he could assume his acceptance, and take for granted their engagement.[151]

To the young wife, looking back upon her years as an unmarried factory girl, that period of free and easy living would soon seem to have been woefully short. Burdened at once with housekeeping and, within a year or so, with children, and generally unprepared for those burdens, she watched as youthful good times vanished along with youthful good looks, acknowledging to herself that routine would now have to sustain her as freedom had done, so short a time before.

> A few years pass, a very few, and these bright girls become apathetic, listless women of whom at 35 it is impossible to guess whether their age is 40 or 50. They are tired out; they toil on, but they have ceased to look forward or entertain any hopes. The contrast between the factory girl and her mother is perhaps the very saddest spectacle that the labour world presents.[152]

# 7 A view of life

EVIDENCE ABOUT THE English working class before the First World War tells us with remarkable persistence that men, women, and children depended upon habit and custom to help them live their lives. Women, as they moved from house to neighbourhood; men, as they geared their existence to the patterns imposed by the factory; children, as they repeated the rhymes and played the games others had played before them, all took comfort in the familiar and set great store by it. The familiar was concrete and personal. And, as Richard Hoggart argues, it was with reference to the concrete and personal that most members of the working class understood their fellow human beings and looked out at the world around them. By 1900 they had begun to experience that bombardment by abstractions which Hoggart maintains they have continued to find so difficult to deal with:

> They are asked to respond to the 'needs of the state', and 'the needs of society', to study 'good citizenship', to have in mind the 'common good'. In most cases the appeals mean nothing, are so many words. They do not think such general calls, for duty, sacrifice, for individual effort, are relevant to them. They are themselves the ground base of society, they know; normally they go on living their own kind of life. When the larger world, society, the world of 'them', needs the mass of the people, why then, they feel, they are quickly told where to go and what to do. For the rest, the local and the concrete world is what can be understood, managed, trusted . . .[1]

People thought in terms of what they already knew well. A woman from Bolton, for instance, described her father's home in the following way:

> He came from Scopey Lane, they called it Labby's Farm . . . They've built down there since, so they call it Tinker Bottom down that way . . . But it was over that water, now whether they've filled that water in I don't know – and there were little narrow bridges you went to this farm. Then me grandma brought nine up on that farm. Yes, they called it Labby's Farm.[2]

The most popular music hall songs were those that drew upon the familiar. Dan Leno's material 'was the sum of all the small things in the life of his class. It was full of baby's bottles, Sunday clothes, pawnshops, lodging, cheap holidays and the like.'[3] 'Just by the Angel at Islington', 'Down at the Welsh 'Arp which is 'Endon Way', 'Knocked 'em in the Old Kent Road': these and other songs were favourites because they evoked particular places an audience might very well know, as 'The Day We Went to Ramsgate, Oh!' might recall the fun and confusion of a factory girl's last holiday, not just in general terms – a good time had by all – but in detail down to the important matter of how much it cost:

> There and back for five and six,
> On board the boat we played some tricks,
> The loudest noisy lot of bricks
> That ever went to Ramsgate, oh![4]

The use of the familiar induced a degree of self-knowledge that made it difficult for working-class people to take themselves too seriously. Self-reverence is a middle-class and not a working-class vice. The middle class, in turn, and particularly that element within the middle class that wished to see the working class better itself, found this preference for the concrete, this disinclination to tackle the abstract, frustrating. Eleanor Rathbone, one of the most sympathetic investigators of the life of working-class women, considered them woefully ill-equipped to place experiences together into the sort of pattern that might better enable them to rise above the everyday. The rich and well-educated, she argued, possessed a kind of 'listening-in apparatus' which gave them this power of reconstruction and transformation. In contrast, the mind of the working woman was occupied solely with 'what is immediately present to her in time and place'. She might not find herself as 'tormented ... by the sense of injustice nor by anxiety about the future', as was her middle-class counterpart. But, in Rathbone's opinion, her limited vision deprived her of both imagination and hope.[5]

One must proceed with extreme caution here. Certainly Reginald Bray, in making the same point as Rathbone, did so to an extreme and with a perjorativeness unwarranted by what we know of the working-class sense of right and wrong. Arguing that reliance upon nothing more than immediate experience left the working class without a framework within which to judge correct behaviour, Bray concluded that families had 'no idea of the meaning of character. Acts and not motives alone count for anything. Their lessons take the form of "do" and "don't", and never reach that higher level where the command is to "be this and not that".[6] Bray, and to a much lesser degree Rathbone, ignored the fact that the 'familiar', against which any particular action might be measured or judged, as often meant habit and tradition as it did the disconnected happenings of the immediate past or present. Nor did they seem to understand the extent to which tradition might itself furnish working-class men and women with a 'listening-in apparatus' on which to pattern their thoughts and thereby reach Bray's 'higher level'. That apparatus was built, however, not of self-generated abstractions but of maxims from the past, whose very concreteness and 'common sense-ness' seemed to guarantee their worth. Hoggart quotes them by the score, and they concerned, as he says, 'the great themes of existence: marriage, children, relations with others, sex':[7] 'I take a man as he is'; 'You can't lay in where bairns are'. And they echo in the refrains of the music halls: 'A little of what you fancy does you good.' They served to reinforce traditional ways: the habits of neighbourhood, the expectations of respectability. They could bring an argument, soaring dangerously into the abstract, back to ground again, to the realm of what was believed to be true because it had so long been so handily available as truth. To argue in terms other than these was to 'talk', to indulge in empty chatter. Middle-class sympathizers, exasperated with that attitude, failed to understand how the familiar and common-sensical might itself become a 'value' to someone who looked to it for security. When they charged the working class with an inability to think abstractly, they were often lamenting its unwillingness to think in abstractions akin to their own.

Educational bureaucrats found themselves equally frustrated when attempting to instil 'traditional' – that is, 'middle-class' – patriotism into the working-class consciousness. Board schools tried their best to inspire children with an understanding of their duty to king and country. Robert Roberts describes the particular efforts expended upon the annual occasion of Empire Day: 'We drew Union Jacks, hung classrooms with flags of the dominions and gazed with pride as they pointed out those massed areas of red on the world map. "This, and this, and this," they said, "belong to us." '[8] The lessons implanted in childhood would, it was hoped, encourage in later life a sense of duty accompanied by a willingness to enlist, or at the very least a sense of pride strong enough to cheer England lustily from the sidelines in any sort of international contest of will or of arms. Critics of the lessons accused those who taught them of fostering the jingoism spawned in what J. A. Hobson described as 'the neurotic temperament generated by town life'. Such a temperament, he warned, 'seeks natural relief in stormy sensational appeals and the crowded life of the streets. ... A coarse patriotism, fed by the wildest rumours and the most violent appeals to hate and the animal lust of blood, passes by quick contagion through the crowded life of cities, and recommends itself everywhere by the satisfaction it affords to sensational cravings.'[9]

Hobson does not specify just who those contagious unfortunates were; we are left to assume that they were probably members of the urban working class. But evidence suggests that the workers' distaste for abstraction and respect for common sense protected them from the sensationalism Hobson so sensationally described. Richard Price, in his recent study, *An Imperial War and the British Working Class*, argues that the working class was not prey to the excessive, mindless patriotism Hobson deplored. It was middle-class, not working-class, patriots who disrupted pro-Boer demonstrations. Working-class lads who joined the army did so, not out of zeal, but because they could find jobs nowhere else. And working-class families, if they cheered with the rest of the country upon the occasion of the relief of Mafeking, celebrated because relatives they knew were a part of the fight, and because the fight had become for them a personal one. The Trades Union Congress, throughout the period of the Boer War, was loathe to spend time debating the 'principle' of participation. No more did the common soldier try to persuade himself he was at war for 'the greater good'. Instead, as a former warehouseman wrote back to his Workingman's Club *Journal*,

I did not care tuppence about the merits of the dispute, and the rubbish about 'fighting for the dear old flag', and our desire to kill Boers or anything else ... the best part of the men went away from the same cause ... it was to escape for a time the monotony of existence, and if other volunteers were only to speak the truth they would tell you the same thing.[10]

And if the soldier died, he died not for king and country, as his superiors constantly tried to convince him, but because he had had the rotten luck to be at the wrong place at the wrong time. As far as the working class was concerned, there was no more to be made of it than that. Grief was real, but its boundaries were personal. Alan Sillitoe, writing of a tough working woman whose son was killed in Korea in the early 1950s, described the limits of those boundaries when he declared of her that 'there was nothing on the face of the earth that would have made her say: "It was worth it. That's a good thing to die for." '[11]

The same boundaries prevented the working class from appreciating the German menace in the way the middle class wanted it to. Workers needed to rely on nothing more than memory to see, in the institution of a territorial army, not a counter to the threat of invasion but a weapon that might easily be turned against militant strikers.[12] To them, a more serious menace than the Germans was the aliens willing to work longer and for less than Englishmen, thereby taking jobs from them. The English worker was no more free from unattractive chauvinism than was the English shopkeeper. The difference lay in the shopkeeper's highly developed skill in disguising prejudice as national interest. The working man simply declared what his experience convinced him was common sense: foreigners, because they threatened his livelihood and the stable life in his neighbourhood, were not to be trusted, should be kept out, and, wherever possible, sent home.[13]

Bound as they were to tradition, the familiar, and the concrete, and hard-pressed in many cases to survive, working-class men and women spent little time speculating about the future. Experience prepared them to expect more of the same; they refused to torment themselves by trying to plan ahead for something different. However well laid the plans, the odds appeared depressingly heavy against their success. Better to spend the extra shilling or two now and be certain of at least some limited pleasure. 'Rainy days' came with an accepted regularity that precluded the hope of saving for shelter against them. Even those fortunate enough to have money to lay by might realize that planning implied change, an implication they would find less an inducement than an inhibition. Change was threatening; if you had a chance for more, it was tempting simply to reach for more of what you knew.

Not surprisingly, this unwillingness to look ahead, to sacrifice the present on behalf of the future, was one further working-class trait annoying to middle-class critics and sympathizers alike. How were the poor to improve if they were unwilling to improve themselves? Alexander Paterson despaired: 'It is only people who shut their eyes to the future who could ever borrow money so generally as the poor are in the habit of doing at 500 per cent.' Later in his study, *Across the Bridges*, he unwittingly provides the explanation for this habit he so deplores when he remarks, of 'the average boy engaged in unskilled work', that 'the most prevalent impression seems to be that tomorrow will in all probability be very like today, that next year, save for a slight rise in wages, will be but a repetition of the present.'[14] When the present is grim, and there is every chance that the future will amount to nothing more than the present, why not borrow to make life today a bit more bearable? Planning ahead, under those circumstances, amounts to little more than self-delusion and is certainly self-torture. Will Thorne made the point in his autobiography:

> There are few rosy patches, if any, in the fight for bread in the lives of the manual labourer with little skill or education. Just long years of drudging work in the past and in the future. One can dream and hope, and if by chance God gives such a one imagination, it is more of a curse than a blessing. Much wisdom, it is said, brings much suffering, and while I may not be a very wise man I have suffered much in mind and soul just thinking of tomorrow and tomorrow's morrow, as well as the physical sufferings and hunger that have been my lot and which are the lot of my people.[15]

Many resorted to a kind of fatalism. Few despaired as totally as George Gissing's character, Sidney Kirkwood, a London worker burdened with a disfigured wife and complaining family. 'If there were hope,' he declared, 'I might fret under the misery.'[16] Most accepted events as they came: acquiescent, mildly hedonistic, concerned with the question of how life should be, but generally only within the manageable dimensions of their own family's daily conduct. Beyond those limits, they were ready to take what came, to believe in something – the hand of God or the hand of fate – if only to use belief in self-defence. They sought a rationale for the life wished upon them, a life for which they saw no reason to shoulder the blame.

Working-class leaders struggled against this fatalistic impulse, convinced that they and their fellow workers must assume responsibility for their future. Keir Hardie, Ben Tillett, John Burns, Ernest Bevin, Arthur Henderson, Ramsay MacDonald, Tom Mann, Philip Snowden, whatever their individual differences and peculiar strengths or weaknesses, emerged from somewhere within the background we have been considering, and thought in terms broader and grander than the traditional, the personal, and the concrete. Driven by a belief in the need for change, their compulsion, it is true, derived from their experience. It was shaped, however, if not by 'abstractions', then by a vision that clearly transcended past and present. That vision derived in some cases from religious conviction; in others, from attachment to the theories of secular socialism; in still others, from the belief that socialist and Christian goals were akin to each other, that the kingdom of God was an end as worthy of pursuit in this world as in the next.[17]

Our particular interest here lies not with the leadership but with the rank and file. And the admittedly patchy evidence we possess carries us a good distance from the heroic vanguard of the labour movement. Religion, after it had helped the working class to define the seasons, and had, through the institution of the Church, offered its limited range of social services in return for nominal loyalty, provided little further sustenance to the majority. Its strength remained greatest in smaller communities in the north. In the great cities, in London particularly, it had lost hold of the working class forever.[18] There was little atheism or outright secularism; instead, as one exasperated clergyman reported to Booth, a ready willingness 'to believe in a God to whom they ascribe their own vague humanitarian impulses and their own lax moral standards'.[19] But the religious conviction that fired the social thinking of men such as Keir Hardie or George Lansbury was not common.

As for socialism, its convinced and practising working-class converts, though increasing in number, remained a small portion of the whole. The anger that drove Robert Tressell to write his novel was directed ultimately against his 'ragged trousered' fellow workers, whose unwillingness even to consider a socialist remedy for their distress turned them into unwitting 'philanthropists' in the service of their middle-class masters:

> They were the enemy. Those who not only quietly submitted like so many cattle to the existing state of things, but defended it, and opposed and ridiculed any suggestion to alter it . . . It was because they were indifferent to the fate of *their* children that he [Owen, the socialist hero] would be unable to secure a natural and human life for *his*. It was their apathy or active opposition that made it impossible to establish a better system of society under which those who did their fair share of the world's work would be honoured and rewarded.

For every Frank Owen there were many more willing to say, along with the reactionary housepainter Bob Crass: 'Never mind about supposing things wot ain't true. Let's 'ave facts and common sense.' The truculence supports Stedman Jones's assertion that the prevailing tone of working-class culture 'was not one of political combativity but of an enclosed and defensive conservatism'.[20] The surprise is not that there was a multitude of Crasses, but that there were as many Owens as there were.

Working-class men and women relied upon habit to protect themselves from changes they either feared or found difficult to understand. During the years before the First World War, changes nevertheless rained down upon them in perplexing and threatening profusion. We have already examined some of the most pressing: the sharpened sense of class consciousness; the altered relationship between skilled and unskilled worker; the continuing disruption of urban migration. At least three additional challenges tested the willingness of the working class to respond creatively to change, to come out from the shelter of tradition and to move beyond the apathy for which Tressell derided it. One, in large part the product of organization and agitation by the working class itself, was the foundation of an independent political movement. The second, the work of middle-class reformers, was the conception of a welfare state. The third, the result of economic forces no one appeared able to control, was a sharp increase in the cost of living. Some urged support of the first, or acceptance of the second, as a means of defeating the third. Others argued as vehemently against them. The working class found itself bombarded not only by change but by advice about how best to meet it. Some heeded one group; some another. Many tried listening for a time and then gave up, retreating as best they could into the time-tested world of the familiar, a refuge which others had never bothered to leave. Workers were not the only ones facing changes. All classes recognized threats of one kind or another and went on the defensive. The result was confusion, bitterness, and a heightened sense of general unrest.

Until the 1890s, working-class politics had meant junior partnership in a Lib-Lab confederacy that left Labour with little say in matters of any real importance. Those economic circumstances which produced increased class division after 1880, however, and the so-called employers' counter-attack in the 1890s,[21] led labour leaders and working-class socialists to join forces, first in the Independent Labour Party of 1893, and then in the Labour Representation Committee of 1900. Thereafter the leadership pressed members of the working class to come alive politically, as they had not before, on behalf of this first party founded specifically to further the interests of working men and women. To aid their effort, they relied on volunteers whose willingness belied Tressell's pessimism. Many of them were largely self-educated, like Tressell's hero Owen, possessing both a library and a willingness to stay up half the night to devour its contents: '[We would] read between ten and one o'clock in the morning . . . We'd both sit and read and we had to read something if it was only *Comic Cuts*, he'd take something from me, but he had to read.'[22] The hard work of these local workers paid off in terms of elections contested and, with increasing frequency, won. In 1913, 353 Labour candidates were nominated for positions on urban district, rural district, and parish council elections, and 196 were successfully returned, a gain of 68 over the previous year. In town and borough council elections 494 candidates stood for office and 196 were returned, a gain of 85.[23] These, in addition to more notable gains since 1900 in Parliament, fed the ambitions and hopes of Labour Party strategists.

As important as winning elections was the task of building a sense of 'movement' within the working class, the sort of spirit displayed in a letter from the secretary of a local Yorkshire ILP to Ramsay MacDonald in 1907, inviting him to come up from London to address the enthusiastic faithful: 'I am writing just to let you know what a splendid lot of comrades we have,' he began. 'We want time to well advertise [the hoped-for visit] and the boys here can advertise. We have comrades who do poster writing and don't forget they put up some startlers.'[24] Here, however, the organizers faced their most difficult task, and the rank and file its particular challenge. In urging the working class as a whole to ally itself with this new adventure, Labour Party leaders were asking not just for a change of political allegiance, but for an alteration of time-honoured habits of mind. The majority of those who could vote, and who were old enough to have been voting for some time, had always been Liberals, attracted to the party by its reformist image locally, acknowledging a debt for attentions paid nationally, and revering it for its stern yet appealing leader, Gladstone.

Nor must one forget the number of workers who, for reasons either of self-interest or deference, continued to vote Tory. Employees in munitions firms, or in clothing factories which supplied the army, voted Conservative in the belief that Conservatives generally favoured a larger military budget. Henry Pelling in his study, *The Social Geography of British Elections*, illustrates the manner in which a Conservative might easily hold a working-class district with the example of Seymour King's control of Kingston-upon-Hull Central. Vague pronouncements in favour of social reform, denunciation of alien immigration, continuing support of free trade: these plus treats and the habits of a deferential electorate kept him in office.[25] A fear of reprisals if they voted against the interests of an employer, or the belief that 'people with money could rule a country better than those that hadn't':[26] these were the habits of mind that kept workers voting for both Liberal and Conservative candidates, while Labour Party organizers despaired at their continuing willingness to do so.[27]

Deference was by no means the only habit organizers tried to break. A working-class tradition of politics as recreation meant that voting days were festivals, voters and non-voters alike sporting party rosettes, awaiting news as they might await the results of an afternoon's horse race, swapping the latest tips or laying a bet on a favourite. The Labour Party broke in upon these customary rituals with a challenge many traditionalists found annoying; the result was often the kind of ridicule that would discourage a commitment to the unfamiliar red rosette. The son of a free-thinking socialist iron moulder remembered going to school at election time: 'And the boys were flouting their rosettes and chidding me because I hadn't one. And I asked for one [at home] and was sent with a red one. "What is that?" "Oh, that's a Socialist." "Well there is no such thing." You know, and in that sense I was an odd man out.'[28]

Another source for the tradition of politics as leisure had been the workingmen's clubs, many of which, during the 1870s and 1880s, bred a tough and independent-minded membership in the course of evening programmes of discussion. John Taylor reports the institution of 'sharp practice' nights, at which the chairman would pull a topic for deliberation from a hat, testing the membership's 'sharpness' by asking it to debate the topic forthwith. By the turn of the century most of the overtly political clubs had succumbed to the temptation of direct party affiliation – either Liberal or Conservative, while the remainder had generally chosen to substitute entertainment for politics.[29] The result was the drying up of a vein of thoughtful independent activism which the Labour Party might otherwise have drawn upon to accustom working-class voters to a new set of political circumstances.

Politics as sport meant that crowds were easily come by. A torchlight procession of 10,000 had celebrated the victory of two Labour candidates in the Barking School Board election of 1889.[30] To sustain the enthusiasms of the movement, however, took a perseverance on the part of dedicated party workers which tested both their abilities and their patience. 'My people can be galvanized into jerky and evanescent excitement in any direction,' a discouraged London rector reported to Booth. 'They are ready to "demonstrate" at any time and for almost any object. They will insist vehemently on Labour Representation and Progressive programmes, but do not take the trouble to turn out even to vote.'[31] Ramsay MacDonald expressed the same dilemma in a 1912 speech:

> We can talk for twenty years about the matter [in this instance national insurance]; we can have exhibitions and special conferences, wars against poverty, and columns in the newspapers . . . But still what happens? For a week everybody is interested; next week the interest begins to wear off. The people are absorbed in a football match, or a horse race, or an excursion to London with fares paid to break windows . . .[32]

A part of the difficulty lay in the exceedingly complex mechanism of registration, which effectively disenfranchised many eligible and interested voters, and discouraged many more. Chiozza Money estimated the number of adult males in 1910 at 12 million; the number of enfranchised males at a little more than half that figure.[33] An excerpt from an instructional pamphlet written to assist Labour Party canvassers goes a good way towards explaining why:

> If a man rents a room at 32 More St and pays 4s a week rent for six months and then takes two rooms in the same house and pays 6s per week rent for another six months and the rent started before July 15, 1905 and continued till July 15, 1906, he would be entitled to claim as a lodger [and therefore qualify to vote in Parliamentary, Parish and District Council and Board of Guardian elections, but not in County Council or Town and Borough Council elections]; but if he lived at 32 More St from July 14, 1905 till December 1905 and rented one room at 4s unfurnished or 5s furnished and then moved to 33 More St next door and took two rooms and paid 6s rent, he would lose his vote both as a lodger and a householder; he must either be a lodger and rent rooms in one and the same house for the whole twelve months stated; or a householder and rent the whole of a house, or a part of a house that is *separate and complete in itself*, and then he claims for one, two, or more houses, or parts of houses that are dwellings separate and complete in themselves, and the successive houses lived in during the period July 15–July 15 may be in different districts or wards of the same Borough and in the case of County Divisions, in different parts of the same county.[34]

Pity the conscientious canvasser attempting to sort out puzzle after puzzle as he went the length of a working-class street. And sympathize with the busy housewife who declared she had no time to retrace her family's history in the necessary detail.

Regulations encouraged apathy, normally diagnosed in direct ratio to poverty: the poorer the family, the less its concern with problems beyond those of immediate survival.[35] Political commitment demands a consciousness that change is both desirable and possible – a consciousness foreign to most men and women trapped at the level of 25 shillings a week. Concern seldom tended to move beyond the immediate and the concrete: 'Ah understands nowt about politics and nowt Ah want to understand. But Ah do understand a load o' coal.'[36] The attitude bred the maxims: 'Politics never did anybody any good'; 'Of course, all politics are crooked'; 'There's nowt to choose between 'em [of political parties]'.[37] Women were particularly difficult to rouse.

Lady Bell found few Middlesbrough wives conversant with the Free Trade controversy, though most of their husbands had expressed an opinion. The reason, as Margery Spring Rice wrote of working-class wives some thirty years later, was by no means difficult to fathom. Poor women had no time to spare for 'immediately irrelevant' considerations such as politics or schemes for social improvement: 'They are not themselves going to be given the second chance, whatever reforms may be introduced, and meantime they have their twelve or thirteen or fourteen hours' work to do every day and their own day to day life to lead.'[38]

The more recent analysis of two sociologists may provide further explanation of the unwillingness of so many to commit themselves. Reinhard Bendix and Seymour Martin Lipset have discovered a relationship between social mobility and political activism which argues that the greater the mobility, either upward or downward, the stronger the impulse to remain politically quiescent: 'The mobile individual, who is in many ways a marginal man, retaining old ties and experiences, is more likely to be subject to cross pressure than the non-mobile person,' and hence more likely to react 'by withdrawal from conflict'.[39] If this is indeed so, and if we recall the extent to which workers in the period before the First World War were experiencing transposition at the hands of technological innovation from one level of the social order to another, we can better understand why not only the poorest but many others within the working class remained outside the political fray. Confronting the unavoidable change induced by social and economic redefinition, they may have had little psychological strength left to contend with a fundamental political reorientation.

Their confusion was further compounded by the fact that by 1914 a sizeable minority within the leadership of the Labour movement had begun to express disenchantment in varying degrees both with the Labour Party and with the institution of Parliament itself. No convocation during those years was complete without discussion, if not formal debate, as to what the Party had done wrong and what it had left undone. The election victory of 1906, and even more the series of welfare measures passed in the ensuing years, appear to have taken many Labour politicians by surprise. They had campaigned on an essentially old-fashioned radical platform: recognition of trade unions, elected school boards, free trade. The 'modern' reforms of Churchill and Lloyd George threw them off balance. Dished by those fast-acting Liberals, they wondered just what it was they had been elected to accomplish, and whether they were condemned to continue taking their cue from the Liberal leadership. If that was the case, how did they

differ from the self-effacing Lib-Labs they had been sent to replace?
With their attention focused on problems of Parliamentary manoeuvre,
they failed to define a clear role for themselves at a time when the
country's political temper continued to reflect increasing division
along class lines.[40] Ben Tillett, in a pamphlet entitled *Is the Parliamentary Labour Party a Failure?*, lambasted Ramsay MacDonald for
allowing temperance reform to take precedence over the problem of
unemployment. Trade unionists held the Party to blame for what they
considered a weak-kneed Parliamentary response to the Osborne
judgment, which threatened to deprive them of their political funds.
What was such hesitation worth? James Gribble of the Boot and Shoe
Operatives declared to his fellow members in 1911 that it was not
worth much at all: 'We have spent thousands of pounds on the Labour
Party, with absolutely no return.' The time had come, he argued, to
strike politics from the rule book and turn to industrial action.[41]

The uncertainty and frustrations of party politics resulted in many
cases in a general revulsion against Parliament as well, an institution
apparently designed, like the law, by a ruling class for its own particular
ends. 'What is this great Parliament to whom we have entrusted our
liberties composed of,' asked George Baker, a member of the Miners'
National Executive, during the 1912 coal strike:

> It consists of six hundred and seventy men, six hundred and thirty
> who were capitalists and landowners, and it will be the death knell
> to the liberties of this movement if we hand them over to a body of
> this character, therefore I say we cannot hope to get much from those
> who represent those great interests of the country.[42]

Parliament provided members with valets to assist them into their
dinner jackets, Fred Jowett complained, but not with clerks to help
them draft legislation: 'The Statute Book has been strewed by generations of lawyer members of Parliament with pitfalls for the unwary
plain man, and unless you can afford to pay for expert assistance you
must flounder as best you can.' Jowett stood with Keir Hardie, Philip
Snowden and others in denouncing the whole game of parliamentary
politics. 'All this jiggery-pokery of party government,' he told the
ILP in 1909, 'played like a game for ascendancy and power, is no
use to us.'[43] The ways of party and Parliament were not the ways of
the working man. Such a pronouncement could not help but increase
the uncertainty of the working class in confronting the political challenge of the infant party that was so assiduously soliciting its support.

The uncertainty with which the Labour Party greeted the progressivism of Liberal legislation after 1906 reflected the difficulties workers generally were experiencing in coming to terms with changing attitudes toward concepts of social service. The years between 1890 and 1914 witnessed the beginning of a struggle between the theories of the social-service state and the welfare state. Victorian England was a social-service state, in which the upper and middle classes, through their own or through the government's agency, extended helping hands to the so-called deserving poor. Modern England is a welfare state, in which the government professes to offer 'all citizens without distinction of status or class ... the best standards available in relation to a certain agreed upon range of social services.'[44] The Charity Organization Society, a sophisticated rationalization of older attitudes, divided the country in two, then demanded efficiency of those who gave and moral rectitude of those who received. The Webbs' minority report of the Poor Law Commission, a daring blueprint for the new, argued against continued division between 'haves' and 'have nots', against the stigmatization of an entire segment of the population as 'pauper', preaching instead a programme of national efficiency grounded in social services available equally to all.

Working-class men and women had chafed in the subservient roles assigned them by Victorian philanthropists. Experience none the less taught them to look warily at schemes advertising partnership, designed by others who claimed to know where the workers' best interest lay. Their apprehension stemmed as well from mistrust of centralization and government intervention, bound to increase as social services increased, and just as bound to let loose armies of middle-class inspectors and reporters, responsible to boards and authorities of a kind already viewed by the working class with apprehension. State power, the foundation of any national welfare system, had expressed itself in the nineteenth century in Housing Acts, Education Acts, and, most particularly, in the Poor Law. All had been designed by the middle and upper classes with the declared aim of assisting workers and their families. All had, to some degree at least, operated to the workers' detriment and, in so doing, had met with their indifference, their hostility, or both.[45] Bureaucracy bred rationalization that made particularly strenuous demands upon the working class.

George Sturt, when he wrote of rural labourers wrestling with the paper work of a modern industrial state, was describing struggles urban workers had experienced, too, over the course of half a century: 'Whether he would join a benefit society, or obtain poor-law relief, or insure the lives of his children, or bury his dead, or take up a small holding, he finds that he must follow a rationalized or standardized procedure set forth in language which his forefathers never heard spoken and never learned to read.'[46]

The working-class mother increasingly found herself cast as her family's representative when confronting or cooperating with the agencies of an increasing bureaucracy. She answered to the authorities when her children stayed away from school or appeared in class with a dirty scalp or without their shoes. Pember Reeves reported the plight of a deserted mother who depended on an invalid child to mind the baby all day while she went out to work at 12s a week. A school inspector discovered the situation and insisted that the mother hire a sitter for 2 shillings. Whether or not the inspector was justified in doing so, one can well understand the mother's resentments and fears at the order. '. . . Her experience of State guardianship of her children', Pember Reeves remarks, 'may be that Public Authority, without troubling as to whether or not fulfilment be in her power, forces further duties and responsibilities on her shoulders in respect of those children – through the threatened medium of the police, with all the horrors of prison in the background.'[47]

Particularly vexatious to the impoverished working-class mother was the matter of free school meals. The Education (Provision of Meals) Act of 1906 had empowered, though it did not require, local authorities to provide meals to necessitous children. It replaced an order of the previous year, which had authorized similar aid through the agency of local Poor Law guardians, and which, as a result of administrative tangles and a dread on the part of parents that acceptance of meals might label them as paupers, probably resulted in the public feeding of fewer rather than more children. The 1906 Act was, from the point of view of social reformers, a distinct improvement over the Order that had preceded it. In 1912–13, nearly 100,000 were being fed in the county of London, and 258,000 throughout the rest of the country. But because the provision of meals remained a voluntary undertaking, and one for which local counties might rely both on private charity and parental payments, as well as on the rates, administration was often frustratingly contradictory, much to the annoyance of the many working-class mothers who were expected to master the intricacies of local regulations. Most communities left it to school teachers to decide who needed the meals, an administrative technique that frequently resulted in surprise inquiries among the children as to the nature of their parents' employment, and the quality and quantity of their daily meals. Teachers who favoured the Act might encourage pupils to accept aid. Those who disapproved, or who worried that too many children on the rolls might brand the school as a paupers' institution, discouraged applications.[48] In some communities, authorities required parents to sign statements pledging repayment of the cost of meals once an unemployed father returned to work. In others, children were expected to present daily notes testifying to their desire to continue the feeding.[49]

All of this – the questioning, the prying, the paying – made the programme less than appealing to many of those for whom it had been designed. Investigators verified wages with employers; in some cities, Leeds and Leicester, for example, a family's total earnings were weighed against its needs; in others, those of the principal wage earner only. Earnings were then measured against an established scale to determine if an applicant deserved help. The system as it operated in Bristol, and as described in a booklet published by the city in 1914, suggests why its appeal was limited:

> Parents who wish their children to be supplied with meals make a personal application at convenient centres which are opened for this purpose on two evenings a week. The attending officers, who are present, furnish the committee with particulars regarding the circumstances of the family, etc. A 'Poverty Scale' has been adopted, and should the net income of the family be above that scale the meals are not granted unless there are exceptional reasons.
>
> When it has been decided to supply the food, a book of tickets, covering a period of four weeks for each child, is sent to the Headmaster of the Day School. Before the end of that time renewed application must be made by the parents for a continuance of the tickets, and if no improved change has taken place, further meals are allowed.[50]

The procedures outlined made good sense to middle-class administrators, anxious to keep poor children from starving yet responsible for the level of the rates. But the regulations, demanding a willingness to open one's life to others and an ability to master the 'rational', 'standard' language and rhythms of bureaucracy, undoubtedly deterred many respectable mothers from applying. What they feared most was the stigma attached to participation in such a programme. The middle class urged them to send their children to be fed, not only for their children's sake, but for the eventual efficiency and well-being of the nation. A working-class mother's vision seldom stretched ahead that far. She knew that by participating she would lose caste in her neighbours' eyes, and knowing that, she lost caste in her own eyes as well. The result, as Margaret McMillan complained, was that far too many parents in straitened but not poverty-stricken circumstances were denying their children a chance to grow up healthy. 'Independent and self-respecting parents' stayed away, and only those in most dire need, the 'poor, ragged, and neglected', were being gathered together 'to intensify their dirt and misery, and without the leaven of cleanly humanity, which might act as an example and an encouragement.'[51]

When the Liberals introduced school medical inspections in 1907, the programme appears to have been hampered not so much by the unwillingness of working-class families to participate, as by the inability of both parents and staff to master the logistics imposed by its scope and by the initial inexperience of those charged with its implementation. Because of the number of children to be examined, the examinations themselves tended to become perfunctory. Parents summoned to attend with their children to learn of any defects often waited for as long as two or three hours for an interview that took no longer than five or ten minutes. Often more vexing for the working-class mother was the question of what to do when informed that her child was in need of further treatment. Dr Marion Phillips, who surveyed the effectiveness of the medical inspection programme in 1913, reported numerous cases in which distance to the hospital had kept parents from taking their children for treatment, or in which the costs of treatment, once undertaken, had worked a severe and unexpected hardship on the entire family:

> A mother took her daughter to hospital with a subscriber's letter for astigmatism. She had to wait there two hours. She has been twice so far, and has to go again. The cost for these two visits, in addition to a 'voluntary' contribution in the hospital box is: glasses, 5s 6d; fares, 6s 8d; substitute for work, 2s 6d; food while away, 9d; total, 15s 5d. This mother thinks 'many people are frightened and put more in the hospital box than they can afford'.

> At [a] London hospital, to which a child was taken for ear trouble, the mother first went on the wrong day, and when she went again had to be there from 10.30 a.m. to 5.25 p.m. These two visits cost her, besides 3d to the hospital and 4d for the fare, 9s for *three* days' work, as on the second day another woman was put in her place. She is threatened with loss of work altogether if she goes again, but the child is not yet cured.[52]

Those cases, and the sixty or so additional ones Phillips details, must be read against a background of late Victorian economic uncertainty, when the loss of 15 shillings or three days' pay could push an entire family to the edge of real deprivation for at least a week, and when tradition and experience both argued in a woman's mind against putting oneself into the hands of doctors or trusting in their advice. Medicine, like the law, was a middle-class institution, full of unfamiliar words and phrases and almost always costly in terms of time and money. A mother who had received an inspector's report with the single word 'eyes' imprinted thereon, and had arranged to take her child to a hospital, only to be told once she had come that the little girl's 'blepharitis' had vanished and that there was nothing in fact the matter, might wonder why she should express her thanks to a government for providing her with this arcane and apparently not very useful 'benefit'.

Her attitude might reflect her own unhappy past experiences with doctors and hospitals. Letters sent to the Women's Cooperative Guild for inclusion in *Maternity* often include descriptions of indignities suffered at the hands of rude or incompetent practitioners. A woman reported that when on the point of miscarriage she had been sent first to one hospital and then another. At the second she was examined, declared fit to go home, and 'bullied' for having come in the first place. 'All the time she was in the greatest pain and vomiting blood; she is now at home and will have to be taken to the first hospital at the end of the week, if nothing happens before.'[53] Rather than attempt to cope with that sort of professionalism and officialdom, working-class wives preferred to trust a midwife known to be competent and sympathetic. Here again the government, in an attempt to regulate and improve the practice of midwifery through licensing, succeeded for a time in further inconveniencing the lives of those most in need of their services. Lady Bell reports that since many Middlesbrough midwives either neglected or refused to pay their guinea registration fee, the practical result of this well-intentioned reform was to reduce the number of the town's practitioners.[54]

Working-class reaction to the National Insurance Act of 1911 remained a mixed one. Families fortunate enough to receive thoughtful, expert assistance appreciated the services rendered them. Those whose experience of the Act was nothing more than filling in forms or out-witting nosey 'sick visitors' were less enthusiastic. The secretary of the Bolton Card and Ring Room Operatives' Association explained to the Webbs how these 'spies', as he called them, harassed married women workers who refused to allow their illness to curtail their housework. ' "Sick Visitor" (really a spy) sent round to see women are not doing any work when taking sick pay,' the Webbs note of their conversation. 'Women dodge her quite successfully, e.g., by getting up early and doing work before Visitor is round, or by taking their soiled clothes to a neighbour's house and doing them there. Secretary thinks Visitors are too "conscientious" which in this case means hard on the people drawing benefit.'[55]

Unions had further quarrels with the Insurance Act, particularly with Part II which dealt with unemployment. The provision allowing workers to insure themselves through union agency, while gratifying in terms of increased membership, soon proved correspondingly burdensome in terms of the clerical strain imposed upon union bureaucracies. Unions welcomed the chance to grow, and publicly resented attempts on the part of insurance companies to 'steal' clients away from them. 'The vast sums spent by these societies for advertising and other expenses', Will Thorne complained at the 1912 TUC Conference, 'must have come mainly out of the people's pence . . . This is digging the grave of organized labour with a vengeance.'[56] But though the unions were keen to have the new members which National Insurance promised them, they were uncertain how to come to terms with the increased administrative responsibilities that were part of that same promise. Annual reports after 1911 reflect the general confusion and occasional resentments of both leadership and rank and file. Most unions found it necessary to enlarge their staffs: the Ironfounders, for example, in August 1912, reported the addition of two organizers, three junior assistant secretaries 'for Trade Union work', and a clerk to handle insurance problems.[57] Workers at branch level begrudged expenditure on functionaries of this kind. E. L. Poulton, general secretary of the Boot and Shoe Operatives, had to reprimand his membership for its shortsightedness in this regard. It was a waste of valuable experience, he wrote, that officers should be kept at work on routine matters 'when by the expenditure of a few extra shillings per week upon competent clerical assistance the officers could be doing work which would mean not only greater efficiency, but would in the aggregate mean hundreds of pounds extra yearly going into the pockets of the members . . .'[58]

Union officials chafed at governmental bureaucracy much as rank and file chafed at union officialdom. Particular wrath descended upon the umpire whose task it was to decide what class of worker was to be permitted association under the Act. 'The Act has installed this gentleman as a law unto himself,' the general secretary of the Sheet Metal Workers declared in his annual report for 1913. 'Consequently *he cannot be appealed against* but he has the power to review his own decision upon what may be regarded by him as fresh evidence. We have therefore to grin and abide until we can satisfy him.'[59] Reaction was not all negative. While Ben Tillett thundered against the Act because it denied workers a share in its control, others admitted its benefits, in terms both of payments made and domestic disaster averted, and of a broader and younger, if not necessarily more committed, membership.[60]

The nature of the reaction is of less importance than the fact that events demanded reaction of some sort. Historians can debate the extent to which the working class welcomed social reform. Certainly, with the exception of old-age pensions, all the welfare schemes enacted in the years before the First World War encountered at least some measure of working-class opposition when proposed; confusion followed by disappointment when enacted; and gradual acceptance as time taught men and women what, and what not, to expect. What historians must acknowledge is that by 1914 working men in factories, their wives at home, and their children at school, were being pressed to come to terms with the blessings and demands of social legislation, to accept new material benefits along with new social duties. The worker had to be weaned from the belief that he might in some way be corrupted by having received assistance, and made to see that the country might be the stronger if he would only accept his government's support. Throughout the nineteenth century the English middle class did its best to make him learn that first lesson; now, in the twentieth, its reform-minded heirs encouraged him to understand the second. That their task of re-education was arduous and frustrating speaks eloquently of the thoroughness with which Victorian middle-class statesmen and philanthropists had catechized their working-class pupils.

They had taught them more than one lesson, however. While devising one set of regulations to help the worker live his life a bit more comfortably and securely as a worker, they had devised another to insure that his chance to live his life as something other than a worker would never amount to much. What the working class learned of authority at the hands of the Victorian middle class made it cherish its independence all the more. The state – its police and its inspectors, its directives and its circulars – threatened the working class in a way the middle class never fully understood. The state was part of 'them', an alien imposition which workers and their families had tried their best to fend off or ignore. Circumstance was now forcing the working class to face directly the implications of massive middle-class intervention. The middle class, anticipating a welcome, was surprised at the frequency with which it encountered confrontation. To expect anything else was to expect the working class to unlearn the experiences of the past one hundred years.

213

That experience had included a general increase in real wages during the second half of the nineteenth century for a majority of the English working class. The economist Leone Levi estimated in 1885 that working-class real income had risen by 59 per cent since 1851.[61] As income improved, a significant drop in the cost of living and the importation of large quantities of cheap food combined to provide a decent life for at least some families, leading them to take an improving standard of living for granted.

Very suddenly, shortly after the beginning of the century, the pattern changed. Real wages began an irregular decline. Board of Trade figures for the years 1905 to 1912 showed that among skilled and unskilled workers in the building, engineering, and printing trades, the mean percentage increases in rates of wages in 88 towns and cities surveyed were a meagre 1·9 per cent and 2·6 per cent for builders; 5·5 and 3·9 for engineers; and 4·1 for compositors. These figures compared unfavourably with those for previous years. Chiozza Money estimated that whereas actual earnings had increased generally by from 15 to 18 per cent from 1886 to 1906, they had remained constant for the four following years. Further Board of Trade statistics published in 1912 recorded the fact that of the 916,366 workers reported to the Board as affected by wage changes in 1911, 399,362 had sustained decreases, as against 507,207 who had experienced increases and 9,797 who had remained at the same level.[62]

Meanwhile, prices rose sharply from 1907 to 1913. The Board of Trade's comparative figures for 1905 and 1912 showed a mean percentage increase of 1·8 in rent, 13·7 for food and coal, and 11·3 for rent, food, and coal combined. The reporters remarked that

> ... the rise in the cost of living, so far as the articles covered by the present Enquiry enter into the total expenditures of the working classes, is then shown to have been very marked in so short a period as 1905–1912, and if the comparison is extended back to the year of lowest prices, namely, 1896, the increase in food prices up to the year 1912 would appear to have been about 25 per cent.[63]

In 38 of the 88 towns surveyed, food prices had risen by anything from 13 to 15 per cent in eight years. Beef had increased in cost by 9·5 per cent; bacon by 32·1 per cent; cheese by 18·8 per cent; potatoes by 46·1 per cent; flour by 15·1 per cent; and coal by 22·5 per cent. Only tea and sugar cost less than they had – 3·8 and 0·2 per cent respectively.[64]

The result was a decline in real wages and, therefore, for many, in their general standard of living. Chiozza Money took the railway worker as a case in point. Earning an average of 25s 3d in 1899, he was making but 1½d more in 1909, while rising prices meant that he must in fact earn 27s 6d if he was to take home the real equivalent of his 1899 pay packet.[65] Railwaymen were probably among the most poorly dealt with both by their employers and by the economy. Other workers claimed to feel the pinch just as severely. 'Do you realize', asked the secretary of the Hollow-Ware Workers in a 1909 issue of *The Metalworker*, 'that you have suffered reductions to the tune of from 10 to 40 per cent, and that taking the extra cost of living into account you are now from 25 to 55 per cent worse off than you were [in 1889]?'[66] Chiozza Money argued in his 1912 book, *Things That Matter*, that Seebohm Rowntree's poverty line of 21s 8d, established in 1899 and representing the barest minimum upon which a family of five could be expected to exist, would need readjustment to 24s 1d if it was to reflect the current cost of living.[67] By 1914, two years later, wages had begun to catch up with prices. But the race was uneven, and especially exasperating for the general worker who, if he bothered himself at all with statistics, took little consolation from the fact that the worst was over, the worst having left him economically exhausted and a good deal poorer than he thought he ought to be.[68]

Economists might point out to him that he and his family lived better than his grandfather – or even his father – had. The lesson was cold comfort to men and women victimized by rising expectations. Chiozza Money argued that the time had come to acknowledge those expectations with a new 'poverty line' which would afford men, women and children not just necessities but an opportunity to enjoy life and to partake occasionally of its pleasures. His suggested weekly sum of 41 shillings included 1s 3d for amusements and holidays and 1s 6d for drink, tobacco, newspapers and books.[69] The suggestion reflected the fact that workers were growing increasingly unwilling to live a less than decent, comfortable life. More and more they held, as E. H. Phelps Brown has written, 'that the payment of a wage determined not by supply and demand but by human needs and common decency should be a first charge upon their industry'.[70] Social workers were discovering, Seebohm Rowntree reported, that young slum dwellers were experiencing a 'deepening discontent' as they contemplated the possibility of a future no brighter than their fathers'. 'When they marry they want to take their wives to better houses, away from the wretched environments in which they were brought up.'[71] Having learned to take gradual improvement for granted, they naturally resented an economic bind that now destined them to less, as they continued to look for more.

Their frustration must be squared with that apparently contradictory fatalism characteristic of so many within the working class. 'Rising expectations' did not include the hope of sudden riches or of dramatic change. They generally extended no further than the price of the family's food or the condition of its lodgings. Meat three times a week, rather than twice; three bedrooms for six people, rather than two: these were the normal hopes. Their modest extent reflected the limited goals of the men and women who had grown accustomed to taking them for granted. Their very modesty produced correspondingly greater disappointment and anxiety when they were not reached. 'Working-class women have grown more refined,' wrote one of the most articulate contributors to *Maternity*. 'They desire better homes, better clothes for themselves and their children, and are far more self-respecting and humble than their predecessors. But the strain to keep up to anything like a decent standard of housing, clothing, diet, and general appearance, is enough to upset the mental balance of a Chancellor of the Exchequer.'[72]

When personal anxiety turned to anger, many assumed that anger was fuelling the working-class unrest which marked the years before the First World War in England. 'The causes of this unrest are not far to seek,' the president of the Amalgamated Society of Railway Servants declared in a characteristic address of 1911:

> The great rise in the cost of living has not been met by a corresponding increase of wages – indeed, in many cases the earnings have been less. When there has been an increase it has been so small as not seriously to alter the balance in favour of the workers.[73]

The Parliamentary Labour Party agreed, introducing a resolution in 1913 'that this House is of opinion that the recent industrial disturbances are caused by a deplorable insufficiency of wages, which has persisted notwithstanding a great expansion of national wealth and a considerable increase in the cost of living'.[74]

The explanation appeared logical at the time, serving to justify to spokesmen for the working class and, they hoped, to the world in general the extraordinary spate of agitation that seemed to have labour in its grip. Statistics suggest the extent of the unrest, and its intensity. Union membership during the years 1911 to 1914 expanded markedly, with 1911 and 1913 experiencing the greatest percentage of growth (22 per cent and 21 per cent, respectively). Total membership in all unions rose by over 60 per cent from 1910 to 1914; membership in the 'new unions' – dockers, transport workers, general labourers – increased by far greater proportions. Membership in the Workers' Union increased from 5,000 to over 20,000 in six months.[75]

The tremendous surge in membership was not due entirely to increased militancy; the national insurance scheme accounted for much of the sudden expansion. But national insurance did not explain the spread of strike activity which, during the 1911–14 period, was as marked as was the growth of the unions which called their men out. From an average of 480 strikes per year for the years 1907 to 1910, the figures leap upward: 872 in 1911, 834 in 1912, 1,459 in 1913, and 972 in 1914 (a number that would have been much higher had not England gone to war in August). Figures for the total number of working days lost are more erratic, though they are generally higher from 1911 to 1914 than from 1907 to 1910.[76]

Observers at the time were prepared to believe that the activity and the unrest stemmed primarily from the fact that living costs had risen faster than wages. Sir George Askwith, the Liberal government's peripatetic negotiator, attributed the workers' discontented mood to economic distress:

> Trade had been improving, but employers thought too much of making up for some lean years in the past, and of making money, without sufficient regard to the importance of considering the position of their workpeople at a time of improvement of trade. Prices had been rising, but no sufficient increase of wages and certainly no general increase, had followed the rise.[77]

The argument has continued to convince most historians, though few have troubled to discover the extent to which the strikes were a conscious and direct reaction to increased living costs. Strikes that workers may have considered aggressive – demands for more take-home pay – may have been unconsciously defensive reactions to a decline in real wages of which the workers were themselves only dimly aware. Henry Pelling, who considers the question thoughtfully in an essay on the pre-war labour unrest, concludes by putting little stock in the rising cost-of-living thesis. He suggests, instead, that the low unemployment figures for the years 1911 to 1914 (never higher than 3·3 per cent) explain the increased pressure of working-class demands.[78] The masters needed the men, and the men took advantage of that need to press their claims. We can agree with Pelling without dismissing as irrelevant the factor of a decline in real wages. The related factors of the decline and the low unemployment rate gave workers both their grievance and their power to articulate it.

Other historians seeking explanations for the militant mood have attempted to link it with Continental syndicalism and with efforts by political activists such as Tom Mann to bring the movement to England.

Few, however, have pressed the suggestion much further than George Dangerfield, who, in *The Strange Death of Liberal England*, contents himself with the observation that syndicalism was 'a convenient expression for a new energy'.[79] The expression was Continental in accent, if not in intent. It borrowed its theory and its tone from Europe. Yet, though syndicalism did appeal to some younger trade unionists and enjoyed a measured success within the railway unions, it did so on English, rather than Continental terms. Lacking a revolutionary vocabulary of their own, English radicals used syndicalists' words to demand not *syndicates* but industrial unions and more militant anti-capitalism. They spoke with the kind of generalized rhetoric employed by W. C. Anderson, chairman of the ILP, in his annual address in 1912:

> The cause of the labour unrest is Labour's subjection to capitalism and the growth of social consciousness. Great monopolies, making huge profits, sweat and starve their workpeople. Rent and dividend take bigger and bigger slices of the national income, wages stand still or go back, the cost of living goes up, and employment is precarious and insecure. The pomp and arrogance of wealth and luxury was never so marked and cynical as in our own day; the contrast between wealth and poverty never so vivid and arresting.[80]

To say that the syndicalists made little permanent headway is not to say that the working class remained aloof from agitation or indeed from occasional violence. Though some historians have expressed surprise that both England and Europe did not experience greater unrest, in view of the sharp check on earning power sustained by the working class in the pre-war years, the surprise of many alive at the time was at the extent and bitterness of the disorders. Askwith, dispatched in the summer of 1911 to mediate at Hull, reported the remark of a town councillor who had experienced Paris during the Commune 'and had never seen anything like this ... he had not known there were such people in Hull – women with hair streaming and half nude, reeling through the streets, smashing and destroying.'[81] Those with a sense of the past might have derived consolation from the memory that working-class history in the nineteenth century was marked by violence: Captain Swing, plug plots, Sheffield outrages, Bloody Sunday. The disturbances of 1911 and after seemed to possess a quality of their own, however. Something – the ever-increasing numbers involved, the restless never-ceasing pattern of agitations – fused them into an expression of mass dissatisfaction and mass uncertainty that lent them an unprecedented and alarming quality. 'Nothing of the kind has ever happened before on such a gigantic scale since the world began,' the Workers' Union trumpeted in its 1911 *Annual Report*.[82] And so it seemed to many.

A belief that the world had never seen the like before contributed to the general confusion which appears to have been a further hallmark of the period. Historians have remarked upon the almost haphazard way in which railwaymen, miners, and transport workers formed their Triple Alliance. As E. H. Phelps Brown notes, the agreement laid the members 'under no obligation to strike together, or indeed to do anything save to consult one another before proceeding with a major issue. . . . Nonetheless, it was understood to have pledged all to back the cause of each. Nothing could have been less thought out.' How to explain the thoughtlessness? Phelps Brown continues:

> That [the alliance] should ever have been adopted can be explained only by the amount of unemployment among railwaymen and the transport workers that the coal strike had caused in 1912, prompting the thought that if all must be in it together in practice they might as well go in with a will; and by the sense of an impending general clash, a civil war between capital and labour, that was strong at that time of so many clashes.[83]

'The sense of an impending clash' is the sense of the evidence. It must be read along with that almost apocalyptic sense of occasion which was persuading men and women to consider their situation unique, and that further sense of confusion leading them to react without knowing quite what it was they were doing. The mood was one that needs to be explained by more than reference to a loss of spending power on the part of the working class as a whole, or to a heightened political militancy on the part of a few spokesmen. Explanation rests upon an understanding of the extent to which the working class depended upon tradition, and then upon a recognition of the challenges tradition faced in this period. All the pressures we have analysed – those of a redefined class consciousness and of continuing urban migration, of expanding political opportunity and of increasing state intervention, of higher prices and lower wages – all these pressures threw men and women back upon tradition for psychological shelter, while at the same time forcing them to discard the very habits of mind and action they needed to sustain themselves.

Confused by the challenge to traditions they had relied upon, working-class men and women were not at all sure what to do. Some contented themselves with doing little or nothing. Those who did something, did many apparently contradictory things at once: they sent unions their dues and resisted their union's leadership; they hid from the state while collecting its pensions; they voted Labour and agreed that Labour accomplished nothing.

There was little joyous anticipation in them as they surveyed their strange-seeming world. Dangerfield is mistaken when he describes them as 'wanting to live, to take chances, to throw caution to the winds'.[84] Instead, they felt themselves trapped, and would willingly have joined a St Helens glassworker of 1970 in his angry, frustrated shout: 'People are getting so that they want to burst out of their skins and take a swipe at somebody for having pressure put on them.'[85] One does catch the sense of *élan* Dangerfield evokes in the memoirs of some of the middle-class intellectual rebels of the time. Leonard Woolf describes the excitement of taking part 'in the springtime of a con-scious revolt against the social, political, religious, moral, intellectual, and artistic institutions, beliefs, and standards of our fathers and grand-fathers'. 'It seemed', he writes, 'as though human beings might really be on the brink of becoming civilized. It was partly the feeling of relief and release as we broke out of the fog of Victorianism.'[86] The past had provided Woolf with security enough to allow him to cast it aside as dead weight. Working-class men and women were not so anxious to disencumber themselves. Their past, which had left most of them insecure and uncertain, seemed to them their best anchor against an even more uncertain future.

# Chapter references

## 1 The working class

1 E. P. Thompson, *The Making of the English Working Class* (London, 1963), pp. 9–11.

2 George Dangerfield's *The Strange Death of Liberal England* (New York, 1961; 1st ed., 1935), remains the starting point for any analysis of Edwardian attitudes and beliefs.

3 Gareth Stedman Jones, 'Working-class Culture and Working-class Politics in London, 1870–1900: Notes on the Remaking of a Working Class', *Journal of Social History*, VII (Summer, 1974), p. 498.

4 Guy Routh, *Occupation and Pay in Great Britain, 1906–60* (London, 1965), pp. 4–5.

5 In their survey of Swansea, Colin Rosser and Christopher Harris found that 23 per cent of the manual workers questioned called themselves middle class. Of the non-manual workers, 32 per cent called themselves working-class. *The Family and Social Change* (London, 1965), p. 92.

6 Richard Hoggart, *The Uses of Literacy* (London, 1957), p. 70.

7 Geoffrey Gorer, *Exploring English Character* (London, 1955), p. 34.

8 John Foster, 'Nineteenth-century Towns – a Class Dimension', *The Study of Urban History*, H. J. Dyos, ed. (London, 1968), pp. 281–99; and *Class Struggle and the Industrial Revolution* (London, 1974). He lists a homogeneous working-class population and the presence of a resident bourgeoisie as necessary for the establishment of a potent working-class political force. Harvey Mitchell has suggested the same conclusion with respect to French working-class politics. See Harvey Mitchell and Peter Stearns, *Workers and Protest* (Itasca, Ill., 1971), p. 51.

9 Words and music by C. W. Murphy, 1902. Reprinted in *Music Hall Song Book*, Peter Gammond, ed. (Newton Abbot, 1975), pp. 75–7.

10 Colin MacInnes, *Sweet Saturday Night* (London, 1967), p. 149.

11 See Eric Hobsbawm's essay on the labour aristocracy for percentages of workers in skilled trades earning wages at this level or above in 1906. 'The Labour Aristocracy in Nineteenth Century Britain', *Labouring Men* (London, 1964), p. 288.

12 Both Robert Roberts and Walter Greenwood, authors respectively

of the autobiographical *The Classic Slum* (Manchester, 1971), and *There Was A Time* (London, 1969), had shopkeeper parents. Yet both obviously consider that they led working-class lives as children and grew up possessing working-class consciousnessses.

*13* See Part One, 'The Liberty Tree', E. P. Thompson, *The Making of the English Working Class*.

*14* George Bourne [George Sturt], *Change in the Village* (London, 1966, 1st ed., London, 1912), pp. 71–72.

*15* See Ch. 7 for a discussion of working-class attitudes toward religion.

*16* H. A. Clegg, Alan Fox, and A. F. Thompson, *A History of British Trade Unions Since 1889* (Oxford, 1964), I, 309. These decisions are treated in detail on pp. 308–311

*17* 'The effect was to render actionable any communication even of the most peaceable kind, except by letter, between strikers and men whom the employer was seeking to engage.' *Ibid.*, p. 309.

*18* B. C. Roberts, *The Trades Union Congress* (London, 1958), p. 173, n. 1.

*19* *Annual Report*, Dock, Wharf, Riverside and General Labourers' Union, 1895 (London, 1896), p. 11.

*20* See Henry Pelling, 'Trade Unions, Workers and the Law', *Popular Politics and Society in Late Victorian Britain* (London, 1968), pp. 62–81.

*21* E. A. Parry, *The Law and the Poor* (London, 1914), p. 53.

*22* Anna Martin, *The Mother and Social Reform* (London, 1913), p. 25.

*23* *Ibid.*, p. 27.

*24* *Ibid.*, p. 28. Hoggart observes that the atmosphere of the courtroom itself was most intimidating to the poor: 'It so often has an air of sour, scrubbed, provincial puritanism and mortification ... The magistrates' clerk may be one who likes to "run people around a bit"; the figures on the bench seem to peer down from a distant world of middle-class security and local importance.' *The Uses of Literacy*, p. 64. In a short story, however, William Pett Ridge called attention to another aspect of the legal fray, its excitement: 'The great advantage ... is that, whether one wins or loses, there has been, for a space, the limelight, and a chance of playing a leading part, and, moreover, a holiday from domestic and other duties.' 'Court-Martial', *London Types* (London, 1926), p. 38.

*25* Paul Thompson and Thea Vigne, 'Family Life and Work before 1918' Project. Interview No. 126, p. 41; No. 237, p. 51. Hereafter cited as 'T and V interviews'.

*26* Walter Greenwood, *Love On the Dole* (London, 1972), p. 13.

*27* Christopher Pulling, *They Were Singing – and What They Sang About* (London, 1952), p. 97. John Taylor has discovered that in workingmen's clubs in the 1880s and 1890s a favourite winter entertainment was 'Judge and Jury class', in which cases were tried in mock solemnity. One of Charles Booth's informants called the practice a 'nasty and pernicious institution', presumably because of the number of affiliation and breach of promise cases tried. John Taylor, *From Self-Help to Glamour, The Workingman's Club, 1860–1972* (Oxford, 1971), pp. 34–35.

28 George Lansbury's acid assessment of Toynbee Hall: '[Its] one solid achievement ... has been the filling up of the bureaucracy of government and administration with men and women who went to East London full of enthusiasm and zeal for the welfare of the masses, and discovered the advancement of their own interests and the interests of the poor were best served by leaving East London to stew in its own juice while they became members of Parliament, cabinet ministers, civil servants ... My sixty years' experience in East London leaves me quite unable to discover what social influence Toynbee Hall or any other similar settlement has had on the life and labour of the people.' *My Life* (London, 1928), pp. 129–131.

29 Richard Price, 'The Workingmen's Club Movement', *Victorian Studies*, XV (December, 1971), p. 130. The working men had deposed their middle-class directors by the mid-1880s.

30 H. B. Phillpott, *London at School* (London, 1904), p. 294.

31 Robert Roberts, *The Classic Slum*, p. 109.

32 *Daily Herald*, January 2, 1913, p. 2.

33 T and V interviews, No. 253, p. 52.

34 Gordon Allport, *The Nature of Prejudice* (New York, 1958), p. 143.

35 Richard Hoggart, *The Uses of Literacy*, pp. 64–65.

36 Evidence for this abounds in the Thompson and Vigne interviews.

37 T and V interviews, No. 117, p. 22.

38 T and V interviews, No. 356, p. 62.

39 Eric Hobsbawm, 'The Labour Aristocracy in Nineteenth Century Britain', *Labouring Men*, p. 274.

40 S. J. Chapman, F. J. Marquis, 'The Recruiting of the Employing Classes From the Ranks of the Wage-Earners in the Cotton Industry', *Journal of the Royal Statistical Society*, LXXV (1912), p. 305.

41 E. Collet, M. Robertson, *Family Budgets: Being the Income and Expenses of Twenty-Eight British Households, 1891–1894* (London, 1896), pp. 23–25.

42 Robert Roberts, *The Classic Slum*, p. 2. Roberts's father was a skilled mechanic who used his wife's legacy to buy a grocer's shop in Salford.

43 C. V. Butler, *Domestic Service* (London, 1916), p. 38.

44 *Ibid.*, p. 37.

45 Clementina Black, 'London', *Married Women's Work*, Clementina Black, ed. (London, 1917), p. 17.

46 Eric Hobsbawm, 'The Labour Aristocracy in Nineteenth Century Britain', *Labouring Men*, p. 297.

47 Charles Booth, *Life and Labour of the People in London* (London, 1891, 3rd ed.), V, 101. Yet writing in 1904, he expressed a belief that 'social influences' would prevail to draw workers and clerks closer together. Third series (London, 1904), VII, 400.

48 *The Club and Institute Journal*, July 6, 1892, quoted in John Taylor, *From Self-Help to Glamour: The Workingman's Club, 1860–1972*, p. 24.

49 See below, pp. 134–142. Also Eric Hobsbawm, 'The Labour Aristocracy in Nineteenth Century Britain', *Labouring Men*, p. 289.

50 L. G. Chiozza Money, *Riches and Poverty* (London, 1905, 3rd ed.), pp. 53, 161.

51 *The Woman Worker*, 10 February 1909. p. 131.

52 In Postgate, *The Builders' History* (London, 1923), p. 343.

53 T and V interviews, No. 185, p. 53.

54 Eric Hobsbawm, 'The Labour Aristocracy in Nineteenth-Century Britain', *Labouring Men*, p. 273.

55 Skilled workers expressed the threat they felt from the semi-skilled in their battles to maintain wage differentials between themselves and their 'inferiors'. In this they were largely successful during the pre-war period, due to trade union pressure and the continued operation of custom. See J. W. F. Rowe, *Wages in Practice and Theory* (London, 1928), pp. 106–111.

56 Shoes, their condition or their lack, could serve as a caste mark. The daughter of a Liverpool wool-sampler in one of the T and V interviews identifies 'the lower type' as those whose children went without shoes. T and V interviews, No. 46, pp. 55–56.

57 *Ibid.*, No. 206, p. 27.

58 *Ibid.*, No. 312, p. 31. The informant's father was a miner; her mother a laundress, in Stoke-on-Trent.

59 *Ibid.*, No. 253, p. 64.

60 Report on Children in Receipt of ... Poor Law Relief, Parliamentary Papers (1910–11), LII, Cd. 5037, 32.

61 T and V interviews, No. 87, p. 15. Thompson and Vigne record an instance in which a boy reproved his mother for swearing at his stepfather: 'I had to tell her about her bad language ... because being a choirboy I didn't like it. And from then on I don't think I ever heard her use a bad word while we were in the house, but she could Lord Mayor ['swear' in rhyming slang] if she went off. Oh, she was a real cockney.' No. 417, pp. 49–50.

62 The widow of a tin-shearer, born in 1887, quoted in Colin Rosser and Christopher C. Harris, *The Family and Social Change*, p. 84.

63 Arthur Morrison, 'To Bow Bridge', *Tales of Mean Streets* (New York, 1921; 1st ed., London, 1894), p. 54.

64 *The Woman Worker*, 14 April 1909, p. 342. Mrs M. S. Pember Reeves echoes the plea in her survey of London working-class households: 'The women who do

not insist upon doing the impossible, and fretting themselves and everybody else because it is impossible, often arrive at better results – with regard at least to the human beings around them – than the women who put furniture first and the peace of the family second . . . The mother who is not disturbed by a little mud on the floor has vitality left to deal with more important matters.' *Round About a Pound a Week* (London, 1914), p. 19.

65 'Respectability did not mean church attendance, teetotalism, or the posssssion of a Post Office savings account [i.e. middle-classness]. It meant the possession of a presentable Sunday suit and the ability to be seen wearing it.' Gareth Stedman Jones, 'Working-class Culture and Working-class Politics', *Journal of Social History*, VII (Summer, 1974), p. 475. See also Geoffrey Crossick, 'The Labour Aristocracy and its Values: a Study of Mid-Victorian Kentish London', *Victorian Studies*, XIX (March, 1976), pp. 306–7.

## 2 House, neighbourhood and kin

1 T. R. Marr, *Housing Conditions in Manchester and Salford* (Manchester, 1904), p. 43. In 1902, although there were by that time 45,686 water closets within the city, there remained 73,915 pail closets, 20,532 midden privies, 10,598 wet middens, and 740 dry middens. *Ibid.*, p. 45.

2 Bristol Adult School Union, *The Facts of Bristol's Social Life* (Bristol, 1915), p. 1; A. Wohl, 'The Housing of the Working Classes in London, 1815–1914', *The History of Working-Class Housing*, Stanley D. Chapman, ed. (Newton Abbot, 1971), p. 35.

3 Reginald A. Bray, 'The Boy and the Family', *Studies of Boy Life in Our Cities*, E. J. Urwick, ed. (London, 1904), p. 13.

4 Charles Booth, *Life and Labour of the People in London*, Third Series, final volume, 89.

5 Reginald Bray, 'The Boy and the Family', *Studies of Boy Life in Our Cities*, E. J. Urwick, ed., p. 20.

6 Some fastened corks on the end of the wires, to soften the blow against the bedroom window. See H. Crapper, 'Reminiscences of a Woolsorter' (1967), typescript in the Bradford Public Library [B 677.31042.CRA], p. 6.

7 Alexander Paterson, *Across the Bridges* (London, 1918; 1st ed. 1911), p. 7.

8 Clementina Black and Adele Meyer, *Makers of Our Clothes* (London, 1909), pp. 11–12.

9 Winifred Blatchford, 'The Borough', *The Woman Worker*, September 1, 1909, p. 199.

10 Charles Booth, *Life and Labour of the People in London*, IV, 91.

11 W. G. Hoskins, *The Making of the English Landscape* (London, 1971), p. 228.

12 Manchester Diocesan Conference, *Report* [on] *the Housing of the Poor* (Manchester, 1902), p. 8;

George Haw, *The Englishman's Castle* (London, 1906), p. 8; Charles Booth, *Life and Labour of the People in London*, IX, 6–9.

13 B. Seebohm Rowntree, A. C. Pigou, *Lectures on Housing* (Manchester, 1914), pp. 4, 13.

14 T. R. Marr, *Housing Conditions in Manchester and Salford*, p. 35.

15 M. S. Pember Reeves, *Round About a Pound a Week*, p. 49.

16 B. Seebohm Rowntree, A. C. Pigou, *Lectures on Housing*, pp. 8–9, 12. In other cities, Coventry and Nottingham, for example, the existence of open fields, owned in common and hence almost impossible to sell to developers, choked off expansion for years, and helped guarantee an overcrowded city centre, even after the fields were finally developed. See Roy Church, *Economic and Social Change in a Midland Town* (London, 1966), p. 162; John Prest, *The Industrial Revolution in Coventry* (Oxford, 1960), pp. 22–24.

17 John Whitburn, *The Housing Problem in Newcastle and District* (Newcastle, 1902), p. 10; Sidney Pollard, *The History of Labour in Sheffield* (London, 1959), p. 89; E. Wilkinson, *The Town That Was Murdered* (London, 1939), pp. 72–74.

18 See M. Kaufman, *The Housing of the Working Classes and the Poor* (London and Edinburgh, 1907), p. 51.

19 See J. C. Thresh, *Enquiry into the Causes of the Excessive Mortality in No. 1 District, Ancoats* (Manchester and Salford, 1889), p. 11.

Arthur Morrison's story, 'All That Messuage', tells of the unsuccessful attempt of a working-class landlord to make a go of it. He ends in the poorhouse.

20 In Leeds, it was by no means the poorest alone who lived in back-to-backs. In 1895, 53,000 such houses – an estimated two-thirds of the total in the borough – were inhabited by 214,000 men, women, and chidren. E. Bowmaker, *The Housing of the Working Classes* (London, 1895), p. 19. See also, M. W. Beresford, 'The Back-to-Back House in Leeds, 1787–1937', in *The History of Working-Class Housing*, Stanley D. Chapman, ed., pp. 93–132.

21 J. C. Thresh, *Enquiry . . .* , p. 31.

22 B. Seebohm Rowntree, A. C. Pigou, *Lectures on Housing*, p. 4.

23 B. Seebohm Rowntree, *Poverty, A Study of Town Life* (London, 1910; 1st ed., 1901), p. 166.

24 S. D. Chapman, J. N. Bartlett, 'The Contribution of Building Clubs and Freehold Land Society to Working-Class Housing in Birmingham', *The History of Working-Class Housing*, Stanley D. Chapman, ed., pp. 232–234. Rooms in model houses built in and around Newcastle after the turn of the century were somewhat larger: living rooms, 13 by 15 feet (although in this case there was no parlour, only a 9' by 7' scullery); bedrooms, 13' by 11' and, in one case 10' by 15'. *North of England Exhibition of Model Cottages* (Darlington, 1908).

25 Walter Besant, *East London* (London, 1901), p. 119.

26 Reginald A. Bray, 'The Boy and the Family', *Studies of Boy Life in our Cities*, E. J. Urwick, ed., pp. 19–20.

27 *Ibid.*, pp. 17–18.

28 T and V interviews, No. 30, p. 3. The informant was a boilermaker from Stoke-on-Trent. Later the family was able to move to a three-bedroom house.

29 M. S. Pember Reeves, *Round About a Pound a Week*, pp. 31–32.

30 M. L. Eyles, *The Woman in the Little House* (London, 1922), p. 40. Robert Roberts claims that 'any tenants daring to use a colour gaily different would have been damned as playing "baby house", a serious indictment in a world where the activities of childhood and maturity were strictly separated.' *The Classic Slum*, p. 18.

31 Reginald A. Bray, 'The Boy and the Family', *Studies of Boy Life in Our Cities*, E. J. Urwick, ed., p. 34. Bray lived for several years in East London.

32 M. S. Pember Reeves, *Round About a Pound a Week*, pp. 38–39.

33 The best surveys of model tenement building are two books by John N. Tarn: *Working-Class Housing in Nineteenth Century Britain* (London, 1971); and *Five Per Cent Philanthropy* (Cambridge, 1973).

34 John Whitburn, *The Housing Problem in Newcastle and District*, p. 32. Whitburn estimated that the cost per room of a tenement was £116, of a cottage, £56. His figures included the price of land and assumed that the tenement would be 'centrally located'.

35 See E. Bowmaker, *The Housing of the Working Classes*, p. 80; [City and County of Newcastle], *The Housing of the Poor* (Newcastle, 1890), p. 4. Booth, in his discussion of model dwellings in London, lists rents ranging from 2s 9d to 'about' 4s 3d per room per week. (*Life and Labour of the People in London*, II, 254–256.) See also, A. S. Wohl, 'The Housing of the Working Classes in London', *The History of Working-Class Housing*, Stanley D. Chapman, ed., p. 39. Rent for a three-room London County Council flat in 1914 ranged from 6s 7½d to 12s 3d. *Ibid.*, p. 41.

36 Charles Booth, *Life and Labour of the People in London*, II, 272–275.

37 For a typical set of regulations, see [City of Manchester] *The Housing of Working Classes* (Manchester, 1904), pp. 44–46.

38 Paul Thompson, *Socialists, Liberals, and Labour: The Struggle for London, 1885–1914* (London, 1967), p. 123. George Gissing described the Farringdon Rd buildings in London in the same fashion: 'Vast, sheer walls, unbroken by even an attempt at ornament; row above row of windows in mud-coloured surface, upwards, upwards, lifeless eyes, mirky openings that tell of barrenness, disorder, comfortlessness within ...' *The Nether World* (London, 1889), III, 58.

39 Charles Booth, *Life and Labour of the People in London*, II, 265.

40 Reginald Bray, 'The Boy and the Family', *Studies of Boy Life in*

*Our Cities*, E. J. Urwick, ed., pp. 37–38. Thomas Bell, however, argues that tenement life in Glasgow helped to draw workers together and radicalize them. *Pioneering Days* (London, 1941), pp. 18–19.

41 B. Seebohm Rowntree, May Kendall, *How the Labourer Lives* (London, 1913), p. 11. The population of Birmingham increased from 400,757 in 1881 to 525,960 in 1911; that of Leeds from 309,126 to 445,568; that of Liverpool from 552,425 to 746,566; that of Manchester from 341,508 to 712,427; that of Middlesbrough from 55,288 to 104,787; that of St Helens from 57,234 to 96,566. Parliamentary Papers, 1881, XCIV; 1911, LXXI.

42 Arthur Redford, *Labour Migration in England* (Manchester, 1964), p. 189.

43 Will Thorne, *My Life's Battles* (London, 1925), pp. 52–54. Will Crooks, another trade unionist, was forced to leave London when he was blacklisted as an agitator in the 1870s. He found cooperage work in Liverpool and sent for his wife and child. Upon the latter's death, however, Mrs Crooks persuaded her husband to return with her to London, which they did, walking the seven miles from Euston station to their lodgings in Poplar. George Haw, *The Life Story of Will Crooks* (London, 1917), pp. 46–47. The Thompson and Vigne interviews contain numerous references to this sort of long-range migration:

A Shropshire labourer and his sister who move to Keighley, Yorkshire, in search of work; a Manchester moulder who, within a year of his daughter's birth, had moved from Manchester to Sheffield, to Darlington. T and V interviews, No. 162, pp. 70–71; No. 168, p. 2.

44 Clara Collet, 'Women's Work in Leeds', *Economic Journal*, I (1891), 471–472.

45 The number of agricultural labourers decreased from 807,608 to 583,751 between 1881 and 1901. B. Seebohm Rowntree, May Kendall, *How the Labourer Lives*, p. 16.

46 See J. W. House, *North-Eastern England. Population Movements and the Landscape Since the Early Nineteenth-Century* (Newcastle, 1954), p. 48.

47 Alfred Williams, *Life in a Railway Factory* (London, 1915), p. 115.

48 T and V interviews, No. 187, p. 1. Booth noted, however, that few workers in some of the newer, mechanical trades – bicycles, sewing machines, etc. – appeared willing to follow firms out of London, for fear that they would end up earning less, and despite the fact that the cost of living was almost invariably lower: 'And so the *work* goes, and with the exception of a few foremen or leading hands, retained at old rates because indispensable, the workmen do *not* follow.' Charles Booth, *Life and Labour of the People in London*, V, 297.

49 J. W. House, *North-Eastern England*, p. 14.

50 E. M. Sneyd-Kynnersley, *H.M.I. Some Passages in the Life of One of H. M. Inspectors of Schools* (London, 1908), p. 56.

51 Raymond Williams, *The County and the City* (London, 1973), pp. 189–190.

52 G. N. Barnes, *From Workshop to War Cabinet* (London, n.d.), p. 24. His friend eventually emigrated to South Africa.

53 See Michael Anderson, *Family Structure in Nineteenth Century Lancashire* (Cambridge, 1971), p. 26.

54 Charles Booth, *Life and Labour of the People in London*, VII, 123. 'It is the result of conditions of life in great towns, and especially in this the greatest town of all, that muscular strength and energy get gradually used up,' Booth wrote in a previous volume. 'The second generation of Londoner is of lower physique and has less power of persistent work than the first, and the third generation (where it exists) is lower than the second.' I, 553.

55 Gareth Stedman Jones, *Outcast London* (London, 1971), pp. 142–151. He argues that it was not degeneration that kept so many native-born Londoners on relief roles. Instead, their appearance there 'can be attributed to the critical condition of the traditional London crafts, and to the drying up of alternative casual sources of employment'. p. 146.

56 T and V interviews, No. 399, p. 1.

57 Mona Wilson, E. G. Howarth, *West Ham* (London, 1907), p. 35.

58 City and County of Newcastle, *The Housing of the Poor*, p. 3.

59 M. Kaufman, *The Housing of the Working Classes and of the Poor*, pp. 24–25.

60 A woman in Bethnal Green pronounced on the advantages of such a situation in an interview with Michael Young and Peter Willmott in the 1950s: 'If [her husband] has words with the boss or doesn't like anything, he can walk out and get into another firm. In Lancashire there was only one firm in his trade.' *Family and Kinship in East London* (London, 1957), p. 92.

61 Robert Roberts, *The Classic Slum*, p. 116.

62 *Bradford Pioneer*, May 16, 1913, p. 1.

63 A. S. Wohl, 'The Housing of the Working Classes in London, 1815–1914', *The History of Working-Class Housing*, Stanley D. Chapman, ed., p. 33. An attempt to assess with any accuracy the exact degree to which workers and their families were moving from older into newer working-class areas must await detailed census studies of the sort Anderson has undertaken for Preston. Statistical evidence readily available, however, does support the thesis of movement away from the city centre. Census returns record a general decline in the population of older working-class districts. In Whitechapel, the population dropped from 78,768 in 1901 to 67,740 in 1911; in Poplar, from 168,822 to 162,442;

in St Saviour's, Southwark, from 23,319 to 19,351; in Ancoats, Manchester, from 44,040 to 40,206; in St Martin's, Birmingham, from 66,019 to 55,208. A working-class community such as South Shields, however, continued to grow – from 107,729 to 118,099. *Census of England and Wales, 1911* (London, 1912), pp. 11, 12, 264, 206, 320. Figures such as these help to explain the situation H. J. Dyos has discovered in Camberwell, his data confirming the fact of increasing migration from the central districts to the suburbs, and the additional fact that these suburban slums were becoming 'settling tanks for submerged Londoners'. His studies also support the impression of a constant turnover in inhabitants. See H. J. Dyos, 'The Slums of Victorian London', *Victorian Studies*, XI (September, 1967), pp. 30–31.

64 On this point, see Gareth Stedman Jones, *Outcast London*, p. 88.

65 Paul de Rousiers, *The Labour Question in Britain* (London, 1896), p. 297.

66 M. S. Pember Reeves, *Round About a Pound a Week*, pp. 39–40.

67 Michael Anderson, *Family Structure in Nineteenth Century Lancashire*, p. 40.

68 See *ibid.*, p. 159, for a discussion of this practice.

69 *Ibid.*, pp. 57–58.

70 *Ibid.*, p. 154.

71 *Ibid.*, p. 3. In this, I think Anderson perhaps fails to deal as thoroughly as he might have with the psychological advantages to be gained by such a relationship.

72 Madeline Kerr, *The People of Ship Street* (London, 1958); Colin Rosser, Christopher Harris, *The Family and Social Change*; J. M. Mogey, *Family and Neighbourhood* (Oxford, 1956). For further material, see Ferdynand Zweig, *The Worker in an Affluent Society* (New York, 1961); and Elizabeth Bott, *Family and Social Network* (London, 1971, 2d ed.).

73 Michael Young, Peter Willmott, *Family and Kinship in East London*, p. 104.

74 Doris Rush, 'Spare Time in the Black Country', *Living in Towns*, Leo Kuper, ed. (London, 1953).

75 Madeline Kerr, *The People of Ship Street*, p. 25.

76 Michael Young, Peter Willmott, *Family and Kinship in East London*, p. 104.

77 Madeline Kerr, *The People of Ship Street*, pp. 102–103.

78 J. M. Mogey, *Family and Neighbourhood*, p. 94.

79 Madeline Kerr, *The People of Ship Street*, p. 24.

80 Michael Young, Peter Willmott, *Family and Kinship in East London*, p. 116.

81 C. F. G. Masterman, 'The Problem of South London', *The Religious Life of London*, Richard Mudie-Smith, ed. (London, 1904), p. 214.

82 Women's Cooperative Guild, *Maternity* (London, 1915), pp. 56, 160, 69–70, 83, 102, 105–106, 112.

83 'The domestic result of [frequent migration] is that young women are separated from the mother on whom, in case of illness, they are often as touchingly dependent as in the earliest days of their lives, and have to meet their time of trial in towns where they have no relatives and probably no friends, and nothing to rely upon but the uncovenanted mercies of their landlady.' M. Loane, *From Their Point of View* (London, 1908), p. 139. Loane was a district nurse in London.

84 J. M. Mogey, *Family and Neighbourhood*, p. 87.

85 *Idem*. Suzanne Keller has found that 'as [working-class] families become more self-reliant and independent of group influences in matters pertaining to child-rearing, style of life, and interests, they rely even less on neighbours'. *The Urban Neighborhood* (New York, 1968), p. 34.

86 Mrs M. L. Eyles, a social worker, commented in 1922: 'The communism of the old days, for mutual protection, has given place to an unnatural individualization.' *The Woman in the Little House*, p. 87. The evidence of Young and Willmott and others argues that an almost instinctive neighbourliness, bred into working-class communities over time, in turn succeeded the individualization which Eyles deplores.

87 N. Elias and J. L. Scotson, *The Established and the Outsiders* (London, 1965), p. 39.

88 Robert Roberts, *The Classic Slum*, p. 10.

89 M. Loane, *From Their Point of View*, p. 23.

90 Michael Young, Peter Willmott, *Family and Kinship in East London*, pp. 161–162.

91 Madeline Kerr, *The People of Ship Street*, p. 116.

92 J. M. Mogey, *Family and Neighbourhood*, pp. 75–76. This tolerance assumes an economically homogeneous neighbourhood and relatively benign economic climate.

93 Suzanne Keller, *The Urban Neighborhood*, p. 24.

94 T and V interviews, No. 399, p. 38.

95 Robert Tressell, *The Ragged Trousered Philanthropists* (London, 1955), p. 79.

96 T. R. Marr, *Housing Conditions in Manchester and Salford*, p. 61.

97 Robert Roberts, *The Classic Slum*, pp. 4–6.

98 T and V interviews, No. 125, p. 37.

99 *Ibid.*, No. 417, p. 7.

100 Alexander Paterson, *Across the Bridges*, p. 6.

101 Edwin Pugh, 'A Small Talk Exchange', originally published in *A Street in Suburbia* (London, 1895), and reprinted in *Working-Class Stories of the 1890s*, P. J. Keating, ed. (London, 1971), pp. 101, 105. For a description that tallies with Pugh's fictional account, see Edward Cadbury, *et al.*, *Women's Work and Wages* (London, 1906), pp. 176–178.

102 *Ibid.*, No. 215, p. 42.

103 *Ibid.*, No. 126, p. 57.

104 T and V interviews, No. 86, p. 17; No. 8, p. 27; No. 237, p. 88.

105 For further discussion on this point, see Peter Willmott and

Michael Young, *Family and Class in a London Suburb* (London, 1960), pp. 128–129; Suzanne Keller, *The Urban Neighborhood*, pp. 10, 21.

106 Celia Reiss, 'Reading', *Married Women's Work*, Clementina Black, ed. (London, 1915), p. 214 (the data was collected in 1909–1910).

107 Margaret L. Davies, *Cooperation in Poor Neighbourhoods* ([n.p.], 1899), p. 9.

108 E. Collet and M. Robertson, *Family Budgets*, p. 20. The brother, however, refused to come to the plumber's house because, in the plumber's words, 'Being a simple man and a little better off, he thinks as my place ain't quite good enough for him.' p. 22.

109 T and V interviews, No. 51, p. 43.

110 *Ibid.*, No. 54, p. 27.

111 Charles Booth, *The Aged Poor* (London, 1894), pp. 325–326.

112 *Ibid.*, p. 326; Booth noted that while most children were willing to see their parents receive outdoor relief, almost all would do whatever they could to keep their aged parents from the workhouse.

113 *Ibid.*, p. 327.

114 M. L. Eyles, *The Woman in the Little House*, p. 49.

115 M. Loane, *From Their Point of View*, p. 37.

116 The Thompson and Vigne interviews contain a great deal of material on funerals. One informant recalls his mother's willingness to spend a third of her husband's £9 legacy on a dark suit for her son (interview No. 14, p. 26); another recalls collecting in the neighbourhood for funeral wreaths and then placing them outside the house of the bereaved on a chair 'so all the neighbours ... as they walked backwards and forwards could look at it and see what they bought with it' (interview No. 334, p. 39). Arthur Morrison's 'On the Stairs' is the story of a woman who is willing to deny her son medicine in order that she can provide him with both mutes and plumes at his funeral. Her neighbour, who buried her husband with £12 insurance received from the Odd Fellows, spurs her on: 'I 'ad a oak caufin an' a open 'earse. There was kerridge for the family an' one for 'is mates – two 'orses each, an' feathers, an' mutes; an' it went the furthest way round to the cimitry. "Wotever 'appens, Mrs. Manders," says the undertaker, "you'll feel as you've treated 'im proper, nobody can't reproach you over that." ' *Tales of Mean Streets*, pp. 156–157.

117 Louis Wirth, 'Urbanism As a Way of Life', *On Cities and Social Life*, Louis Wirth, ed. (Chicago, 1964), pp. 74–75.

118 Talcott Parsons, 'The Social Structure of the Family', *The Family: Its Function and Destiny*, Ruth N. Anshen, ed. (New York, 1949), pp. 192, 200–201.

119 C. F. G. Masterman, 'Realities at Home', *The Heart of the Empire*, C. F. G. Masterman, ed. (London, 1902), p. 8.

120 E. J. Urwick, *Studies of Boy Life in Our Cities*, p. 266.

121 T and V interviews, No. 31, p. 14.

122 Arthur Morrison, *Tales of Mean Streets*, p. xix.

## 3 Women at home

1 Peter Townsend, *The Family Life of Old People* (London, 1957), p. 113.

2 Madeline Kerr, *The People of Ship Street*, p. 15.

3 Peter Townsend, *The Family Life of Old People*, p. 27.

4 J. M. Mogey, *Family and Neighbourhood*, p. 78.

5 Colin Rosser, Christopher Harris, *The Family and Social Change*, p. 13.

6 T and V interviews, No. 281, pp. 91–92.

7 Robert Roberts, *The Classic Slum*, p. 27. Loane deplored the fact that networks so consistently developed only within the matriarchal connection: 'The poor waste nearly half the strength and sweetness of family life by a tendency to ignore all relationships but those on the mother's side.' M. Loane, *From Their Point of View*, p. 34.

8 Alexander Paterson, *Across the Bridges*, p. 22.

9 BBC Archives. LP 26422, X20298; T and V interviews, No. 237, p. 15; No. 8, p. 2; Jack Jones, *My Lively Life* (London, 1928), p. 16; George Haw, *The Life Story of Will Crooks*, p. 3.

10 Peter Townsend, *The Family Life of Old People*, p. 98.

11 Robert Smillie, *My Life For Labour* (London, 1924), p. 10.

12 Josephine Klein, *Samples from British Culture* (London, 1965), I, 39.

13 Robert R. Dolling, *Ten Years in a Portsmouth Slum* (London, 1896), p. 42.

14 T and V interviews, No. 12, p. 56. The speaker eventually found his future wife at the local W.E.A.

15 *Ibid.*, No. 117, p. 14.

16 Walter Greenwood, *Love on the Dole*, p. 125. A tabulation made by Rowntree of working-class marriages in York in 1898–1899 showed the largest percentage of women marrying at 21, with far fewer doing so in the years immediately before that age than in the years immediately after. Only 2·56 per cent of skilled women workers and 5·23 per cent of the unskilled, for example, married at 18. Rowntree discovered a marked difference in the ages at which skilled and unskilled males married: nearly one-third of the latter married before age 23, while only one-fifth of the former did so. B. Seebohm Rowntree, *Poverty*, pp. 400, 139.

17 T and V interviews, No. 417, pp. 35–36. In this instance, the speaker's stepfather slept apart from his wife, on her orders, 'owing to his habits getting a little bit – I suppose – out of hand', p. 38. See also M. Loane, *The Queen's Poor* (London, 1906), p. 7.

18 Charles Booth, *Life and Labour of the Poor in London*, Third Series, final volume, 41–42; Women's Cooperative Guild, *Working Women and Divorce*

(London, 1911), p. 8. Women complained that although a husband could divorce his wife for one act of unfaithfulness, a wife was forced to put up with continued unfaithfulness if unaccompanied by cruelty and desertion. Even when a husband brought another woman into the house to live, wives had no grounds to proceed against him. The Women's Cooperative Guild recommended that grounds for divorce include cruelty and desertion by themselves, refusal to maintain, and serious incompatibility. 'No other subject in the life of the Guild has aroused such immediate response and elicited such strength and earnestness of feeling.' pp. 4, 14, 20.

19 Richard Titmus, *Essays on the 'Welfare State'* (London, 1963, 2d ed.), p. 110.

20 Elizabeth Bott, *Family and Social Network*, p. 64.

21 Alfred Williams, *Life in a Railway Factory*, pp. 256–257.

22 Words by Albert Chevalier, music by Charles Ingle, 1893. Reprinted in *Music Hall Song Book*, Peter Gammond, ed., pp. 40–42.

23 T and V interviews, No. 162, p. 52.

24 Geoffrey Gorer, *Exploring English Character*, p. 125.

25 Robert Roberts, *The Classic Slum*, pp. 27, 74.

26 Richard Hoggart, *The Uses of Literacy*, p. 83.

27 T and V interviews, No. 162, p. 44; No. 51, p. 7; No. 39, p. 16.

28 Women's Cooperative Guild, *Maternity*, p. 30; T and V interviews, No. 213, p. 52; *Maternity*, pp. 187–188.

29 T and V interviews, No. 92, p. 16.

30 Robert Roberts, *The Classic Slum*, pp. 37–38.

31 Women's Cooperative Guild, *Maternity*, pp. 9–10. Booth suggested that infant mortality was in itself a cause of further pregnancies: 'The death of a child, especially if it be a baby, does tend to bring about the birth of another. If child mortality could be checked the birth rate would certainly be reduced, and a terrible waste of every kind would be prevented.' Charles Booth, *Life and Labour of the People in London*, Third Series, final volume, 20.

32 Women's Cooperative Guild, *Maternity*, pp. 60–61.

33 Walter Greenwood, *There Was a Time*, p. 50. See also Robert Roberts, *The Classic Slum*, pp. 34, 100; M. L. Eyles, *The Woman in the Little House*, p. 159. Margaret Bondfield reported that by 1910 the practice of abortion was 'fairly widespread' among low-wage textile workers in Yorkshire. *A Life's Work* (London, 1949), p. 40.

34 M. S. Pember Reeves, *Round About a Pound a Week*, p. 9.

35 Women's Cooperative Guild, *Maternity*, p. 37.

36 'We were all allotted a task, and we did the shopping, and she'd [Mother] teach somebody how to do the cooking, or Father would help with the cooking, at the weekends, certainly.' T and V

interviews, No. 75, p. 28. About one-third of the women who responded to the Women's Co-operative Guild mention their reliance upon a nurse for at least a short period following confinement.

37 Women's Cooperative Guild, *Maternity*, p. 89.

38 *Ibid.*, pp. 172–173, 29, 44, 119. Out of 800 households surveyed by Lady Bell in Middlesbrough, 275 had experienced the loss of one child or more. *At the Works* (Newton Abbot, 1969; 1st ed., London, 1907), p. 193.

39 Women's Cooperative Guild, *Maternity*, p. 32. This account is confirmed by the report, published as well by the Guild, of conditions in 1875. 'In some instances the poor unfortunate patient was not allowed to have her face and hands washed for days. I remember hoping I should never have a baby if I could not be washed.' *Life as We Have Known It*, Margaret L. Davies, ed. (London, 1931), p. 31.

40 Elizabeth Bott, *Family and Social Network*, p. 73.

41 Women's Cooperative Guild, *Maternity*, pp. 27–28.

42 M. L. Eyles, *The Woman in the Little House*, p. 142.

43 More typical, in this regard: 'I am pleased to tell you that I am fortunate in having a considerate husband, which of course is something to be thankful for. My heart aches when I think of women who have brutes to contend with.' Women's Cooperative Guild, *Maternity*, p. 139.

44 Statistics on 'average' wages were normally calculated on an assumption of a 'full normal week'. A. L. Bowley reckoned, on that basis, that the median wage in 1906 was 29s 4d. Fifty-one per cent of all workers, excluding miners and agricultural labourers, earned less than 30 shillings a week in that year. Average earnings, again in 1906, in textiles were 22·9 shillings; in printing, 27·2; in metal manufacture, 28·1; in building, 27·4. A. L. Bowley, *Wages and Income in the United Kingdom Since 1860* (Cambridge, 1937), pp. 42, 51.

45 Charles Booth, *Life and Labour of the People in London*, I, 197.

46 B. Seebohm Rowntree, *Poverty*, p. 44.

47 H. A. Mess, *Casual Labour at the Docks* (London, 1916), p. 44.

48 Robert Tressell, *The Ragged Trousered Philanthropists*, pp. 54–58.

49 *Trade Unionist*, February 6, 1892, p. 4.

50 T and V interviews, No. 51, p. 48. Lady Bell discovered that in over one-third of the houses she visited in Middlesbrough, the wife did not know how much her husband earned, the implication being that in at least that many instances, the husbands paid over a portion of their wages and withheld the rest. Lady Bell, *At the Works*, p. 78. For further observations see Geoffrey Gorer, *Exploring English Character*, p. 132; Ferdynand Zweig, *Labour, Life and Poverty* (London, 1949), p. 11; Michael Young, Peter

Willmott, *Family and Kinship in East London*, pp. 26–27.

51 A. L. Bowley, 'Earners and Dependents in English Towns in 1911', *Economica*, I (May, 1921), 110.

52 B. Seebohm Rowntree, *The Human Needs of Labour* (London, 1918), p. 34.

53 Robert Roberts, *The Classic Slum*, p. 61. Margaret L. Davies paints a rather different picture: 'I have by me one of these "books", and a pathetic history may be read between the various little items marked down each week ... The constant entries are: lard, 4d or 2d; tobacco, 1½d or 3d; bread, 4d or 8d; and pork occasionally, 1s 1d. The first addition in this book, with the balance owing from the previous one, amounts actually to £5 4s 6½d. At the end of each week's account you find a partial paying up, entered as "cash", the amount varying from 8s 11d to 6s. After this has gone on for many weeks, the debt always remaining at about £5, there is a change in the entries. The woman has been told she will be summoned if she doesn't pay up the whole amount. No more purchases are recorded – but instead "cash 1s", "cash 1s", all down the pages.' Davies ends with a satisfied note that the woman paid up the debt and is now a co-operator. Margaret L. Davies, *Co-operation in Poor Neighbourhoods*, p. 11.

54 Charles Booth, *Life and Labour of the People in London*, Third Series, final volume, 82.

55 T and V interviews, No. 137, p. 42. Walter Greenwood has much to say about the life of a pawnshop proprietor in *There Was a Time* and *Love on the Dole*.

56 Mrs Pember Reeves fulminated against the loan sharks but admitted there was little to be done about them: '[The housewife] does not know the law, and she could not afford to invoke its aid if she did know it. She goes on being bled because it is the locally accpted rate of a "lender".' *Round About a Pound a Week*, p. 73. See also Charles Booth, *Life and Labour of the People in London*, Third Series, final volume, pp. 82–83.

57 M. S. Pember Reeves, *Round About a Pound a Week*, pp. 22–23.

58 B. Seebohm Rowntree, A. C. Pigou, *Lectures on Housing*, p. 7; A. L. Bowley, A. R. Burnett-Hurst, *Livelihood and Poverty. A Study in the Economic Conditions of Working-Class Households in Northampton, Warrington, Stanley, and Reading* (London, 1915), pp. 23–24. Rowntree found that in York the very poorest spent up to 29 per cent of their income on housing. *Poverty*, p. 165.

59 Henry Studniczka, *Industrial Conditions in Europe*, Part I (Washington, 1910), p. 13; E. Bowmaker, *The Housing of the Working Classes*, pp. 71–72; T. R. Marr, *Housing Conditions in Manchester and Salford*, pp. 57–58; A. L. Bowley, A. R. Burnett-Hurst, *Livelihood and Poverty*, p. 19.

60 F. W. Laurence, 'The Housing Problem', *The Heart of the Empire*, C. F. G. Masterman, ed., p. 64; A. S. Wohl, 'The Housing of the Working Classes in London', *The History of Working-Class Housing*, S. D. Chapman, ed., pp. 37, 39.

61 B. Seebohm Rowntree, *The Human Needs of Labour*, p. 94. In his study of York, Rowntree's estimates were lower: 3s 3d a week for a man; 2s 9d a week for a woman; 2s 7d a week for a child over 8; 2s 1d for a child under 8. *Poverty*, p. 105. Booth's figure for the average amount spent for food per male adult per week in his lowest category was 2s 4½d. Charles Booth, *Life and Labour of the People in London*, I, 132.

62 L. G. Chiozza Money, *Things That Matter* (London, 1912), p. 267.

63 M. S. Pember Reeves, *Round About a Pound a Week*, pp. 81–83, 21.

64 Anna Martin, *The Married Working Woman* (London, 1911), p. 16.

65 *Ibid.*, p. 15.

66 Lady Bell, *At the Works*, p. 62.

67 T and V interviews, No. 187, p. 15.

68 Ben Turner, *About Myself* (London, 1930), p. 46.

69 T and V interviews, No. 43, p. 9.

70 Anna Martin, *The Married Working Woman*, pp. 14–15; see also T and V interviews, No. 320, p. 12.

71 J. C. Drummond, Anne Wilbraham, *The Englishman's Food* (London, 1939), p. 382.

72 Robert Roberts, *The Classic Slum*, p. 88.

73 M. S. Pember Reeves, *Round About a Pound a Week*, p. 79.

74 M. L. Davies, *Co-operation in Poor Neighbourhoods*, p. 12.

75 Alexander Paterson, *Across the Bridges*, p. 25.

76 M. L. Eyles, *The Woman in the Little House*, p. 74.

77 Robert Roberts, *The Classic Slum*, p. 87.

78 M. S. Pember Reeves, *Round About a Pound a Week*, p. 144.

79 *Ibid.*, p. 99. Milk cooperatives, started in St Helens, Liverpool and Battersea in 1903, charged 1s 6d a week for new babies and up to 2s a week for infants over seven months old. *Cooperative News*, January 24, 1903, p. 106.

80 Robert Tressell, *The Ragged Trousered Philanthropists*, pp. 52–3.

81 C. E. B. Russell, *Manchester Boys* (Manchester, 1905), p. 16.

82 D. J. Oddy, 'Working-Class Diets in Late Nineteenth-Century Britain', *Economic History Review*, XXIII, No. 2 (August, 1970), p. 321.

83 *Ibid.*, p. 320.

84 B. Seebohm Rowntree, *Poverty*, p. 234; D. N. Paton, J. C. Dunlop, Elsie Inglis, *A Study of the Dietaries of the Labouring Classes in Edinburgh* (Edinburgh, 1901), pp. 61–62; W. A. McKenzie, 'Changes in the Standard of Living in the United Kingdom, 1860–1914', *Economica*, I (October, 1921), p. 227.

85 B. Seebohm Rowntree, *Poverty*, p. 281.

86 *Ibid.*, pp. 393–399.

87 B. Seebohm Rowntree, *The Human Needs of Labour*, p. 127.

88 'Accounts of Expenditures of Wage-Earning Women and Girls', Parliamentary Papers, 1911, LXXXIX, Cd. 5963, 45.

89 B. Seebohm Rowntree, *Poverty*, p. 395.

90 A. L. Bowley, A. R. Burnett-Hurst, *Livelihood and Poverty*, p. 119; M. S. Pember Reeves, *Round About a Pound a Week*, p. 63.

91 The cotton winder who lived with her mother owned three blouses and a skirt that had been made at home, either by herself or her mother. 'Accounts of Expenditures', p. 45.

92 Robert Roberts, *The Classic Slum*, p. 23; H. Crapper, 'Reminiscences of a Woolsorter', p. 4.

93 T and V interviews, No. 136, p. 10. For further details see No. 206, p. 5; No. 176, p. 7; No. 137, p. 5.

94 M. Loane, *The Next Street But One* (London, 1907), p. 38.

95 M. L. Eyles, *The Woman in the Little House*, p. 98.

96 Ben Turner, *About Myself*, pp. 63–64.

97 M. S. Pember Reeves, *Round About a Pound a Week*, p. 51.

98 Joseph Rowntree, A. J. Sherwell, *The Temperance Problem and Social Reform* (London, 1900, 7th ed.), pp. 16–20. Seebohm Rowntree, in his study of York, discovered that comparatively large sums of money were being spent by the working class on gambling and betting as well. *Poverty*, pp. 143–144.

99 M. L. Davies, *Co-operation in Poor Neighbourhoods*, pp. 11–12. Lady Bell discovered that of 700 Middlesbrough workmen interviewed, 380 belonged to a sickness club, 80 belonged to two clubs, and 270 to none. *At the Works*, p. 119. In 1898, 34 Friendly Societies boasted a joint membership of 2,351,150 members. Bentley B. Gilbert, *The Evolution of National Insurance in Great Britain* (London, 1966), p. 170.

100 B. Seebohm Rowntree, *Poverty*, p. 272.

101 *Ibid.*, pp. 133–134. Note the remark of a Lancashire member of the Women's Cooperative Guild: 'If you want a saucepan, or a blanket, or a pair of clogs, you've either got to go without or save out of the food.' M. L. Davies, *Co-operation in Poor Neighbourhoods*, p. 9.

102 T and V interviews, No. 25, p. 8.

103 *Ibid.*, No. 113, p. 7; No. 47, p. 11. One Londoner recalls buying stale bread at a rate of four loaves for 2d. Bread normally sold for a bit under 3d a loaf. *Ibid.*, No. 399, p. 10.

104 M. S. Pember Reeves, *Round About a Pound a Week*, pp. 108–109.

105 Charles Booth, *Life and Labour of the People in London*, I, 142.

106 M. S. Pember Reeves, *Round About a Pound a Week*, p. 58.

107 T and V interviews, No. 75, p. 14.

108 See T and V interviews, No. 14, p. 15; also No. 184, p. 10: 'We'd all sit down together. Till the boys started working. Then of

course – we'd all sit down in penny numbers [separately] more or less because their times were different.'

109 *Ibid.*, No. 399, p. 27. The same man recalled walking by the restaurant where his mother worked and lowering a shopping bag on a string to the basement kitchen window, where his mother would fill it with food for the next day's meal. Once he was caught by a policeman, but his mother fixed the matter with sandwiches and cocoa for the bobby. *Ibid.*, p. 8.

110 Anna Martin, *The Mother and Social Reform* (London, 1913), pp. 15–16. See T and V interviews, No. 117, p. 11: 'Well to tell you the truth she'd so many of us [8] that when she gave us all food I don't even remember her sitting down and eating with us.' The speaker's father was dead; his mother a laundress.

111 Walter Greenwood, *Love on the Dole*, p. 11.

112 M. L. Eyles, *The Woman in the Little House*, p. 45; T and V interviews, No. 187, p. 10; No. 168, p. 35.

113 The older members of the household, particularly the males, might, instead, avail themselves of public baths.

114 T and V interviews, No. 126, p. 12.

115 Alexander Paterson, *Across the Bridges*, p. 8.

116 *Cotton Factory Times*, October 6, 1905, p. 8. One of Thompson and Vigne's informants recalled the Durham 'Spiritualist herbalist' for whom he had worked as odd

job lad: 'They had to keep a doctor really in case of an emergency and that sort of thing, you see, because she couldn't write any death certificate out . . . But on the general run of business she was as fine a lady as anybody may wish to meet . . .' T and V interviews, No. 266, p. 79.

117 *Ibid.*, No. 162, p. 12; No. 124, p. 13; No. 136, p. 60; No. 237, p. 11; No. 237, p. 37; No. 168, p. 17. See also Robert Roberts, *The Classic Slum*, pp. 97–100.

118 Lady Bell, *At the Works*, p. 232.

119 Both Rowntree and Bell mention horse-race betting as a fact of life with working-class women. Bell lamented her inability to persuade a woman with a £5 win to her credit to gamble no more: 'In the face of the £5 suddenly falling from the skies in the midst of a hard winter into a household earning 30s a week, it was difficult to persuade the winners that the chances were that it would not happen again.' *At the Works*, p. 257. See also *Betting and Gambling*, B. Seebohm Rowntree, ed. (London, 1905) pp. 72–73, 77.

120 Charles Booth, *Life and Labour of the People in London*, Third Series, VII, 277.

121 Lady Bell, *At the Works*, p. 162.

122 *Home Companion*, January 17, 1903, p. 16; June 27, 1903, p. 1.

123 *Reynolds's*, May 2, 1909, p. 9.

124 Richard Hoggart, *The Uses of Literacy*, pp. 105–106.

125 *Cotton Factory Times*, January 6, 1905. By 1911, however, the paper was running a story about labour unrest entitled 'A Girl of

Grit, or the Heroine of Downham Mills. A Story of Stress and Strife.' June 9, 1911.

126 Lady Bell, *At the Works*, p. 167.

127 T and V interviews, No. 253, p. 120.

128 Charles Booth, *Life and Labour of the People in London*, Third Series, final volume, 63.

129 *Ibid.*, p. 60.

130 Joseph Rowntree, A. J. Sherwell, *The Temperance Problem and Social Reform*, p. 85.

131 Charles Booth, *Life and Labour of the People in London*, Third Series, final volume, 62. Monday was often cited as the day when most women drank too much: 'We have our fling; we like to have a little fuddle on Monday.' *Idem.*

132 M. L. Eyles, *The Woman in the Little House*, p. 81.

133 Anna Martin, *The Mother and Social Reform*, p. 19.

## 4 Working wives and mothers

1 D. C. Marsh, *The Changing Social Structure of England and Wales* (London, 1958) p. 126. Figures are from the 1901 census, and include all females aged ten and over. The total of unemployed women was 9,018,000.

2 A. L. Bowley, 'Earners and Dependants in English Towns in 1911', *Economica*, II (May, 1921), p. 110. Bowley used 1911 census figures and the survey, *Livelihood and Labour*, which investigated Bolton, Warrington, Northampton, Reading, and Stanley. B. L. Hutchins, *Women in Modern Industry* (London, 1915), p. 234.

3 William Beveridge, *Changes in Family Life* (London, 1932), p. 76.

4 *Women in the Printing Trades*, J. R. MacDonald, ed. (London, 1904), p. 108; B. L. Hutchins, 'Yorkshire', *Married Women's Work*, Clementina Black, ed., p. 140.

5 T. R. Marr, *Housing Conditions in Manchester and Salford*, p. 13.

6 John Robertson, The Birmingham M.O.H.: 'Mortality in summer diarrhoea in 1904 was in the whole population about 30 times greater among bottle-fed children than among breast-fed children.' City of Birmingham Department of Health, *Report on Industrial Employment of Married Women and Infant Mortality* (Birmingham, 1910), p. 17. See also C. B. Hawkins, *Norwich: A Social Study* (London, 1910), p. 95. Yet W. Elkin, investigating the question in Manchester, reported that infant mortality appeared to be no greater in those families where the mother was at work than in those where she remained at home: 'The general condition of the town must be largely responsible, and again the question arises whether, when the income is small, the disadvantages of married women's employment are counteracted or not by the additional comfort derived from their wages.' W. Elkin, 'Manchester', *Married Women's Work*, Clementina Black, ed., p. 176.

7 B. L. Hutchins, 'Yorkshire', *Ibid.*, p. 136.

8 *Women's Trade Union Review*, January 1894, pp. 1–2.

9 W. Elkin, 'Manchester', *Married Women's Work*, Clementina Black, ed., p. 173. Figures in a similar survey support the conclusion that income was an important determinant of the cleanliness of houses. They argue as well, however, that houses managed by women who did not work were generally 'cleaner, tidier, and more comfortable' than the houses of women who did. The greater comfort might have reflected a husband's steady and adequate weekly wage, which would have made it unnecessary for his wife to supplement the family income. Again, the importance of money. Edward Cadbury, *et al.*, *Women's Work and Wages*, pp. 222–223.

10 207 per 1,000 births as opposed to 190 per 1,000 births. Department of Health, City of Birmingham, *Report on Industrial Employment of Married Women and Infant Mortality*.

11 B. L. Hutchins, 'Yorkshire', *Married Women's Work*, Clementina Black, ed., p. 142.

12 Department of Health, City of Birmingham, *Report on Industrial Employment of Married Women and Infant Mortality*, p. 8.

13 B. L. Hutchins, 'Yorkshire', *Married Women's Work*, Clementina Black, ed., p. 138.

14 Add the 4·2 per cent claiming their husbands were not giving them a large enough share of their earnings, the 5·3 per cent citing their husbands' drinking habits, the 8·4 per cent separated from their husbands, and the 6·3 per cent who were widows, and the case becomes all the more striking. *Ibid.*, p. 135.

15 Department of Health, City of Birmingham, *Report on Industrial Employment of Married Women and Infant Mortality*, p. 11.

16 W. Elkin, 'Manchester', *Married Women's Work*, Clementina Black, ed., p. 165.

17 *Cotton Factory Times*, February 3, 1905, p. 3.

18 Clementina Black, 'Introduction', *Married Women's Work*, p. 4.

19 T and V interviews, No. 284, p. 3.

20 *Women in the Printing Trades*, J. R. MacDonald, ed., p. 67.

21 T and V interviews, No. 162, p. 67.

22 Edward Cadbury, *et al.*, *Women's Work and Wages*, pp. 63, 70, 76–77.

23 See W. Elkin, 'Manchester', *Married Women's Work*, Clementina Black, ed., p. 168.

24 L. W. Papworth, 'Charwomen', *Ibid.*, pp. 111–112.

25 See, e.g., Charles Booth, *Life and Labour of the People in London*, II, 319. Booth reports that women who took home work for West End tailors could earn up to 20 shillings a week during 'the season'; at other times, their earnings fell to from 5 to 8 shillings. See also Clementina Black, *Sweated Industry and the Minimum Wage* (London, 1907), p. 29.

26 Edward Cadbury, *et al.*, *Women's Work and Wages*, p. 147: 'It is so frequently asserted that the married women work [at home] for pocket-money or "to pass the time", that it was surprising to find that only ·04 per cent did so.' See also Clementina Black, 'London', in *Married Women's Work*, p. 103. Clara Collet, who surveyed women's work for Booth, found few married women engaging in home-work for pocket money. Wages were in most cases too paltry. 'Whenever I have found women who said they worked at very low rates they have been working for their living and for that of their children; their husbands have always been men disabled or out of work.' Charles Booth, *Life and Labour of the People in London*, I, 451. Of a group of home-working box makers she surveyed, Clementina Black observed: 'There does not appear to be one woman in this group whose work was not necessary if the family was to be kept above the barest level of subsistence; and there were several without whose earnings even that could not be attained.' *Married Women's Work*, p. 60.

27 B. L. Hutchins, *Women in Modern Industry*, pp. 216, 218, 225, 226.

28 Edward Cadbury, *et al.*, *Women's Work and Wages*, pp. 122–123; Mona Wilson, E. G. Howarth, *West Ham*, p. 158, 167.

29 Clementina Black, *Sweated Industry and the Minimum Wage*, pp. 27–28. Of the 107 sheets ex-amined in the first week, 78 recorded wages in the 5 to 10 shilling range; of the 98 examined in the second week, 64 fell within the same range.

30 *Handbook of the 'Daily News' Sweated Industries Exhibition*, Richard Mudie-Smith, ed. (London, 1906), pp. 74–75.

31 *Ibid.*, p. 53.

32 Clementina Black, Adele Meyer, *Makers of Our Clothes*, p. 151.

33 Edward Cadbury, *et al.*, *Women's Work and Wages*, p. 138.

34 Charles Booth, *Life and Labour of the People in London*, I, 469–471; *Women in the Printing Trades*, J. R. MacDonald, ed., p. 105.

35 W. Elkin, 'Manchester', *Married Women's Work*, Clementina Black, ed., p. 167.

36 B. L. Hutchins, 'Yorkshire', *Ibid.*, pp. 130–131.

37 *Women in the Printing Trades*, J. R. MacDonald, ed., pp. 50–51.

38 B. L. Hutchins, 'Yorkshire', *Married Women's Work*, Clementina Black, ed., p. 131.

39 Annual Report, Trade Union Congress, 1900 (London, 1900), p. 86.

40 Margaret Bondfield, *A Life's Work*, p. 38.

41 B. L. Hutchins, 'Yorkshire', *Married Women's Work*, Clementina Black, ed., p. 133.

42 *Women in the Printing Trades*, J. R. MacDonald, ed., p. 65.

43 Edward Cadbury, *et al.*, *Women's Work and Wages*, p. 39.

44 Barbara Drake, *Women in the Engineering Trades* (London, 1917), pp. 7–8.

45 Edward Cadbury, *et al.*, *Women's Work and Wages*, p. 40.

46 C. B. Hawkins, *Norwich: A Social Study* p. 43.

47 Annie Abram, 'Newcastle', *Married Women's Work*, Clementina Black, ed., p. 195. In Leek and Macclesfield, where the tradition of women's employment was more firmly established, 'only one or two of the husbands object to their wives working, and among these the most decided opinions are attributed to one long dead'. Margery Lane, 'Leek and Macclesfield', *Ibid.*, pp. 212–213.

48 LSE. Webb, Trade Union Documents, A. XLVII, f. 1. Total membership was 3,281,881.

49 *Women's Trade Union Review*, January, 1900, p. 5.

50 *Women in the Printing Trades*, J. R. MacDonald, ed., p. 29; *Women's Trade Union Review*, January, 1900, p. 13.

51 Mary Agnes Hamilton, *Mary Macarthur* (London, 1925), p. 36.

52 Alan Fox, *History of the National Union of Boot and Shoe Operatives, 1874–1957* (Oxford, 1958), pp. 309–311.

53 Annual Report, Manchester, Salford, and District Women's Trade Union Council, 1911, pp. 7ff.

54 Annual Report, Women's Trade Union League, 1901, p. 5.

55 LSE. Webb, Trade Union Documents, A. XLVII, ff. 38–39. Mary Macarthur wrote of experiences reflecting the same attitude. When working to organize a union 'I was very enthusiastic, and perhaps I gave it to them in too glowing terms. They believed me, and gave me their names to join the union. Ten days afterwards the girls looked more inclined to mob me than anything else, and I asked them what was the matter. "Oh, we've been ten days in the Union and our wages haven't gone up yet." ' Mary Agnes Hamilton, *Mary Macarthur*, p. 35.

56 LSE. Webb, Trade Union Documents, A.XLVII, f. 248.

57 *Ibid.*, ff. 49, 234. Isabella Ford of the Leeds Tailoresses Union wrote in 1897: 'It is a common excuse amongst the girls with whom we have to do that they do not join the union because their fathers do not urge them or care for them to do so.' *Women's Trade Union Review*, July, 1897, pp. 19–20.

58 *Ibid.*, January 15, 1892, p. 4.

59 LSE. Webb, Trade Union Documents, A. XLVII, f. 111.

60 Clementina Black, Adele Meyer, *Makers of Our Clothes*, p. 145. In 1905 a total of 151 inspectors served a total of 255,000 registered work places. L. G. Chiozza Money, *Riches and Poverty*, p. 115.

61 *Women's Trade Union Review*, October, 1894, p. 6; July, 1899, p. 5; April, 1900, pp. 22–23; January, 1904, pp. 1–2; July, 1912, pp. 12–13.

62 Annual Report of the Chief Inspector of Factories and Workshops, 1911. Parliamentary Papers, 1912–1913, XXVI, Cd. 6259, 89–90.

63 T and V interviews, No. 47, p. 21.

64 *Women's Trade Union Review*, October, 1898, p. 20.

65 Clementina Black, *Sweated Industry and the Minimum Wage*, pp. 25–26.

66 Gertude Tuckwell, 'The Regulation of Women's Work', B. L. Hutchins, *Women in Modern Industry*, p. 7.

67 Annual Report, Women's Trade Union League, 1909, p. 12.

68 T and V interviews, No. 87, p. 36.

69 Walter Greenwood, *There Was a Time*, p. 31.

70 *Women's Trade Union Review*, April, 1901, p. 9.

71 *Ibid.*, October, 1898, p. 22; Annual Report, Women's Trade Union League, 1908, pp. 9–10; Annual Report of the Chief Inspector of Factories and Workshops, 1911. Parliamentary Papers, 1912–1913, XXV, Cd. 6239, 138.

72 Charles Booth, *Life and Labour of the People in London*, I, 466.

73 Edward Cadbury, *et al.*, *Women's Work and Wages*, pp. 194–195; Priscilla Moulder, 'Factory Morals', *Woman Worker*, February 24, 1909, p. 169; Margaret Bondfield, *A Life's Work*, p. 41.

74 LSE. Webb, Trade Union Documents, A. XLVII, f. 45.

75 Jessie Boucherett, Helen Blackburn, *The Condition of Working Women and the Factory Acts* (London, 1896), p. 10. See also Lilian Harris, *Abolition of Overtime for Women* (Manchester, 1896); *Women in the Printing Trades*, J. R. MacDonald, ed., p. 87.

76 Labour Party Archives, LRC 31/173., n.d.

77 Independent Labour Party, *Labour Laws for Women* (London, 1900), n.p.

78 *Handbook of the 'Daily News' Sweated Industries Exhibition*, Richard Mudie-Smith, ed., pp. 30–31. Pay was 3s 6d per gross for the best flowers; 1s 4d per gross for button roses, to include, as well, a gross of small buds.

79 Clementina Black, *Sweated Industry and the Minimum Wage*, pp. 3–6.

80 *Life As We Have Known It*, Margaret L. Davies, ed., p. 87. The commentator was a Stockport hat worker.

81 Walter Greenwood, *There Was a Time*, p. 54.

82 'L.D.', 'Wage-earning Wives in a Slum', *Married Women's Work*, Clementina Black, ed., p. 120.

83 Clementina Black, 'London', *ibid.*, p. 27.

84 Anna Martin, *The Married Working Woman*, pp. 10–11.

## 5 Husbands and fathers

1 T and V interviews, No. 30, tape 2, p. 7.

2 *Ibid.*, No. 34, p. 162.

3 Robert Blatchford, 'His First Wife', *Woman Worker*, March 3, 1904, p. 194: 'What I say is, any woman can manage a good man if she gets about it in a workmanlike way.'

4 Arthur Barton, *Two Lamps in Our Street* (London, 1967), p. 65.

5 T and V interviews, No. 168, p. 7; No. 54, p. 4; No. 253, p. 7;

No. 266, p. 97; No. 187, p. 9; No. 28, p. 20.

6 *Ibid.*, No. 31, p. 10; No. 54, p. 3.

7 Michael Young, Peter Willmott, *Family and Kinship in East London*, p. 27.

8 T and V interviews, No. 43, p. 16; No. 47, p. 16; No. 270, p. 29.

9 *Working Days*, Margaret A. Pollock, ed. (London, 1926), p. 168.

10 Charles Booth, *Life and Labour of the People in London*, Third Series, final volume, 48.

11 Reginald A. Bray, 'The Boy and the Family', *Studies of Boy Life in our Cities*, E. J. Urwick, ed., pp. 48–49.

12 George Gissing, *Thyrza* (London, 1907), pp. 53–54.

13 In some households the tenor of Sunday ritual was determined by religious orthodoxy: 'We daren't touch anything on a Sunday. One day had to be different from the rest.' T and V interviews, No. 117, p. 16.

14 L. V. Shairp, 'Leeds', *Social Conditions in Provincial Towns*, Helen Bosanquet, ed. (London, 1912), pp. 79–80.

15 John Law, *Out of Work* (London, 1888), p. 44.

16 George Haw, *Christianity and the Working Classes* (London, 1906), p. 83.

17 For attitudes toward religion, see below, pp. 199–200.

18 Arthur Morrison, 'Squire Napper', *Tales of Mean Streets*, pp. 182–183.

19 T and V interviews, No. 12, p. 22.

20 Richard Price, 'The Workingmen's Club Movement and Victorian Social Reform Ideology', *Victorian Studies* XV (December, 1971), p. 125.

21 *Club and Institute Journal*, December 17, 1892. Quoted in John Taylor, *From Self-Help to Glamour: the Workingman's Club, 1860–1972*, p. 62. Taylor gives an excellent description of the manner in which the change from politics to sociability took place.

22 Henry Solly, *Working Men's Social Clubs and Educational Institutes* (London, 1904, 2nd ed.), pp. 179–181.

23 T. S. Peppin, *The Club-Land of the Toiler* (London, 1895), pp. 79–83.

24 M. D. Stocks, *Fifty Years in Every Street* (Manchester, 1945), p. 19.

25 B. T. Hall, 'The Rev. Henry Solly: The Harvest of His Work', in Henry Solly, *Working Men's Social Clubs and Educational Institutes*, p. 209.

26 *Ibid.*, p. 206.

27 B. Seebohm Rowntree, *Poverty*, pp. 327–330.

28 T. S. Peppin, *The Club-Land of the Toiler*, pp. 93–94.

29 Joseph Rowntree, A. J. Sherwell, *The Temperance Problem and Social Reform*, pp. 6, 77–78.

30 T. R. Marr, *Housing Conditions in Manchester and Salford*, p. 27.

31 Robert Roberts, *The Classic Slum*, p. 94.

32 Quoted in Joseph Rowntree, A. J. Sherwell, *The Temperance Problem and Social Reform*, pp. 9–10.

33 *Ibid.*, p. 82; Charles Booth, *Life and Labour of the People in London*, Third Series, final volume, 69.

34 *Ibid.*, pp. 70–71; Robert Roberts, *The Classic Slum*, p. 93; C. F. G. Masterman, 'Realities at Home', *The Heart of the Empire*, C. F. G. Masterman, ed., p. 25.

35 B. Seebohm Rowntree, *Poverty*, pp. 316–325.

36 Robert Tressell, *The Ragged Trousered Philanthropists*, p. 315.

37 Robert Roberts, *The Classic Slum*, pp. 93–94.

38 T and V interviews, No. 155 p. 4.

39 Robert Blatchford, *Dismal England* (London, 1899), p. 106.

40 C. Stella Davies, *North Country Bred* (London, 1963), p. 26.

41 Ben Turner, *About Myself*, p. 83; Brian Harrison, *Drink and the Victorians* (London, 1971), p. 332.

42 T and V interviews, No. 52, p. 19.

43 Alfred Williams, *Life in a Railway Factory*, pp. 249–250. Greenwood describes a women's 'beano' in *There Was a Time*, pp. 36–37.

44 T and V interviews, No. 189, p. 41.

45 Charles Booth, *Life and Labour of the People in London*, Third Series, final volume, 57.

46 T and V interviews, No. 22, p. 41. These are Nottingham prices. Tickets at London theatres cost 6d.

47 Robert Roberts, *The Classic Slum*, p. 119.

48 Harry Gosling, *Up and Down Stream* (London, 1927), p. 86; Robert Blatchford, *Dismal England*, p. 36.

49 See Richard Hoggart, *The Uses of Literacy*, pp. 83–84.

50 T and V interviews, No. 36, pp. 52–53.

51 C. V. Butler, *Social Conditions in Oxford* (London, 1912), pp. 50–51.

52 Charles Booth, *Life and Labour of the People in London*, I, 328.

53 Board of Trade, *Labour Gazette*, 1912–1913, XX, XXI. During the same year the board reported 890 cases of lead poisoning. *Ibid.*, XXI, p. 28.

54 *Hansard*, 5th series. XXVII, 260–269. 26 June, 1911.

55 Annual Report of the Chief Inspector of Factories and Workshops. Parliamentary Papers, 1911, 1912–13, XXV, Cd. 6239, 49.

56 L. G. Chiozza Money, *Things That Matter*, p. 113.

57 Rosalind Nash, *Life and Death in the Potteries* (Manchester, 1898), p. 3. Nash describes the effects of lead poisoning as it affected workers: 'Paralysis of certain muscles of the hands, known as "wrist-drop", is one of the commonest consequences of lead poisoning. The hand falls at the wrist, and cannot be raised. The fingers are powerless to grasp anything ... In other cases of paralysis the hands are tightly clenched, so that they will not open, or the feet, legs, or other parts are helpless. It may be attended by great pain. Sometimes the lead causes convulsions and death. Or it may bring on insanity. Or there may be violent pains in the head with dimness of sight, gradually passing into total blindness.' *Ibid.*, p. 7.

58 B. Seebohm Rowntree, Bruno Lasher, *Unemployment: A Social Study* (London, 1911), p. 252;

Arnold J. Freeman, *Boy Life and Labour* (London, 1914), p. 67.

59 T and V interviews, No. 334, p. 13. Williams reported, however, that most men could not resist the extra money overtime work provided: 'The trade unionists are usually as well agreed as the others to work extra time; there is but very little difference between them. No matter how loudly they declaim against the system and advocate the abolition of overtime, should the order be issued they commonly obey it with alacrity.' Alfred Williams, *Life in a Railway Factory*, p. 293.

60 Tom Bell, *Pioneering Days*, p. 65.

61 Lady Bell, *At the Works*, pp. 30–31.

62 Allen Clarke, *The Effects of the Factory System* (London, 1913, 3rd ed.), p. 43.

63 *Ibid.*, pp. 64–65.

64 Alfred Williams, *Life in a Railway Factory*, pp. 251–255.

65 Annual Report of the Chief Inspector of Factories and Workshops. Parliamentary Papers, 1911, 1912–13, XXV, Cd. 6239, 73.

66 Alfred Williams, *Life in a Railway Factory*, p. 33.

67 See, for example, the 1911 Annual Report of the Factory Inspector, p. 6.

68 Tony Lane, Kenneth Roberts, *Strike at Pilkingtons* (London, 1971), p. 41. The lesson: 'Treat your workers as if they are people and then perhaps they will not notice that they are commodities.'

69 Lady Bell, *At the Works*, p. 44.

70 James B. Jeffreys, *The Story of the Engineers* (London, 1946), p. 123.

71 Paul de Rousiers, *The Labour Question in Britain*, p. 53.

72 *The Trade Unionist*, January 30, 1892, p. 8.

73 See Alan Fox, *History of the National Union of Boot and Shoe Operatives, 1874–1957*, pp. 20–21.

74 Robert Blauner, *Alienation and Freedom* (Chicago, 1973, 1st ed., 1964), p. 20.

75 Tom Bell, *Pioneering Days*, pp. 72–73.

76 Alfred Williams, *Life in a Railway Factory*, pp. 183–186.

77 *Ibid.*, pp. 304–305.

78 Whereas 5 per cent of all engineering and boilermaking workers worked to the payment-by-results system in 1886, 27·5 per cent did so by 1906. Among turners and machine-men the figures had reached 46 and 47 per cent by 1914 and 1913 respectively. Eric Hobsbawm, 'Custom, Wages, and Workload in Nineteenth-Century Industry', *Labouring Men*, p. 360.

79 Allen Clarke, *The Effects of the Factory System*, p. 53.

80 H. J. Fyrth, H. Collins, *The Foundry Workers* (Manchester, 1958), p. 114. Employers countered increasing accident figures with the argument that they represented the result of closer accounting procedures required by the Workmen's Compensation Act of 1906; the union denied that claim by pointing to the fact that the figures had begun to rise before 1906. *Idem.*

81 *The Iron Founders' Monthly Report*, May, 1908, p. 37.

82 Huw Beynon, *Working For Ford* (London, 1973), p. 98.

83 Arthur Kornhauser, 'Human Motivations underlying Industrial Conflict', *Industrial Conflict*, Robert Dubin, Arthur M. Ross, eds. (New York, 1954), p. 87.

84 Speech of J. V. Stevens. Annual Report, Trades Union Congress, 1897 (London, 1898), p. 27.

85 Annual Report, 1912, General Union of Braziers and Sheet Metal Workers (Liverpool, 1913), p. 7.

86 *The Iron Founders' Monthly Report*, July, 1910, p. 169.

87 Quarterly Report, Ship Constructive and Shipwright's Association, January–March, 1909, p. 10.

88 Quoted in Joan Thomas, 'A History of the Leeds Clothing Industry', *Yorkshire Bulletin of Economic and Social Research*, 1955, p. 50.

89 J. W. F. Rowe, *Wages in Practice and Theory*, pp. 88, 97–101.

90 Arnold J. Freeman, *Boy Life and Labour*, p. 165.

91 'Youths and even girls were doing work once done by men. Boys were being put on to machines with no prospect before them [i.e., they, too, would be laid off once they reached the stage where they could demand higher wages]. Differential rates and prices for similar work were becoming more prevalent than ever according to the varying facilities of machines and tools of different manufacturers.' W. A. Dalley, *The Life Story of W. J. Davis, M.P.* (Birmingham, 1914), p. 163.

92 *The Transport Worker*, December, 1911, p. 100.

93 Henry Pelling, *Popular Politics and Society in Late Victorian Britain*, p. 53.

94 ILP, *The Abolition of Destitution and Unemployment* (London, 1910), p. 2.

95 J. W. F. Rowe, *Wages in Practice and Theory*, pp. 90, 98; N. B. Dearle, *Problems of Unemployment in the London Building Trades* (London, 1908), pp. 48–49.

96 J. Swift, 'Engineering', *Workers and Their Industries* (London, 1896), p. 111.

97 See below, p. 211.

98 H. J. Fyrth, H. Collins, *The Foundry Workers*, p. 85.

99 Amalgamated Society of Engineers, *Journal and Monthly Record*, January, 1897. Quoted in H. A. Clegg, Alan Fox, A. F. Thompson, *A History of British Trade Unions Since 1889*, I, 162.

100 Alan Fox, *A History of the National Union of Boot and Shoe Operatives*, p. 207.

101 *The Metal-Worker*, March, 1909, p. 65.

102 *Annual Report*, United Patternmakers Association (London, 1913), p. 4.

103 Raymond Postgate, *The Builders' History*, p. 378.

104 D. C. Cummings, *A Historical Survey of the Boilermakers and Iron and Steel Ship Builders' Society* (London, 1905), pp. 204–207.

105 *Annual Report*, Boilermakers and Iron and Steel Ship Builders' Society (London, 1907), p. vii.

106 *The Iron Founders' Monthly Report*, June, 1908, p. 16.

107 Ben Turner, *About Myself*, p. 131.

108 Annual Report, Trade Union Congress, 1911 (London, 1912), p. 229; Harry Gosling, *Up and Down Stream*, p. 146.

109 Alan J. Fox, *A History of the National Union of Boot and Shoe Operatives*, pp. 331–333.

110 Beatrice and Sidney Webb, *The History of Trade Unionism* (London, 1920), p. 469.

111 *Annual Report*, Boilermakers and Iron and Steel Ship Builders' Society (London, 1907), p. vi.

112 Will Hay *et al.*, *The Miners' Next Step* (Tonypandy, 1912), p. 14.

113 N. B. Dearle, *Problems of Unemployment in the London Building Trades*, p. 157.

114 Ben Tillett, *History of the London Transport Workers' Strike* (London, 1911), p. vii.

115 *The Iron Founders' Monthly Report*, April, 1908, pp. 18–31.

116 *Annual Report*, United Pattern-makers Association (London, 1913), pp. 28–29.

117 *The Metal-Worker*, January 1909, p. 3.

118 Tony Lane, Kenneth Roberts, *Strike at Pilkingtons*, p. 252.

119 'A stated goal of higher wages may veil unverbalized strivings for self-respect and dignity or vague hostilities toward the boss, the machine, and the entire industrial discipline. The unstated motivations may be inferred at times from the fact that the dis-content continues after the wage increase is granted ...' Arthur Kornhauser, 'Human Motivations underlying Industrial Conflict', *Industrial Conflict*, Robert Dubin, Arthur M. Ross, eds., pp. 64–65.

120 T and V interviews, No. 215, pp. 34–35.

121 R. A. Leeson, *Strike* (London, 1973), p. 36. The speaker was Sid Fineman, branch secretary of the National Union of Furniture Trade Operatives.

122 See below, pp. 216–219.

123 The unemployment rate was particularly high in 1904–1905, when it moved above 7 per cent and only at the end of that period dropped below 5 per cent. It rose again in 1908, reaching levels of 8 and 9 per cent in the winter of 1908–1909, and not falling again below 5 per cent until April 1910. Board of Trade, *Labour Gazette* XII, XIII, XVII. The figures were based on reports from trade unions only and therefore take no account of the unemployed who did not belong to unions.

124 Paul de Rousiers, *The Labour Question in Britain*, p. 282–283. Rowe estimates that unemployment and short time together resulted in a general reduction of from 5 to 10 per cent in the weekly wage rates of men employed in the mining, building, cotton, and engineering trades. *Wages in Practice and Theory*, p. 63.

125 Gareth Stedman Jones, *Outcast London*, p. 43.

*126* W. H. Beveridge, *Unemployment: A Problem of Industry* (London, 1909), p. 76.

*127* Charles Booth, *Life and Labour of the People in London*, IX, 368–369.

*128* Alfred Williams, *Life in a Railway Factory*, p. 18.

*129* N. B. Dearle, *Problems of Unemployment in the London Building Trades*, p. 94.

*130* B. Seebohm Rowntree, Bruno Lasher, *Unemployment: A Social Study*, p. 255.

*131* See George Orwell, *The Road to Wigan Pier* (London, 1937), p. 87.

*132* B. Seebohm Rowntree, Bruno Lasher, *Unemployment: A Social Study*, p. 135.

*133* The trades insured included building, shipbuilding, mechanical engineering and ironfounding.

*134* E. Collet, M. Robertson, *Family Budgets*, p. 18.

*135* T and V interviews, No. 126, p. 13; No. 213, p. 4.

*136* R. A. Leeson, *Strike*, p. 45.

*137* George Haw, *The Life Story of Will Crooks*, pp. 10–11.

*138* Robert Blatchford, *Dismal England*, p. 209.

## 6 Children

*1* See Winifred Blatchford, 'A London Letter', *The Woman Worker*, June 2, 1909, p. 509: 'I never saw so many children . . . We threaded our way through them, dodged them, and stepped over them.'

*2* A. L. Bowley, 'Earners and Dependants in English Towns in 1911', *Economica*, II (May, 1921) pp. 108–109; B. Seebohm Rowntree, *Poverty*, pps. 80–81; E. H. Phelps Brown, *The Growth of British Industrial Relations*, pp. 4–6. On middle-class family planning see J. A. Banks, *Prosperity and Parenthood* (London, 1965); and J. A. and Olive Banks, *Feminism and Family Planning* (London, 1964).

*3* Second Report on Infant and Child Mortality (Local Government Board). Parliamentary Papers, 1913, XXXII, Cd. 6909, 73.

*4* Department of Health, City of Birmingham, *Report on the Industrial Employment of Married Women and Infant Mortality*, p. 3; M. S. Pember Reeves, *Round About a Pound a Week*, pp. 194, 28.

*5* A. L. Bowley, A. R. Burnett-Hurst, *Livelihood and Poverty*, p. 47.

*6* B. Seebohm Rowntree, *Poverty*, pp. 211–212. The Birmingham survey disclosed that in families in which the income ranged between 10 to 20s a week, babies at twelve months weighed an average of 17·5 lb; in families with incomes of from 20 to 30s, 18·3 lb. Department of Health, City of Birmingham, *Report on the Industrial Employment of Married Women and Infant Mortality*, p. 18.

*7* Women's Cooperative Guild, *Maternity*, p. 90.

*8* M. S. Pember Reeves, *Round About a Pound a Week*, p. 178.

*9* Arnold J. Freeman, *Boy Life and Labour in London*, p. 83. See M. S. Pember Reeves, *Round*

*About a Pound a Week*, p. 179: 'There is no doubt that the healthy infant at birth is less healthy at three months, less healthy still at a year, and often by the time it is old enough to go to school it has developed rickets or lung trouble through entirely preventible causes.'

10 C. V. Butler, *Social Conditions in Oxford*, p. 160.

11 During the years 1893–1902, 34·6 per cent of those volunteering were rejected upon initial physical inspection. (234,914 out of 679,703). In 1901, 593·4 per thousand were under the previous standard height of 5 feet 6 inches and 511·8 were under the chest measurement of 34 inches. Inter-departmental Commission on Physical Deterioration, Parliamentary Papers, 1904, XXXII, Cd. 2175, I, 96; A. Watt Smyth, *Physical Deterioration* (London, 1904), pp. 21–22.

12 G. A. N. Lowndes, *Margaret McMillan, 'The Children's Champion'* (London, 1960), p. 57.

13 Alexander Paterson, *Across the Bridges*, p. 27.

14 [Isabella Ford] *Tom Maguire, A Remembrance* (Manchester, 1895), p. vii. Maguire composed a 'Nursery Rhyme for Old Kids' on the same theme (p. 66):

Jack Frost – Jack Frost –
   take a walk in space,
Skim the Milky Way,
   kiss the moon's cheese face;
Go to Mars or Jupiter,
   stay with each a year,
Then go anywhere you like
   that's further still from here.

15 One is reminded of Michael Anderson's discussion of the same sort of calculus which determined whether or not working-class townspeople sought the assistance of relatives in the early years of industrialization. See above, p. 46. See also the remarks of S. F. Jackson in 'The New Scholar', a chapter in *The Young Wage Earner*, J. J. Findlay ed. (London, 1918): 'The [wage-earning] youth demands, not formally, but none the less explicitly, to be treated as a senior … leaving school is his emancipation. His mother anticipates and grants his demands, and the rest of the seniors, where there are any, follow suit. They expect him to behave as one of them.' pp. 40–41.

16 Alexander Paterson, *Across the Bridges*, p. 38; Paul de Rousiers, *The Labour Question in Britain*, p. 35.

17 Robert Roberts, *The Classic Slum*, p. 33.

18 T and V interviews, No. 54, p. 11a; No. 75, p. 15.

19 Elizabeth Bott, *Family and Social Network*, p. 137.

20 Reginald A. Bray, 'The Boy and the Family', *Studies of Boy Life in Our Cities*, E. J. Urwick, ed., pp. 81–83.

21 T and V interviews, No. 253, p. 23; No. 3, p. 13; No. 28, p. 10; No. 12, p. 30.

22 Charles Booth, *Life and Labour of the People in London*, IX, 435. Reginald Bray bears him out, in 'The Boy and the Family', *Studies*

*of Boy Life in Our Cities*, E. J. Urwick, ed., p. 81.

23 T and V interviews, No. 126, p. 16; No. 252, p. 18; No. 187, p. 24.

24 *Ibid.*, No. 252, p. 18.

25 *Ibid.*, No. 39, p. 8. See Thea Vigne, 'Parents and Children, 1890–1918: Distance and Dependence', *Oral History*, III (Autumn, 1975), pp. 6–13.

26 T and V interviews, No. 162, p. 8.

27 *Ibid.*, No. 54, p. 23.

28 *Ibid.*, No. 155, p. 38.

29 Roberts remarks: 'It came as a curious shock to one who revered the Old School when it dawned upon him that he himself was a typical sample of the "low cads" so despised by all at Greyfriars. Class consciousness had broken through at last.' *The Classic Slum*, p. 128.

30 T and V interviews, No. 215, p. 38; No. 284, p. 22; No. 124, p. 23.

31 *Ibid.*, No. 92, p. 29.

32 Walter Besant, *East London*, p. 174.

33 Madge and Robert King, *Street Games of North Shields Children* (Tynemouth, 1926), I, 23.

34 *Ibid.*, II, 28.

35 T and V interviews, No. 71, p. 29. See Walter Greenwood, *There Was a Time*, p. 23.

36 *Ibid.* pp. 33–34.

37 T and V interviews, No. 417, pp. 27–28.

38 *Ibid.*, No. 162, p. 28.

39 *Ibid.*, No. 208, p. 28.

40 *Ibid.*, No. 28, pp. 17–18; Robert Roberts, *The Classic Slum*, p. 120.

41 T and V interviews, No. 252, pp. 45–46.

42 *Ibid.*, No. 54, p. 18. Another informant recalled regular walks with friends of from ten to twelve miles. (No. 31, p. 15).

43 Reginald Bray, 'The Boy and the Family', *Studies of Boy Life in Our Cities*, E. J. Urwick, ed., pp. 73–74.

44 J. R. Hall, *The Elswick Works Schools* (Newcastle, 1912), p. 17.

45 M. D. Stocks, *Fifty Years in Every Street*, pp. 29–30.

46 C. E. B. Russell, Lilian Rigby, *Working Lads' Clubs* (London, 1908), pp. 338, 349. Though clubs for girls were not organized on the scale of the Lads' Clubs, most cities offered recreational facilities to both boys and girls. Oxford girls' clubs in 1911 numbered 20, and a union of 45 clubs with a membership of over 4,000 existed in Birmingham. C. V. Butler, *Social Conditions in Oxford*, p. 179; Edward Cadbury, et al., *Women's Work and Wages*, pp. 274–275.

47 C. E. B. Russell, *Manchester Boys*, pp. 65, 61; C. E. B. Russell, *Social Problems of the North* (London, 1914), p. 100.

48 Brian Jackson, Dennis Marsden, *Education and the Working Class*, pp. 106–107. This desire to subvert the establishment is what kept Alan Sillitoe's long-distance runner from winning his race.

49 C. E. B. Russell, Lilian Rigby, *Working Lads' Clubs*, pp. 248, 215.

50 Reginald Bray, 'The Boy and the Family', *Studies of Boy Life in Our Cities*, E. J. Urwick, ed., p. 99; Charles Booth, *Life and Labour of the People in London*, Third Series, II, 87.

51 George Lusk, 'My First Camp', *The Owl* (Bulletin of the Oldham Lads' Club), December, 1903, p. 13.

52 Richard Hoggart, *The Uses of Literacy*, p. 59.

53 Walter Greenwood, *There Was a Time*, p. 35.

54 T and V interviews, No. 31, p. 8.

55 B. Seebohm Rowntree, *Poverty*, pp. 76–77. Rowntree attributed the growth of the custom in York to the fact that a large proportion of this class worked for the railway and was therefore entitled to reduced fares.

56 Colin and Rose Bell, *City Fathers* (London, 1972), p. 134.

57 *The Cotton Factory Times*, 2 June, 1911, p. 7.

58 T and V interviews, No. 28, p. 11.

59 *Ibid.*, No. 184, p. 26.

60 M. S. Pember Reeves, *Round About a Pound a Week*, p. 15; Lady Bell, *At the Works*, p. 162; Robert Roberts, *The Classic Slum*, p. 104.

61 E. H. Phelps Brown cites as 'the most eloquent statistics of the day' those which estimated the increase in the proportion of the population of London within the ages of 25 to 55 which had passed through an "efficient" school: in 1891, 23 per cent; in 1901, 52 per cent; in 1911, 78 per cent. *The Growth of British Industrial Relations*, p. 45.

62 Harry Gosling, *Up and Down Stream*, pp. 12–13.

63 In York, the Voluntary schools, educating over half the population of working-class children, were much inferior to the Board schools. The Inspector had found them 'old, and, in most cases poor'. B. Seebohm Rowntree, *Poverty*, p. 335.

64 Reginald Bray, 'The Children of the Town', *The Heart of the Empire*, C. F. G. Masterman, ed., p. 154. Robert Roberts's description of the Voluntary school which served his Salford community is equally grim. *The Classic Slum*, pp. 104–106.

65 R. H. Best, W. J. Davis, C. Perks, *The Brassworkers of Berlin and Birmingham, A Comparison* (London, 1905), p. 5.

66 C. E. B. Russell, *Social Problems of the North*, p. 48.

67 See, for example, the favourable report of Her Majesty's Inspector for York, quoted in B. Seebohm Rowntree, *Poverty*, p. 335.

68 By far the best summary of British educational policy in the late nineteenth century is contained in Brian Simon, *Education and the Labour Movement* (London, 1965). In 1911 and 1912 in Manchester, of the 35,000 elementary school children over the age of 11, 12,613 boys received training in light woodwork and handicraft, 8,089 girls were taught cookery, 3,585 laundering, 572 housewifery, and 5,797 care and feeding of infants. Similar courses were offered in Liverpool, Birmingham, Bradford, Newcastle,

and London. See C. E. B. Russell, *Social Problems of the North*, pp. 40–41; A. Watt Smyth, *Physical Deterioration*, p. 185.

69 Booth pointed out that until 1890, nothing but the three R's and needlework were permitted to be taught children until they had passed a proficiency test in English grammar. *Life and Labour of the People in London*, II, 502. For an account – perhaps overly optimistic – of imaginative teaching techniques employed in London schools, see H. B. Philpott, *London at School*, pp. 54–55.

70 Charles Booth, *Life and Labour of the People in London*, II, 493.

71 T and V interviews, No. 137, p. 59; No. 252, p. 40; No. 253, p. 62.

72 David Rubenstein, *School Attendance in London, 1870–1904* (Hull, 1969), p. 112; H. B. Philpott, *London at School*, p. 87.

73 Charles Booth, *Life and Labour of the People in London*, III, 235.

74 T and V interviews, No. 208, p. 14.

75 *Ibid.*, No. 136. The school was the West Liverpool Street Council School. By way of contrast, the entry for 19 June, 1907: 'James William Stretch completed seven years' unbroken attendance at school. This is the first time in the history of the school that this has been done. The teachers and scholars presented him with a silver watch.'

76 B. Seebohm Rowntree, *Poverty*, p. 60. See also Charles Booth, *Life and Labour of the People in London*, IX, 380–381.

77 Annual Report, Trades Union Congress, 1909 (London, 1910), pps. 91–92. Half-timers' shifts were from 6 or 6.30 a.m. to 12.30 p.m., or from 1 p.m. to 5.30 or 6, with breaks in between. The law forbade their employment for more than 4½ hours per day or 5½ hours at a stretch. Average pay for piecers or doffers in the textile industry was from 2s to 4s 6d per week. C. E. B. Russell, *Social Problems in the North*, pp. 45–46.

78 Annual Report, Trades Union Congress, 1911 (London, 1912), p. 161.

79 *The Woman Worker*, June 2, 1909, p. 510.

80 See, for example, the speech of W. C. Steadman of the Barge Builders, President of the TUC Conference in 1904, urging 'a non-competitive system of maintenance scholarships which will provide a secondary educational scholarship for every child who can reach a certain standard'. Annual Report, Trades Union Congress, 1904 (London, 1905), p. 69.

81 Again, the best account of the struggle appears in Brian Simon, *Education and the Labour Movement*.

82 L. G. Chiozza Money, *Things That Matter*, p. 212. Students could pass out of school at 13 provided they passed a 'labour exam' attesting to their mastery of basic skills in the 3 R's.

83 Interdepartmental Commission on Physical Deterioration, Par-

liamentary Papers, 1904, XXXII, Cd. 2175, II, 25.

84 H. Crapper, 'Reminiscences of a Woolsorter', p. 4.

85 Reginald Bray, 'The Boy and the Family', *Studies of Boy Life in Our Cities*, E. J. Urwick, ed., p. 55.

86 T and V interviews, No. 124, p. 36. Compare these remarks with the discussion of just such open days in contemporary schools in Jackson and Marsden's *Education and the Working Class*. Working-class parents reported themselves intimidated and generally dissatisfied with the treatment they received from the middle-class teachers: 'You'd see this bloody Glen-Smith fellow and he'd look at you and hum and bloody haw and he'd give you no encouragement at all, none whatever, not a bloody bit of encouragement ... We're good citizens aren't we? We might be poor folk around this way, but we've as much bloody right as any other buggers in this bloody town to get the job done properly.' (p. 119.)

87 T and V interviews, No. 228, p. 7.

88 Brian Jackson, Dennis Marsden, *Education and the Working Class*, p. 61.

89 Nettie Adler, 'Child Employment and Juvenile Delinquency', *Women in Industry*, Gertrude Tuckwell, ed. (London, 1908), p. 132.

90 T and V interviews, No. 208, p. 14; No. 229, p. 30; No. 339, p. 15.

91 Walter Greenwood, *There Was a Time*, p. 52.

92 Clementina Black, *Sweated Industry and the Minimum Wage*, pps. 105–106.

93 Bob Gilding, *The Journeyman Coopers of East London* (Oxford, 1971), p. 15.

94 Walter Greenwood, *Love on the Dole*, p. 21.

95 Alan Fox, *A History of the National Union of Boot and Shoe Operatives*, p. 17.

96 Harry Gosling, *Up and Down Stream*, p. 1. Bob Gilding remarks on the fact that 'several of my contemporaries are the sons, grandsons, and great-grandsons of coopers'. *The Journeyman Coopers of East London*, p. 1. See S. J. Chapman, W. Abbott, 'The Tendency of Children to Enter their Fathers' Trades', *Journal of the Royal Statistical Society*, LXXVI (May, 1913), pp. 599–604. The authors, surveying 2,415 Lancashire continuation school students, found that 'the patrimonial system [meaning here the tendency of a child to follow the father's calling] is strongly marked'.

97 See David F. Wilson, *Dockers: The Impact of Industrial Change* (London, 1972), p. 51.

98 N. B. Dearle, *Industrial Training* (London, 1914), pp. 238–9, 240.

99 Arnold T. Freeman, *Boy Life and Labour*, p. 22.

100 *Ibid.*, p. 4.

101 *Ibid.*, pp. 24, 39, 30–31. A Glasgow survey found that the boy who had fewer than six jobs between the ages of 14 and 21 was the exception to the rule. Cases of as many as twelve jobs

were common. Arthur Greenwood, *Juvenile Labour Exchanges and Aftercare* (London, 1911), pp. 7–8.

*102* Sidney and Beatrice Webb, *Industrial Democracy* (London, 1920, 1st ed. 1897), p. 474.

*103* N. B. Dearle, *Industrial Training*, p. 62.

*104* C. E. B. Russell, *Manchester Boys*, p. 13.

*105* 'The workmen generally are in many cases none too favourably disposed towards the lads, for, with the ever-present fear of losing their employment, they are apt to look with jealousy on all possible rivals and competitors, and as such they often regard the lads ...' N. B. Dearle, *Problems of Unemployment*, p. 111.

*106* Arnold J. Freeman, *Boy Life and Labour*, p. 168.

*107* Reginald Bray, *Boy Labour and Apprenticeship* (London, 1911), pp. 114, 123–127.

*108* W. H. Beveridge, *Unemployment: A Problem of Industry*, p. 131.

*109* Arnold J. Freeman, *Boy Life and Labour*, p. 192.

*110* *Women in the Printing Trades*, J. R. MacDonald, ed., p. 60.

*111* Edward Cadbury, *et al.*, *Women's Work and Wages*, pp. 78–79.

*112* T and V interviews, No. 187, p. 55.

*113* Edward Cadbury, *et al.*, *Women's Work and Wages*, p. 72.

*114* *Women in the Printing Trades*, J. R. MacDonald, ed., p. 87.

*115* Charles Booth, *Life and Labour of the People in London*, I, 437.

*116* C. V. Butler, *Domestic Service*, p. 129. The number of indoor domestic servants per 1,000 families had declined from 218 in 1881, to 189 in 1901, to 170 in 1911 (p. 130).

*117* *Ibid.*, p. 74. The number of girls entering service at age 14 declined 17·2 per cent from 1901 to 1911; the number of young women entering service between the ages of 25 to 35 and 35 to 45 increased by 7·3 and 19·3 per cent respectively in the same years. The largest single contingent entering service in 1911 was that between the ages of 15 to 20 – a total of 390,330. *Ibid.*, p. 130.

*118* C. V. Butler, *Social Conditions in Oxford*, p. 63.

*119* *Ibid.*, pp. 73, 32.

*120* *Ibid.*, p. 66.

*121* Edward Cadbury, *et al.*, *Women's Work and Wages*, pp. 114–118.

*122* C. V. Butler, *Domestic Service*, p. 62.

*123* T and V interviews, No. 105, p. 48.

*124* *Ibid.*, No. 105, p. 49.

*125* *Ibid.*, No. 38, p. 57.

*126* *Mrs Beeton's Book of Household Management* (London, 1912), pp. 546–548.

*127* T and V interviews, No. 38, pp. 52–53.

*128* *Ibid.*, No. 105, p. 49.

*129* *Ibid.*, No. 268, p. 67.

*130* *Ibid.*, No. 38, p. 61.

*131* Quoted in Steven Marcus, *The Other Victorians* (New York, 1966), p. 132.

*132* C. V. Butler, *Domestic Service*, p. 64.

*133* D. H. Lawrence makes this limbo the subject of his short story 'Fanny and Annie'.

*134* For a discussion of the fining system, see Margaret Bondfield, *A Life's Work*, pp. 64–65. Girls working in what one team of investigators described as 'first-class shops' could expect to work an average of 60 to 65 hours a week; those in 'second-class shops', 69 to 74 hours; those in 'third-class shops' – often open on Sundays – 75 to 85 hours. J. Hallsworth, R. J. Davies, *The Working Life of Shop Assistants* (Manchester, 1910), p. 62.

*135* *Ibid.*, p. 37.

*136* Barbara Drake, 'The Tea Shop Girl', *Women's Industrial News*, April, 1913, p. 125.

*137* Charles Booth, *Life and Labour of the People in London*, Third Series, IV, 121.

*138* Helen Bosanquet, *Rich and Poor* (London, 1896), p. 104.

*139* S. F. Jackson, 'The New Scholar', *The Young Wage-Earner*, J. J. Findlay, ed., p. 49.

*140* Charles Booth, *Life and Labour of the People in London*, I, 472–473. George Gissing described a girl of the same sort as walking 'with her usual independence, with that swaying of the haunches and swing of the hands with palm turned outwards which is characteristic of the London work-girl.' *Thyrza* p. 113.

*141* Quoted in E. P. Thompson, 'Homage to Tom Maguire', *Essays in Labour History*, Asa Briggs, John Saville, eds. (London, 1960), p. 315. 'Number Three' refers to the Duchess's department.

*142* Edward Cadbury reported that 'the average factory girl buys almost all her clothing through clubs'. He estimated, as well, that she spent something like 2 or 3 shillings a week on her own clothing. Edward Cadbury, *et al.*, *Women's Work and Wages*, pp. 197, 189. For further figures on the amount working girls spent on clothes, see Board of Trade, *Accounts of Expenditure of Wage-Earning Women and Girls* (London, 1911), Cd. 5963.

*143* *The Woman Worker*, May 5, 1909, p. 423; C. E. B. Russell, *Manchester Boys*, p. 18.

*144* Flora J. Freeman, *Religious and Social Work Amongst Girls* (London, 1901), p. 73.

*145* Katharine Dewar, *The Girl* (London, 1921), p. 56.

*146* Arnold J. Freeman, *Boy Life and Labour*, pp. 111, 113, 115.

*147* Robert Roberts, *The Classic Slum*, p. 124.

*148* C. E. B. Russell, *Manchester Boys*, p. 3.

*149* C. E. B. Russell, Lilian M. Rigby, *Working Lads' Clubs*, p. 267.

*150* C. E. B. Russell, *Manchester Boys*, pp. 115–116.

*151* 'There appears to be a deep-seated idea that the two sexes cannot mix in their dwellings with any degree of friendship, or with the knowledge of their parents, without the ulterior motive of marriage.' C. E. B. Russell, Lilian M. Rigby, *Working Lads' Clubs*, p. 266.

*152* Clementina Black, *Sweated Industry and the Minimum Wage*, p. 138.

## 7 A view of life

1 Richard Hoggart, *The Uses of Literacy*, p. 87.
2 T and V interviews, No. 36, p. 3.
3 Harold Scott, *The Early Doors* (London, 1946), p. 176.
4 Christopher Pulling, *They Were Singing*, p. 59.
5 Eleanor Rathbone, *The Disinherited Family* (London, 1924), p. 76.
6 Reginald Bray, 'The Boy and the Family', *Studies of Boy Life in Our Cities*, E. J. Urwick, ed., p. 60.
7 Richard Hoggart, *The Uses of Literacy*, p. 88.
8 Robert Roberts, *The Classic Slum*, p. 112.
9 J. A. Hobson, *The Psychology of Jingoism* (London, 1901), p. 8.
10 Richard Price, *An Imperial War and the British Working Class* (London, 1972), p. 232. See also Henry Pelling, 'British Labour and British Imperialism', *Popular Politics and Society in Late Victorian Britain*.
11 Alan Sillitoe, 'The Good Woman', *The Ragman's Daughter* (New York, 1964), p. 172.
12 See Annual Report, Trades Union Congress, 1907 (London, 1908), pp. 169–170; *ibid.*, 1911 (London, 1912), pp. 176–182.
13 *Ibid.*, 1906 (London, 1907), p. 142. Robert Smillie, introducing a resolution prohibiting foreigners from working in English mines: 'As to foreign workmen, they are chiefly employed because they are more amenable to discipline. They would be willing to work for lower wages and so produce higher profits, if the unions at the present time would permit it.' See also Paul Thompson, *Socialists, Liberals, and Labour. The Struggle for London, 1885–1914*, pp. 29–30, for a description of the anti-semitic, working-class supported Big Brothers' League.
14 Alexander Paterson, *Across the Bridges*, pp. 32, 91.
15 Will Thorne, *My Life's Battles*, p. 24.
16 George Gissing, *The Nether World*, III, 278.
17 Fred Henderson, a socialist, wrote in his 1911 pamphlet, *The Labour Unrest*: 'The simple elementary fact that this is not the devil's world but ultimately and triumphantly God's world, and that whoever falls for a moment under the delusion that it is otherwise is a fool and a simpleton, is the primary underlying fact to be borne in mind in interpreting human history. And since it is to men, in the working out of their human instincts, that the insistence upon God's purpose of order and of justice in the world is committed, the human revolt against the new fools' gospel of getting rich by buying in the cheapest market and selling in the dearest followed naturally and inevitably upon the temporarily successful raid of the powers of darkness by which Mammon-worship superseded Christianity as the established religion of the new capitalist world.' p. 49.
18 'The new city race of workers is developing apart from the influ-

ences of religion; the spiritual world has vanished from their vision; the curtain of their horizon has descended round the little life of toil and struggle which constitutes their immediate universe.' C. F. G. Masterman, 'The Problem of South London', *The Religious Life of London*, Richard Mudie-Smith, ed., p. 199. See also Charles Booth, *Life and Labour of the People of London*, Third Series, *passim*; K. S. Inglis, *Churches and the Working Classes in Victorian England* (London, 1963), esp. 'Epilogue'; and Hugh McLeod, *Class and Religion in the Late Victorian City* (London, 1974), esp. Chapters 3 and 4 for an extended discussion of the same general phenomenon. For an example of the strength of religion in the north, see Beatrice Webb, *My Apprenticeship* (London, 1938; 1st ed., 1926), I, 187, for her description of life among her Nonconformist relatives in Bacup, Lancs.

19 Charles Booth, *Life and Labour of the People in London*, Third Series, VII, 103.

20 Robert Tressell, *The Ragged Trousered Philanthropists*, pp. 46, 27; Gareth Stedman Jones, 'Working-Class Culture and Working-Class Politics', *Journal of Social History*, VII (Summer, 1974), p. 462. In *Outcast London* Stedman Jones notes: 'Brought up to treat life with the fatalism of the gambler, the casual poor rejected the philosophy of thrift, self-denial, and self-help preached to them so insistently by the C.O.S. [Charity Organization Society]. But, by the same token, they rejected qualities which, for different reasons, were also essential to the strength of the labour movement. Dispirited leaders of the new Dockers' Union at the beginning of the 1890s, found it ten times easier to bring men out on strike than to collect union dues.' *Outcast London*, p. 344.

21 See above, p. 24 ff.

22 T and V interviews, No. 12, p. 4. The informant recalled that the reading matter was more often Hood, Shakespeare or Chaucer. Another, whose father was a Liverpool packer, remembered the following books in the family's library: 'A sort of encyclopedic library of science books ... And a Webster's International Dictionary on Indian papers, one volume. That was a gold mine. And there was Blatchford's *Merrie England* and *Britain and the British* and other similar sort of books. And there was novels by Sola and Reader. And others including preference to us like *Little Women* and *Good Wives* for me sister and *Coral Island*, *Gorilla Hunters*, etc., and *The First Men in the Moon* by H. G. Wells and things like that.' *Ibid.*, No. 108, p. 12. For descriptions of the process of self-education, see J. R. Clynes, *Memoirs* (London, 1937), I, 34–37; and Tom Mann, *Memoirs* (London, 1967, 1st ed., 1923), pp. 18–19.

23 Annual Report of the Independent Labour Party, 1914, p. 27.

24 Labour Party Archives, LPC 2.11/420.

25 Henry Pelling, *The Social Geography of British Elections, 1885–1910* (London, 1967), p. 296.

26 One of Thompson and Vigne's respondents, of her Conservative father. T and V interviews, No. 184, p. 31. A Keighley warp dresser told Thompson and Vigne: 'The mill owner expected his hands – his employees to vote – to fall in – his politics. If he was a Liberal his employee was supposed to be Liberal . . . And I think that's why we've all been brought up as Liberals.' *Ibid.*, No. 176, p. 40.

27 Ellen Wilkinson, in her book on Jarrow, *The Town That Was Murdered*, describes the willingness of voters to return Charles Mark Palmer, owner of the Palmer shipyards. In 1892, workers had thrown eggs and flour at the Labour candidate. In this case, the deference was, as much as anything, to the name. (p. 112.)

28 T and V interviews, No. 12, p. 6.

29 John Taylor, *From Self-Help to Glamour: The Working Man's Club, 1860–1972*, pp. 42–43, 53, 56. See also Richard Price, *An Imperial War and the British Working Class*, pp. 67–70.

30 Paul Thompson, *Socialists, Liberals and Labour, The Struggle for London, 1885–1914*, p. 101.

31 Charles Booth, *Life and Labour of the People in London*, Third Series, VII, 104.

32 J. Ramsay MacDonald, *The Labour Party's Policy* (ILP pamphlet) (London, 1912).

33 L. G. Chiozza Money, *Things That Matter*, p. 193: 'The period of qualification seems to have been the aspect of electoral law which most affected the extent of enfranchisement. Where mobility was greatest the voters were fewest. In the city divisions of Manchester, Salford, and Liverpool only about half the adult males were on the register, and those divisions associated with the migratory Irish had the smallest proportion of all.' P. F. Clarke, *Lancashire and the New Liberalism* (Cambridge, 1971), p. 111.

34 G. W. Shreve, *Canvassers' Guide to Registration* (London, 1907), p. 5.

35 Paul Thompson attributes the absence of any Labour Party organization in Bethnal Green, Stepney, and Camberwell to the fact of 'the chronic poverty typical of inner working-class districts, breeding a political apathy which made a labour or socialist movement peculiarly hard to establish'. *Socialists, Liberals and Labour, the Struggle for London, 1885–1914*, p. 239.

36 Walter Greenwood, *Love on the Dole*, pp. 164–165.

37 Richard Hoggart, *The Uses of Literacy*, pp. 86–87.

38 Lady Bell, *At the Works*, p. 233; Margery Spring Rice, *Working-Class Wives* (London, 1939), p. 96.

39 Reinhard Bendix, Seymour Martin Lipset, *Social Mobility in Industrial Society* (Berkeley and Los Angeles, 1959), pp. 68–69.

40 See P. F. Clarke, *Lancashire and*

the New Liberalism, pp. 17–18, 401–402.

41 Alan Fox, *A History of the National Union of Boot and Shoe Operatives*, p. 339.

42 R. Page Arnot, *The South Wales Miners* (London, 1967), pp. 305–306.

43 Fenner Brockway, *Socialism Over Sixty Years, The Life of Jowett of Bradford* (London, 1946), pp. 73, 104.

44 Asa Briggs, 'The Welfare State in Historical Perspective', *Archives Européenes de Sociologie*, II (1961), p. 228.

45 Gareth Stedman Jones writes: 'Historians have generally discussed this question in a rather one-sided and teleological manner. Looking forward to the creation of the welfare state, they have concentrated upon proposals for old-age pensions, free education, free school meals, subsidized housing, and national insurance. They have virtually ignored parallel proposals to segregate the casual poor, to establish detention centres for "loafers", to separate pauper children from "degenerate" parents or to ship the "residuum" overseas. Yet for contemporaries, both sorts of proposals composed parts of a single debate.' *Outcast London*, pp. 313–314.

46 George Bourne [George Sturt], *Changes in the Village*, p. 171.

47 M. S. Pember Reeves, *Round About a Pound a Week*, p. 226.

48 M. E. Bulkley, *The Feeding of School Children* (London, 1914), p. 70.

49 *Ibid.*, p. 110.

50 The Bristol Adult School Union, *Facts of Bristol Social Life, 1914*, p. 10.

51 Margaret McMillan, A. C. Sanderson, *London's Children: How to Feed Them and How Not to Feed Them* (London, n.d.), p. 4. An Act passed in 1914 improved matters somewhat. It granted the Board of Education authority to compel local authorities to feed necessitous children, removed a previous limitation on the amount local authorities might spend, and authorized the use of Board grants-in-aid to supplement local money. It also placed responsibility for the programme in the hands of the school medical officer, thereby, Bentley Gilbert has noted, reasserting the original intent of school feeding: 'That feeding should be undertaken solely for the benefit of the physique and learning ability of children and not considered in any way a measure of poor relief.' The reassertion was undoubtedly clearer in the minds of those who drafted the Bill than in those of the people it was designed to benefit. Bentley Gilbert, *The Evolution of National Insurance in Great Britain*, (London, 1966), p. 116.

52 Marion Phillips, *The School Doctor and the Home* (London, 1913), pp. 22, 25.

53 Women's Cooperative Guild, *Maternity*, p. 21.

54 Lady Bell, *At the Works*, p. 205. Margaret Davies reports the case of a Mrs Layton, a midwife with

much experience, who failed her examination: 'The written examination took place at 9.00 p.m. in a closely packed room. We had two hours to answer the questions, and a fortnight later an oral examination.' *Life as We Have Known It*, Margaret L. Davies, ed., pp. 45–46.

55 LSE. Webb, Trade Union Documents, A. XLVII, f. 251.

56 Annual Report, Trades Union Congress, 1912 (London, 1913), p. 54.

57 *The Ironfounders Monthly*, August, 1912, p. 215.

58 Alan J. Fox, *A History of the National Union of Boot and Shoe Operatives*, p. 325.

59 Annual Report, General Union of Braziers and Sheet Metal Workers, 1912 (Liverpool, 1913), p. 2.

60 For Tillett's reaction, see his remarks in the 1913 Annual Report of the Dock, Wharf, Riverside, and General Workers' Union: 'A Government of capitalist representatives, a Parliament of capitalist representatives, a workers' movement without directions and at times without a just conception of either its powers or rights, a Labour Party without a mandate and without a policy, together with all the activities of all the trade, political and religious as well as party organizations of the employers and capitalists generally; all these stood a solid phalanx against any real sort of democratic control and initiative.' (London, 1914), p. 16. A positive expression appears in the Annual Report of the United Patternmakers' Association, also for 1913: 'It is impossible but to acknowledge that its effect has been distinctly beneficial.' (London, 1914), p. 2. The Patternmakers' reports were generally temperate, if not conservative.

61 Leone Levi, *Wages and Earnings of the Working Class* (London, 1885), p. 55. Levi estimated a decrease of 30 per cent in middle-class income and an increase of 37 per cent in that of the lower middle class.

62 *Report of an Inquiry by the Board of Trade into Working-Class Rents and Retail Prices – Together with the Rates of Wages in Certain Occupations in Industrial Towns of the United Kingdom in 1912*. Parliamentary Papers, 1913, LXVI, Cd. 6955, lix; L. G. Chiozza Money, *Things That Matter*, p. 27; Board of Trade, *Report on Changes in Rates of Wages and Hours of Work*, Parliamentary Papers, 1912, XCII, Cd. 6471, 8. For an analysis of the decline in the increase of Britain's national income, see A. R. Prest, 'The National Income of the United Kingdom, 1870–1946', *Economic Journal* (March, 1948), pp. 31–56; and C. H. Feinstein, 'Income and Investment in the United Kingdom, 1856–1914', *Ibid.*, (June, 1961), pp. 367–385.

63 *Report . . . Parliamentary Papers*, 1913, LXVI, Cd. 6955, vii.

64 *Ibid.*, xii, xlii.

65 L. G. Chiozza Money, 'The Rise

in the Poverty Line', *Things That Matter*, p. 255.

66 *The Metalworker* (November, 1909), p. 254.

67 L. G. Chiozza Money, 'The Rise in the Poverty Line', *Things That Matter*, p. 254.

68 See A. L. Bowley, *The Change in the Distribution of the National Income* (Oxford, 1920), p. 18.

69 L. G. Chiozza Money, 'The Rise in the Poverty Line', *Things That Matter*, pp. 256–257.

70 E. H. Phelps Brown, *The Growth of British Industrial Relations*, p. 313.

71 B. Seebohm Rowntree, A. C. Pigou, *Lectures on Housing*, p. 20.

72 Women's Cooperative Guild, *Maternity*, p. 46.

73 Agenda and Decisions of the Annual General Meeting, Amalgamated Society of Railway Servants (London, 1911), p. 4.

74 Parliamentary Labour Party, *Annual Report* (London, 1913), p. 36.

75 These and subsequent figures from Henry Pelling, 'The Labour Unrest, 1911–14', *Popular Politics and Society in Late Victorian Britain*, p. 149. Pelling's sources for the figures are Committee on Industry and Trade, *Survey of Industrial Relations* (London, 1926), and the *Ministry of Labour Gazette*.

76 Figures in thousands: 2,150 (1907); 10,790 (1908); 2,690 (1909); 9,870 (1910); 18,169 (1911); 40,890 (1912 – the year of the national coal strike); 9,800 (1913); 9,880 (1914). These figures suggest comparison with the findings of Edward Shorter and Charles Tilly, who have concluded that as organizational techniques increase, along with union membership, a strike turns from a test of endurance to a show of strength. Strikes are shorter but more frequent. See 'The Shape of Strikes in France', *Comparative Studies in Society and History*, XIII (1971), p. 67.

77 Lord Askwith, *Industrial Problems and Disputes* (London, 1920), p. 175.

78 Henry Pelling, 'The Labour Unrest, 1911–14', *Popular Politics and Society in Late Victorian Britain*, p. 150.

79 George Dangerfield, *The Strange Death of Liberal England*, p. 233.

80 Independent Labour Party, *Annual Report* (London, 1912), p. 40.

81 Lord Askwith, *Industrial Problems and Disputes*, p. 150.

82 Annual Report, The Workers' Union, 1911, p. 5.

83 E. H. Phelps Brown, *The Growth of British Industrial Relations*, p. 330.

84 George Dangerfield, *The Strange Death of Liberal England*, p. 235.

85 Tony Lane, Kenneth Roberts, *Strike at Pilkingtons*, p. 202.

86 Leonard Woolf, *Beginning Again* (London, 1964), pp. 34, 36.

# Bibliography

Listed below are the sources most often used in the writing of *A Life Apart*. For further references, readers should consult the footnotes.

## Unpublished sources

The most useful material is to be found in the archives of Paul Thompson's and Thea Vigne's 'Family Life and Work before 1918' project at the University of Essex. Other sources consulted include the archives of the Labour Party Library, the Webb Collections at the Library of Economic and Political Science, London School of Economics, and the Sound Archives of the British Broadcasting Corporation.

## Parliamentary papers

In addition to the annual reports of the Chief Inspector of Factories and Workshops, those publications which provided particularly useful information include:

*Report of the Inter-departmental Committee on Physical Deterioration*, 1904, XXXII, Cd. 2175.

*Report on the Condition of Children who are in Receipt of the Various Forms of Poor Relief in England and Wales*, 1910, LII, Cd. 5037.

Board of Trade, *Accounts of Expenditures of Wage-Earning Women and Girls*, 1911, LXXXIX, Cd. 5963.

Board of Trade, *Report on Changes in the Rates of Wages and Hours of Work*, 1912, XCII, Cd. 6471.

*Report of an Inquiry by the Board of Trade into Working-Class Rents and Retail Prices Together with the Rates of Wages in Certain Occupations in Industrial Towns of the United Kingdom in 1912*, 1913, LXVI, Cd. 6955.

Local Government Board, *Report on Infant and Child Mortality*, 1913, XXXII, Cd. 6909.

## Other contemporary newspapers, reports, etc.

*The Cooperative News*
*The Cotton Factory Times*
*The Daily Citizen*
*The Daily Herald*

*The Home Companion*
*Reynolds's*
*The Star*
*The Yorkshire Factory Times*
*The Woman Worker*
Annual reports of various trade unions, especially of the Trades Union Congress, and of the Labour Party and the Independent Labour Party.


## Contemporary surveys

Besant, Walter, *East London* (London, 1901)
Beveridge, W. H., *Unemployment: A Problem of Industry* (London, 1909)
Black, Clementina, *Sweated Industry and the Minimum Wage* (London, 1907)
Black, Clementina, ed., *Married Women's Work* (London, 1915)
Black, Clementina, Meyer, Adele, *Makers of Our Clothes* (London, 1909)
Blatchford, Robert, *Dismal England* (London, 1899)
Booth, Charles, *The Aged Poor* (London, 1894)
Booth, Charles, *Life and Labour of the People in London* (London, 1891, 1902)
Bosanquet, Helen, *Social Work in London, 1869–1912* (London, 1914)
Bowley, Arthur, *The Change in the Distribution of National Income* (Oxford, 1920)
Bowley, Arthur L., Burnett-Hurst, A. R., *Livelihood and Poverty* (London, 1915)
Bowmaker, E., *The Housing of the Working Classes* (London, 1895)
Bray, Reginald, *Boy Labour and Apprenticeship* (London, 1911)
Butler, C. V., *Domestic Service* (London, 1916)
Butler, C. V., *Social Conditions in Oxford* (London, 1912)
Cadbury, Edward, *et al.*, *Women's Work and Wages* (London, 1906)
Chiozza Money, L. G., *Riches and Poverty* (London, 1905, 3rd ed.)
Chiozza Money, L. G., *Things That Matter* (London, 1912)
Collet, Clara, *Women in Industry* (London, 1911)
Collet, E., Robertson, M., *Family Budgets* (London, 1896)
Davies, Margaret L., *Cooperation in Poor Neighbourhoods* (n.p. 1899)
Dearle, N. B., *Industrial Training* (London, 1914)
de Rousiers, Paul, *The Labour Question in Britain* (London, 1896)
Drake, Barbara, *Women in the Engineering Trades* (London, 1917)
Freeman, Arnold J., *Boy Life and Labour* (London, 1914)
Hutchins, B. L., *Women in Modern Industry* (London, 1915)
Kaufman, M., *The Housing of the Working Classes and of the Poor* (London and Edinburgh, 1907)
Levi, Leone, *Wages and Earnings of the Working Classes* (London, 1885)
Loane, M., *From Their Point of View* (London, 1908)
Loane, M., *The Next Street but One* (London, 1907)

MacDonald, J. R., ed., *Women in the Printing Trades* (London, 1904)

Marr, T. R., *Housing Conditions in Manchester and Salford* (Manchester, 1904)

Masterman, C. F. G., *et al.*, *The Heart of the Empire* (London, 1902)

Martin, Anna, *The Married Working Woman* (London, 1911)

Martin, Anna, *The Mother and Social Reform* (London, 1913)

Mudie-Smith, Richard, ed., *Handbook of the 'Daily News' Sweated Industries Exhibition* (London, 1906)

Mudie-Smith, Richard, ed., *The Religious Life of London* (London, 1904)

Parry, E. A., *The Law and the Poor* (London, 1914)

Paterson, Alexander, *Across the Bridges* (London, 1911)

Pember Reeves, M. S., *Round About a Pound a Week* (London, 1914)

Peppin, T. S., *Club-Land of the Toiler* (London, 1895)

Philpott, H. B., *London at School* (London, 1904)

Seebohm Rowntree, B., *Poverty. A Study of Town Life* (London, 1901)

Seebohm Rowntree, B., ed., *Betting and Gambling* (London, 1905)

Seebohm Rowntree, B., Kendall, May, *How the Labourer Lives* (London, 1913)

Seebohm Rowntree, B., Lasher, Bruno, *Unemployment: A Social Study* (London, 1911)

Seebohm Rowntree, B., Pigou, A. C., *Lectures on Housing* (Manchester, 1914)

Rowntree, Joseph, Sherwell, A. J., *The Temperance Problem and Social Reform* (London, 1900, 7th ed.)

Russell, C. E. B., *Manchester Boys* (Manchester, 1905)

Russell, C. E. B., *Social Problems of the North* (London, 1914)

Russell, C. E. B., Rigby, Lilian M., *Working Lads' Clubs* (London, 1908)

Solly, Henry, *Working Men's Social Clubs and Educational Institutes* (London, 1904, 2nd ed.)

Tuckwell, Gertrude, ed., *Women in Industry* (London, 1908)

Urwick, E. J., ed., *Studies of Boy Life in Our Cities* (London, 1904)

Watt Smyth, Aimée, *Physical Deterioration* (London, 1904)

Williams, Alfred, *Life in a Railway Factory* (London, 1915)

Wilson, Mona, Howarth, E. G., *East Ham* (London, 1907)

Women's Cooperative Guild, *Maternity* (London, 1915)

Women's Cooperative Guild, *Working Women and Divorce* (London, 1911)

## Autobiography, biography, and memoirs

Askwith, Lord, *Industrial Problems and Disputes* (London, 1920)

Bell, Thomas, *Pionering Days* (London, 1941)

Bondfield, Margaret, *A Life's Work* (London, 1949)

Brockway, Fenner, *Socialism Over Sixty Years: The Life of Jowett of Bradford* (London, 1946)

Davies, C. Stella, *North Country Bred* (London, 1963)
Gosling, Harry, *Up and Down Stream* (London, 1927)
Greenwood, Walter, *There Was a Time* (London, 1967)
Hamilton, Mary Agnes, *Mary Macarthur* (London, 1925)
Haw, George, *The Life Story of Will Crooks* (London, 1917)
Mann, Tom, *Memoirs* (London, 1923)
Roberts, Robert, *The Classic Slum* (Manchester, 1971)
Thorne, Will, *My Life's Battles* (London, 1925)

## Fiction

Gissing, George, *The Nether World* (London, 1889)
Gissing, George, *Thyrza* (London, 1907)
Keating, P. J., ed., *Working-Class Stories of the 1890's* (London, 1971)
Morrison, Arthur, *Tales of Mean Streets* (London, 1894)
Tressell, Robert, *The Ragged Trousered Philanthropists* (London, 1957)

## Other studies

Anderson, Michael, *Family Structure in Nineteenth Century Lancashire* (Cambridge, 1971)
Bagwell, P. S., *The Railwaymen* (London, 1963)
Chapman, Stanley D., ed., *The History of Working-Class Housing* (Newton Abbot, 1971)
Clegg, H. A., Fox, Alan, Thompson, A. F., *A History of British Trade Unions since 1889* (Oxford, 1964)
Dangerfield, George, *The Strange Death of Liberal England* (London, 1935)
Dyos, H. J., ed., *The Study of Urban History* (London, 1968)
Eyles, M. L., *The Woman in the Little House* (London, 1922)
Fox, Alan A., *History of the National Union of Boot and Shoe Operatives* (Oxford, 1958)
Fyrth, H. J., Collins, H., *The Foundry Workers* (Manchester, 1958)
Gilbert, Bentley B., *The Evolution of National Insurance in Great Britain* (London, 1966)
Harrison, Brian, *Drink and the Victorians* (London, 1971)
Hobsbawm, E. J., *Labouring Men* (London, 1964)
Hoggart, Richard, *The Uses of Literacy* (London, 1957)
Keating, P. J., *The Working Classes in Victorian Fiction* (London, 1971)
McLeod, Hugh, *Class and Religion in the Late Victorian City* (London, 1974)
Pelling, Henry, *Popular Politics and Society in Late Victorian Britain* (London, 1968)
Phelps Brown, E. H., *The Growth of British Industrial Relations* (London, 1959)
Postgate, Raymond, *The Builders' History* (London, 1923)
Price, Richard, *An Imperial War and the Working Class* (London, 1972)

Rowe, J. W. F., *Wages in Practice and Theory* (London, 1928)

Stedman Jones, Gareth, *Outcast London* (Oxford, 1971)

Tarn, J. N., *Five Per Cent Philanthropy* (Cambridge, 1973)

Taylor, John, *From Self-Help to Glamour: The Workingman's Club, 1860–1972* (Oxford, 1971)

Thompson, Paul, *The Edwardians* (London, 1975)

Thompson, Paul, *Socialists, Liberals, and Labour: The Struggle for London, 1885–1914* (London, 1967)

## Recent sociological surveys and commentaries

Bott, Elizabeth, *Family and Social Network* (London, 1968; 2nd ed.)

Gorer, Geoffrey, *Exploring English Character* (London, 1955)

Jackson, Brian, *Working-Class Community* (London, 1968)

Jackson, Brian, Marsden, Dennis, *Education and the Working Class* (London, 1962)

Keller, Suzanne, *The Urban Neighborhood* (New York, 1968)

Kerr, Madeline, *The People of Ship Street* (London, 1958)

Kuper, Leo, ed., *Living in Towns* (London, 1953)

Mogey, J. M., *Family and Neighbourhood* (London, 1956)

Rosser, Colin, Harris, Christopher, *The Family and Social Change* (London, 1965)

Young, Michael, Willmott, Peter, *Family and Kinship in East London* (London, 1957)

# Sources of illustrations

Aerofilms (1); Author's collection (21); Birmingham City Library (4); Gernsheim Collection (13); Guildhall Library, London (10); Leeds City Library (2); Liverpool Corporation, Engineer's Department (7); Manchester City Library (16); Frank Mullineux Collection (14, 18); Radio Times Hulton Picture Library (8, 9, 11, 12, 15, 17, 19, 22); Professor J. N. Tarn (3, 5, 6); Victoria and Albert Museum, London (20).

# Index

adolescence, 190–3; employment, 176ff; street gangs, 192

agricultural labourers, 40

alienation, 136–8

Allport, Gordon, 20

Anderson, Michael, 45, 46, 55, 57

Anderson, W. C., 218

apprenticeship, 179–82

Arch, Joseph, 41

Ashby, Joseph, 41

Ashby, Mabel, 41

Askwith, George, 217, 218

Baker, George, 206

Band of Hope, 164–5

Barnes, George, 149

Beeton, Mrs Isabella, 185, 187

Bell, Colin, 169

Bell, Lady Florence, 77, 91, 131–2, 134, 169, 205, 211

Bell, Rose, 169

Bell, Tom, 131, 137

Bellwood, Bessie, 127, 128

Bendix, Reinhard, 205

Besant, Walter, 163

Bethnal Green, London, 46–8, 51, 60

Beveridge, William, 95, 152, 181

Bevin, Ernest, 199

Birmingham, 25, 40, 75, 96–7, 103, 105, 123, 128, 156, 157, 170, 178, 180

Black, Clementina, 7, 96, 98, 100, 107, 108, 113, 175

Blackburn, 95

Blackpool, 169

Blatchford, Robert, 121, 125, 155

Bloody Sunday, 218

Boer War, 197

boilermakers, 40

Boilermakers and Iron and Steel Ship Builders' Society, 145, 148

Bolton, 105, 109, 128, 171

Bondfield, Margaret, 102, 104, 110

bookbinders, 102

Boot and Shoe Operatives, National Union of, 105, 144, 147

boot and shoe workers, 105, 136, 177

Booth, Charles, 7, 24, 32, 38, 39, 57, 71, 76, 91, 93, 110, 118, 124, 127, 128, 152, 167, 190, 203

Bosanquet, Helen, 190

Bott, Elizabeth, 56, 70, 159

Bourneville, 108

Bowley, A. L., 75, 95, 156

boys' clubs, 166–8

Bradford, 31, 41, 84, 95, 110, 126, 138, 158

Bray, Reginald, 37, 39, 118, 159–60, 167, 170, 174, 180, 195, 196

Bristol, 30, 123

budgets, family, 70ff; and family size, 73; rent, 75–6; food, 76–82; clothing, 82–4

building trades, 135, 141, 142, 145, 214

Burn, W. L., 7

Burnett-Hurst, A. R., 75, 156

Burns, John, 25, 26, 199

Butler, C. V., 128, 183, 184

Cadbury, Edward, 101, 103, 110, 181, 182, 184

Captain Swing, 218

Carnie, Ethel, 28

Charity Organization Society, 207

charwomen, 98

child-care, 114–15

childhood, 87–8, 158ff; discipline, 161, 171; games, 162–3; employment, 175–89

Chiozza Money, L. G., 24, 130, 204, 214, 215

Christmas, 168–9

Churchill, Winston, 205

cinema, 93

Clapham, J. H., 122

Clarke, Allen, 138

class consciousness, 12ff, 19, 23–4, 59, 140–2

clothing, 82–4, 191

Comic Cuts, 207

Conservative Party, 202

cooking, 79, 87

Cooperatives, 11, 74

cost of living, 214–16

Cotton Factory Times, 92, 97, 169

courtship, 62–3, 192–3

Coventry, 151

Crooks, Will, 61, 120, 149, 155

Daily Herald, 20

Daily News, 100

Dangerfield, George, 218, 220
Davies, Stella, 125
Dearle, N. B., 142, 177, 179
death, 58, 85, 95–6, 156
deference, 21, 202
de Rousiers, Paul, 150, 159
Dickens, Charles, 8
diet, 80–2
divorce, 17, 63–4
dockers, 135, 151, 216
domestic service, 23, 183–9
Drake, Barbara, 189
drink, 27, 59, 85, 123–6
Durham, 40, 60, 95

education, 169–76, 196–7, parents' attitudes towards 172–5
Education Act, 1870, 172
Education Act, 1902, 173
Education (Provision of Meals) Act, 1906, 208–9
Empire Day, 196
Engels, Friedrich, 136
engineering, 103, 135, 141, 142, 143, 180, 214
Engineers, Amalgamated Society of, 144, 146

Fabian Women's Group, 68
Factory Acts, 106
factory conditions, 106–11, 128–34; hours, 111, 131; inspection, 111, 133; industrial accidents, 129–30; management, 133
factory girls, 182–3; 190–1
Family, 72–3, 81, 87, 114–15; see also kinship
fatherhood, 117ff, 177, 178
Fenn, Manville, 166
Findlay, J. J., 190
football, 127, 167, 192
Foster, John, 13, 21
Fox, Alan, 147, 177
Freeman, Arnold, 141, 178–9, 182
Freeman, Flora, 191
Friendly Societies, 11, 122
furniture, 35–6, 84

gambling, 27, 59, 127
Gaskell, Elizabeth, 8
Gem, 162
General and Municipal Workers Union, 150
Gissing, George, 8, 119, 199
Gladstone, William E., 202
Glasgow, 139
glassmakers, 135
Gorer, Geoffrey, 65
Gosling, Harry, 128, 146, 170, 177
Greenwood, Walter, 18, 63, 109, 114, 163, 168, 175, 176
Gribble, James, 206

Hall, B. T., 122
Hardie, Keir, 62, 199, 200, 206
Harrison, Brian, 125
Hartog, P. J., 122
Hastings, 53
Hay, George, 155
Henderson, Arthur, 129, 149, 199
Henty, G. A., 166
Hill, Octavia, 38, 39
Hobhouse, L. T., 122
Hobsbawm, Eric, 21, 23, 26
Hobson, Charles, 144
Hobson, J. A., 196, 197
Hoggart, Richard, 9, 13, 20, 66, 92, 168, 194
holidays, 168–9
Home Companion, 92
Houghton, Walter, 7, 10
housecleaning, 88–90
housing, 30, 32–4, 75; 'model' tenements, 37–9, 43
Huddersfield, 126, 167
Hull, 143, 166, 202, 218
Hutchins, B. L., 95, 96, 101, 102

illness, 55, 68–70, 90–1, 107, 157, 210–11
Independent Labour Party, 112, 201, 202, 206, 218
infant mortality, 95–6, 156

Ipswich, 104
ironfounders, 132, 138, 140, 143, 146, 148–9

Jackson, Brian, 167
Jackson, S. F., 190
Jones, Jack, 61
Jowett, Fred, 206

Keller, Suzanne, 52
Kerr, Madeline, 47
King, Seymour, 202
kinship, 46–7, 49, 56–8, 60–1, 177
Kornhauser, Arthur, 139

labour aristocracy, 11, 21–3, 25, 35, 143
Labour Party, 111, 201–6, 216, 220
Lancashire, 95, 156, 172
Lansbury, George, 155, 200
laundresses, 98, 154
law, 16–18, 206
Leeds, 40, 119, 126, 209
Leicester, 142, 144, 209
leisure, 91–3, 118–21, 164–165
Leno, Dan, 127, 195
Levi, Leone, 124, 214
Liberal Party, 205
Lipset, Seymour Martin, 205
literacy rates, 169–70
Liverpool, 32, 43, 47, 51, 55, 105
Lloyd, Marie, 127
Lloyd George, David, 205
Lloyds, 92
Loane, M. L., 84
London, 30, 31, 32, 36, 40, 44, 75, 93, 95, 120, 123, 171
London Board of Guardians, 77
London County Council, 76
London Trades Council, 106

Macarthur, Mary, 104
MacDonald, Margaret, 104

MacDonald, Ramsay, 62
101–2, 111, 142, 181,
182, 199, 202, 203, 206
MacInnes, Colin, 14
Mackenzie, W. A., 81
McMillan, Margaret, 209
*Magnet*, 162
Maguire, Tom, 158, 191
Mallon, J. J., 122
Manchester, 30, 32, 51, 53,
61, 75, 93, 97, 105, 111,
123, 136, 149, 166, 170,
180, 193
Mann, Tom, 72, 199, 217
marriage, 62–70, 97, 116–
17
Marsden, Dennis, 167
Martin, Anna, 17, 115
Marx, Karl, 12
Master and Servant Act,
1867, 16
Masterman, C. F. G., 48,
59, 124, 170
Maternity, 69–70
mealtimes, 87–88
Metal Trades Federation,
144
Middlesbrough, 40, 77,
169, 205, 211
migration, 39–44
Mogey, J. M., 49
Morant, Robert, 173
Morecambe, 169
Morrison, Arthur, 8, 28,
59, 120
motherhood, 60ff
music halls, 14, 18–19, 127,
192, 195, 196

Nash, Rosalind, 130
national insurance, 143,
144, 153, 211–13, 217
neighbourhood, 13, 27,
30ff, 44ff; shops, 53–4,
79–80
Newcastle, 32, 104, 166
*News of the World*, 92
Northampton, 75, 144, 147
Norwich, 103, 104
Nottingham, 157

Oddy, D. J., 81
Ogden, J. W., 173

Oldham, 13, 21, 168
*Oral History*, 9
Osborne judgment, 16, 17,
206
Oxford, 47, 49, 51, 128,
157, 183

Parliament, 205–6
Parsons, Talcott, 58–9
Paterson, Alexander, 90,
158, 159, 198
patriotism, 196–8
pattern makers, 144
Pattern Makers, Society of,
140, 149
pawnshops, 74
Pelling, Henry, 202, 217
Pember Reeves, M. S., 7,
36, 37, 77, 86, 87, 156,
157, 169, 208
Peppin, T. S., 122, 123
Phelps Brown, E. H., 215,
219
Phillips, Marion, 210
Pigou, A. C., 32, 75
police, 18, 163
politics, 15, 201–6; working-class conservatism,
202; apathy, 204
Poor Law, 153, 207–8
Poor Law Commission,
1905, 207
Poplar, London, 53, 120,
155, 191
population, 30, 51
Postgate, Raymond, 145
potters, 107, 130–1, 135
Poulton, E. L., 147, 212
pregnancy, 68–70
premium bonus, 139
Preston, 32, 45, 49, 51, 55
Price, Richard, 197
printers, 135, 179, 182, 214
pubs, 54, 93, 121, 123–4
Pugh, Edwin, 8, 54

Railway Servants, Amal-
gamated Society of, 216
railway workers, 214–15,
218
Rathbone, Eleanor, 195
reading, 91–3
Reading, 75, 157

Redford, Arthur, 40
religion, 15–16, 26, 120,
164, 199–200
rent, 34, 36, 38, 75–6
respectability, 25, 26–9,
31, 35, 67, 94, 98, 171,
191
*Reynolds's*, 92
Rigby, Lilian, 166
Ripon, 169
Roberts, Robert, 9, 22,
37, 44, 45, 51, 53, 61, 66,
67, 73–4, 80, 123, 127,
159, 169, 192, 196
Rowe, J. W. F., 141, 142
Rowntree, Joseph, 84, 93,
123, 124
Rowntree, B. Seebohm, 7,
32, 35, 71, 73, 75, 76, 81,
82, 85, 123, 152, 153, 155,
157, 169, 215
Russell, C. E. B., 166, 180,
192, 193

St Helens, 95
Salford, 14, 37, 166, 171–2
sanitation, 31
Scarborough, 169
schools, 169–76; attend-
ance, 171–2; half-time,
172–3; medical inspec-
tions, 210–11
sexuality, 20, 27, 66–70,
110, 188
sheet metal workers, 140,
212
Sheffield, 34, 75, 123, 128,
218
Shipton, George, 106
shipwrights, 145
shop assistants, 189
shopping, 86
Sillitoe, Alan, 197
Smillie, Robert, 62
Smith, Edward, 81
Snowden, Philip, 199, 206
socialism, 199, 200
Solly, Henry, 19
South Shields, 125
Southampton, 149
Southport, 169
Spring Rice, Margery, 205
Staffordshire, 40

Stanley, 75, 157
Stedman Jones, Gareth, 12, 42, 157, 200
Stephen, Leslie, 10
Stockport, 149
Stoke-on-Trent, 95
strikes, 149–51, 217
Sturt, George, 15, 207
suburbs, 44, 75
Sunday School, 164–5
Swansea, 47
sweating, 100–1, 112–14, 182
Swinton, 155
syndicalism, 217–18

Taff Vale decision, 16
technological change, 134–42
temperance, 125–6, 164, 206
textile workers, 102, 105, 107, 109, 128, 136, 138, 146, 172
Thompson, E. P., 11
Thompson, Flora, 41
Thompson, Paul, 9, 20, 117, 155, 158, 159, 160, 171, 175, 187, 188
Thorne, Will, 40, 106, 199, 212
Tillett, Ben, 17, 148, 150, 199, 206, 212
Townsend, Peter, 60, 61, 62
Toynbee Hall, 19, 59
trade unions, 14, 15, 142–51, 212–13; bureaucracy, 14, 147; women's, 104–6; rank and file, 148; arbitration, 150; membership figures, 216

Trades Union Congress, 25, 139, 149, 173, 197
*Trade Unionist*, 136
transport workers, 216
*Transport Worker*, 141
Tressell, Robert, 8, 52–3, 71–2, 80, 124, 126, 128, 129, 200
Trevelyan, G. M., 122
Triple Alliance, 219
Truck Act, 1897, 108
Turner, Ben, 78, 84, 126, 146
Twain, Mark, 166

unemployment, 77, 141–2, 151–4, 206

Vigne, Thea, 9, 20, 117, 155, 158, 159, 160, 171, 175, 187, 188

wages, 70–71, 98ff, 131, 137, 138, 180, 183, 214
Wales, 40
Wapping, London, 53
Warrington, 75, 157
Weavers, Amalgamated Society of, 106, 173
Webb, Beatrice, 105–6, 111, 147, 173, 179, 207
Webb, Sidney, 105–6, 111, 147, 173, 179, 207
welfare state, 207–13
West Ham, London, 43, 100
Whit Sunday, 84, 165
Whitsun week, 167, 168
widowhood, 100
Williams, Alfred, 40–1, 64, 126, 127, 132–5, 137, 152

Williams, Raymond, 41
Willmott, Peter, 8, 47, 55, 58, 60, 117
Willson, Lizzie, 105
Wirth, Louis, 58–9
*Woman Worker*, 25, 28, 110, 173
women, legal rights, 17–18; budgeting, 70–5; shopping, 86–7; house-cleaning, 88–9, 115; health, 211; politics, 204–5; welfare state, 208–11
women's employment, 95ff
Women's Cooperative Guild, 48–9, 50, 67–70, 211
Women's Industrial Council, 23
Women's Trade Union League, 106, 109
*Women's Trade Union Review*, 96, 104, 107–8
Woolf, Leonard, 220
Workers' Union, 216, 219
workhouse, 154–5
workingmen's clubs, 19, 121–3, 197, 203
Workingmen's *Club and Institute Journal*, 24, 121
Workingmen's Club and Institute Union, 122
workmen's compensation, 130

York, 31, 35, 81, 82, 123, 131, 153, 155, 169
Yorkshire, 40, 95, 101, 156, 172
Young, Michael, 8, 47, 55, 58, 60, 117